TEACHING GENDER

Teaching Gender: Feminist Pedagogy and Responsibility in Times of Political Crisis addresses the neoliberalization of the university, what this means in real terms, and strategic pedagogical responses to teaching within this context across disciplines and region.

Inspired by bell hooks' "transgressive school" and Donna Haraway's "responsibility", this collection promotes a politics of care within the classroom through new forms of organizational practices. It engages with the challenges and possibilities of teaching students about women and gender by examining the multiple pedagogical, theoretical, and political dimensions of feminist learning.

The book revisits how we can reconfigure a feminist politics of responsibility that is able to respond to or engage with contemporary crises. It also conceptualizes crisis and explains how it is transforming contemporary societies and affecting individual vulnerabilities and institutional structures. Finally, it offers practical cases from different European locations, in which crisis and responsibility have served to reformulate contemporary feminist pedagogies, altering curriculums, reframing institutions, and affecting the process of teaching and learning.

Beatriz Revelles-Benavente is a Juan de la Cierva post-doctoral researcher at Universidad de Barcelona.

Ana M. González Ramos is a senior researcher at the Internet Interdisciplinary Institute in the Open University of Catalonia.

TEACHING GENDER

Feminist Pedagogy and
Responsibility in Times of
Political Crisis

*Edited by Beatriz Revelles-Benavente and
Ana M. González Ramos*

ATGENDER

Routledge
Taylor & Francis Group

LONDON AND NEW YORK

First published 2017
by Routledge
2 Park Square, Milton Park, Abingdon, Oxon OX14 4RN

and by Routledge
711 Third Avenue, New York, NY 10017

Routledge is an imprint of the Taylor & Francis Group, an informa business

British Library Cataloguing in Publication Data
A catalogue record for this book is available from the British Library

Library of Congress Cataloguing in Publication Data
A catalog record for this book has been requested

ISBN: 978-1-138-70122-9 (hbk)
ISBN: 978-1-138-70123-6 (pbk)
ISBN: 978-1-315-20416-1 (ebk)

Typeset in Sabon
by Out of House Publishing

MIX
Paper from
responsible sources
FSC
www.fsc.org   FSC® C013056

Printed and bound in Great Britain by
TJ International Ltd, Padstow, Cornwall

CONTENTS

FIGURES

CONTRIBUTORS

Jessie Bustillos is Senior Lecturer in Education Studies at London Metropolitan University, UK. She is currently interested in looking at the theoretical, philosophical, and sociological intersections between education, culture, and new technologies. This teaching feeds into her current research which is an online ethnography exploring young people's experiences as networked public on various social media.

Alexandra Cheira is a researcher at the University of Lisbon Centre for English Studies, Portugal. Her current areas of research include contemporary women's writing, women's studies, and, particularly, gender issues and wonder tales in A. S. Byatt's fiction. She has taught Portuguese and English as a Foreign Language in secondary schools and polytechnic colleges since 1995.

Olga Cielemecka is a postdoctorate at the Unit of Gender Studies, Department of Thematic Studies, Linköping University in Sweden. She holds a PhD in philosophy. She brings together research within the domains of contemporary philosophy, feminist theory, and posthumanism, in an effort to rethink the concepts of the subject, community, and collaboration in times of advanced capitalism and environmental change.

Felicity Colman is Professor of Film and Media Arts at Manchester Metropolitan University, UK. She is the author of *Film Theory: Creating a Cinematic Grammar* (2014), *Deleuze and Cinema* (2011), editor of *Film, Theory and Philosophy: The Key Thinkers* (2009), and co-editor of *Sensorium: Aesthetics, Art, Life* (2007).

Ester Conesa Carpintero is a PhD candidate (Universitat Oberta de Catalunya) working on gender and scientific careers in the GENERA Project. She previously worked as a research assistant on gender and technology (Universitat Rovira i Virgili) and studied Research on Social Psychology (MA, Universitat Autònoma de Barcelona).

Rosa Costa is a historian, youth worker, trainer in adult education, and activist in Vienna. She teaches at different Austrian universities on topics such as gender-reflective pedagogy and feminist critique of science. She is currently working at the Department of Political Science at the University of Vienna.

Verònica Gisbert Gracia is a PhD student at the Department of Sociology and Social Anthropology at the University of Valencia. She completed the GEMMA Erasmus Mundus master's degree in Women's and Gender Studies at the University of Granada (Spain) and Utrecht (Netherlands) and a master's in Human Rights, Democracy, and International Justice at the University of Valencia.

Ángela Harris Sánchez holds a BA in Art History (University of Granada) and an MPhil in Art Therapy (Complutense University, Madrid). She is Initial Research Fellow at the University of Granada and has also contributed to Art Therapy programmes in spaces of social inclusion such as the Gypsy Secretariat Foundation, RAIS Foundation for the Homelesss, and Ventillarte Association for immigrant children in Madrid.

Barbara Mahlknecht is a researcher, curator, and art educator. She is currently a lecturer at the Academy of Fine Arts, Vienna. Her work in research, curating, and art education strongly relates to feminist curatorial practices, socially/politically engaged art, the exhibition as performative space, and critical art education.

Iris Mendel is a social scientist and philosopher based in Graz, Austria. Her research interests include materialist feminism, feminist theories of knowledge production, and critical pedagogy. She is currently working at the Department of Political Science at the University of Vienna.

Monika Rogowska-Stangret is a lecturer and postdoctoral researcher at the University of Warsaw. She is the author of *Ciało: poza Innościąi Tożsamością. Trzy figury ciała w filozofii współczesnej [The Body: Beyond Otherness and Sameness. Three Figures of the Body in Contemporary Philosophy]* (2016) and "Of Other Spaces, of Other Times: Towards New Materialist Politics of Squatting" in *Avant* (2015).

Adelina Sánchez Espinosa is Senior Lecturer in English Literature and Gender Studies at the University of Granada. She is currently Scientific Coordinator for the Erasmus Mundus joint master's degree in Women's Studies and Gender in Europe and Principal Investigator at the University of Granada for the Gender and Cultures of Equality in Europe, a Marie Curie H2020 research and development project. Her current research focuses on textual and visual cultures of equality in Europe.

Esther Sánchez-Pardo is Professor of English at the Universidad Complutense, Madrid. She has published in feminist theory and comparative literature, with volumes including *Cultures of the Death Drive: Melanie Klein and Modernist Melancholia* (2003), and has co-edited *Women, Identities and Poetry* (1999), *Feeling the Worlds* (2001), *Ophelia's Legacy* (2001), and *L'Écriture Désirante: Marguerite Duras* (2015).

Erin K. Stapleton is Honorary Fellow in the School of Historical and Philosophical Studies at the University of Melbourne, where she also teaches Gender Studies. She completed her PhD at the London Graduate School at Kingston University in 2014.

INTRODUCTION

Beatriz Revelles-Benavente and
Ana M. González Ramos

In *Dispossession: The Performative in the Political*, Judith Butler and Athena Athanasiou (2013) critique contemporary society as predicated on a form of neoliberal crisis management which controls subjects based on economic and political premises, as well as moralistic ones. To disrupt this organizational structure, contextualized via universities, philosophical approaches, social movements (and other layers), Butler and Athanasiou propose dispossession as a way to critique recognition and the sovereign subject. Looking through different mass media such as television, internet, and newspapers, we can see many different examples of how this form of neoliberal crisis management is controlling and affecting subjects across the world. If we reflect upon the "flaring" migrant crisis in the Mediterranean (so described by the *New York Times*[1]), during which twenty migrants a day are killed while trying to cross from their country of origin to various points in Europe,[2] we can see a clear example of neoliberal world ordering marked by managerial practices controlling human bodies across frontiers. The number of women and children involved in the migration drama in the Mediterranean is rising gradually, at the same time that the urgency of war, violence, and poverty in their origin countries is growing. This ongoing and intensifying crisis of human migration places women's bodies in the center of the whirlpool: they are the object of trafficking, of harassment during migration, and sometimes of sexual slavery imposed by those who are smuggling them. The migrant crisis also leads to an ecological crisis, since this migration directly contributes to an erosion of coastlines and significant environmental deterioration.[3] On this occasion, the fact that a third of the world's population is migrating across one specific area and destroying habitat there is not a strong enough reason to implement regulatory mechanisms. The addition and overlapping of various types of crisis around our environment provokes what Butler and

Athanasiou (2013) have defined as the acclimatization of a population to insecurity and precarization related to vulnerability, anxiety, and illness.

This is just one of the many manifestations that contemporary crisis is materializing, and a very brief overview of just one specific case of neoliberal regulatory practice. An increasing political orientation to the extreme right in Europe is being enhanced, which only reinforces the aforementioned crisis that transversally affects politics, economics, the environment, feminist values, and education (to mention just a few of the many layers involved). Feminist theory and practice have been fighting against all of these injustices during their entire history; nevertheless, this change in the way knowledge is created and circulated, together with the ways in which hierarchical structures of power are permeating our socio-cultural material discourses, calls for new political strategies that can have an impact on the process while it is being materially enacted and before the results are manifested (Grosz, 2005). In a new era in which the capitaloscene (Haraway, 2016) is the controlling force of subjects (as controlled by the circulation of neoliberal capital), we need to find alternatives to work in and out of the system. bell hooks (1994) promotes the school as the beginning point for installing what we considered "lost" feminist values. With this book, the editors want to follow that premise in order to engage society with theory and teaching with learning, thus producing new forms of organizational practices both intergenerational and interdisciplinary, forms that become radically "response-able" (Haraway, 2008; Barad, 2010) through a politics of care for each other. New feminist approaches are emerging in order to promote a more horizontal approach to teaching, one in which teacher and students are decentralized to promote a co-creation of knowledge. Some examples of these approaches are feminist materialist teaching (Hinton and Teusch, 2015) or affective pedagogies (Hickey-Moody, 2016), approaches inspired by bell hook's transgressive teaching or education for freedom (hooks, 1994). The classroom has historically been a space of rebellion for students and teacher when they are mutually involved in the learning process, but at the same time teaching is often constructed through the reproduction of certain values that at times make it hard to materialize resistance.

The contributors to this volume follow a similar premise: they conceive of education as a central tool for freeing the subject from this neoliberal managerial crisis, and they follow this decentralizing notion of the process of teaching–learning in order to configure a gender pedagogy, or, as the title of the book announces, in order to begin teaching with a feminist politics of responsibility. The Teaching with Gender book series addresses the challenges and possibilities of teaching students about women and gender by discussing the pedagogical, theoretical, and political dimensions of learning and teaching. Teaching a feminist politics of responsibility nowadays means at the same time radically questioning racialized and sexualized epistemologies (Butler and Athanasiou, 2013) and acting against new conservative "rationality". This book aims to shed light upon three particular dimensions of the topic that will structure the book: first, by revisiting how we can reconfigure a feminist politics of responsibility "able to respond" (Haraway, 2008; Barad, 2007) or engage with contemporary crises; second, by conceptualizing crisis and explaining how it is transforming contemporary societies and affecting individual vulnerabilities and institutional structures; and third, by offering practical cases from different European locations in which crisis and responsibility have served to reformulate contemporary feminist pedagogies, altering curriculums, reframing institutions, and affecting the process of teaching and learning. The relevance of the topic cuts across many of the established feminist journals with recent special issues including "Gender and Crisis in Global Politics" (*International Feminist Journal of Politics*, 2013); "Responsibility and Identity Global Justice" (*Hypatia*, 2011); and "Feminism and the Politics of Austerity" (*Feminist Review*, 2015). Nevertheless, this volume asks: what kinds of feminist response are emerging in classrooms?

The editors of this book pursue the analysis of the challenges and look for the possibilities of teaching about women and gender through discussing the pedagogical, theoretical, and political dimensions of learning and teaching. We believe that in times of political crisis (as well as of environmental, of moral, economical, and of other kinds of crisis) a feminist intervention becomes essential to ensure social change and the preservation of women's rights. All in all, this book constitutes a plea for acknowledging not only the multiplicity present in the required areas of knowledge, as well as the necessity to produce relational patterns between them, but also for acknowledging the plethora of scholars defining the different approaches that might be taken into account when engaging theoretically and practically with feminism. Thus, the editors have decided to leave the book without conclusions in order to foster the debate that is being created and enhance the multiplicity that inhabits any act of resistance as an open door to different possibilities created by the contributors. Their chapters stir our reflection on political crisis, neoliberalism in the university, work discipline in intellectual professions, gender identity and technology management, and the use of resistance methodology in the classroom so that the fruitful debate that feminism is proposing can be highlighted.

Gathering the twelve chapters that compose this book, we consider that we have achieved a very useful feminist pedagogy for classrooms at the primary and secondary level as well as for spaces outside classrooms, in places like university departments or collective actions. We foresee our proposal as a very open one which can be reworked iteratively and opened up to explore new possibilities and strategies. Beginning from Donna Haraway's situated knowledges (1988), we believe this pedagogical knowledge is situated, and thus different chapters explore different countries (the United Kingdom, Spain, Poland, Portugal, and Austria), different types of crisis (economic crisis, neoliberal crisis in the universities, political crisis), and the context in which situated knowledges are being applied (universities, high schools, feminist collectives, or even different disciplines). Relying upon the situatedness of each context of study means orientating our research object and recognizing our non-innocent gaze, or as Olga Cielemecka and Beatriz Revelles-Benavente state, it means we must "depart from our own backyard" (Cielemecka and Revelles-Benavente, Chapter 2). Situating our pedagogical strategy prevents us from universalizing feminist ideologies and conceptualizations of gender and allows us to move towards a feminist politics of multiplicity, of openness, and of situatedness by focusing on local problems while retaining a global perspective.

Regardless of what we consider to be progress or regression in universities, hegemonic discourses, or normative cultures, what this book wants to demonstrate is how a feminist politics can be response-able for and with contemporary society in times of crisis, with these concepts differing according to each chapter. Far from pointing towards a relative definition of both, what the authors in this compilation show is the importance of contextualizing, or in Haraway's words *situating*, our work and concerns in order to find "provisional" solutions to urgent problems (Lykke, 2010). Thinking through solidarity and relationality, the contributors to this book aim at engaging with differing feminist pedagogies to pursue a multiple truth-reclaiming knowledge through different disciplines (film studies, feminist science studies at the high school level, feminist philosophy, art therapy, English as a foreign language, and arts). At the same time, this book is reinforcing the need to create independent studies of gender beginning with differing pedagogies. This will provoke tensions around what we mean by sex, gender, and inequalities by promoting an engaged confrontation with biased gender knowledge.

As previously stated, feminist researchers in this book adopt a situated position, which consequently means that most of the chapters are inspired by the work of Donna Haraway. However, the authors diffract (as in Barad's words of reading *with* each other instead of opposing each other) different approaches to Haraway's thought in the current state of permanent political crisis and from varied geographical European regions. According to one of our contributors, this diffraction is "[b]ased on the premise that the local and the global are not defined in terms of physical geography but exist simultaneously and constitute one another" (Sánchez-Pardo, Chapter 4). Globality and locality need to be mutually dependent on each other and intra-acting relationally, which is why one of the premises of this book, in basing chapters in different geographical locations in Europe, was to demonstrate a common need and a common premise that can be oriented despite the multiplicity of contexts that the book shows. Additionally, when in neoliberal times, the kind of subject engaged with these concerns is a knowmadic cognitive force (in Cielemecka's and Revelles-Benavente's words, Chapter 2) which traverses geo-political frameworks. Opening up this multiplicity with the variety of chapters encourages the need to observe problems locally; nevertheless, it does not prevent orientating our political strategies around a common goal, which is what gives our book its title: finding gender pedagogies able to produce a responsible answer for a political crisis from a feminist perspective. This is, following again Haraway's premise to avoid the "God Trick", in order to produce situated and, we would like to add here, *feminist* knowledges (a concept that is further explored in Cielemecka and Revelles-Benavente's Chapter 2).

The tools proposed by the contributors of this book comprise a wide diversity including negotiation, responsibility, relationships between differing women, sorority, alliances, and resistances to normative concepts such as the neoliberal "failure" which favors a free-labor market in academia. As Esther Sánchez-Pardo warns us in Chapter 4, feminism is not a secure ground, which means that moving towards a fixed identity can collapse its force. Thus, she looks into a pedagogy that enhances dialogue or allows for the co-creation of knowledges and curriculums in a context of high precarity, introducing concepts unknown in other regions of Europe such as "zero-hours contracts". These contracts manifest, at times, the precarity at public universities in which temporary contracts with a low charge of hours are favored above permanent contracts or positions, which not only promotes instability but also the difficulty of advancing in your academic career; something geographically situated but also expressed by Monika Rogowska-Stangret (Chapter 1), Ester Conesa Carpintero (Chapter 3), and Olga Cielemecka and Beatriz Revelles-Benavente (Chapter 2).

This book shows the complexity of the contemporary crisis, with its varied layers and manners of response and resistance: pedagogy, human values, solidarity, and the inclusion of new themes and identities. This crisis has encouraged feminist research to pursue a wide and varied vocabulary in order to build up a different political strategy able to face an anthropocentric society like our present one. This vocabulary has problematized not only issues such as the relation between teacher and student, but also the tension between the self and society (situated in universities and other areas of research) that often results in human illnesses such as anxiety (as Rogowska-Stangret and Conesa Carpintero reflect, in Chapters 1 and 3, respectively), as well as the conceptualization of affects as relational forces that make visible things initially appearing materially invisible, as expressed by Barbara Mahlknecht (Chapter 7) and Ángela Harris Sánchez and Adelina Sánchez Espinosa (Chapter 8).

As a consequence, at times the self relating with society as it is presented in this book is a vulnerable one, in Rogowska-Stangret's words (Chapter 1). Focusing on the vulnerability of the self in these neoliberal times, Rogowska-Stangret presents a relational subject who needs to share vulnerabilities in order to find companionship with others and survival in the accelerated academy, and argues through her definition of the ethics of this self via four "unruly edges" that will "reveal its relational character" that vulnerability is the basis for necessary feminist alliances (Rogowska-Stangret, Chapter 1). These unruly edges or movements towards unpacking the notion of the self have to do with its identity, its normativization and classification, the necessity to situate the self in time and space, and the self's recognition of social, political, economic, and environmental entanglements, all of which contribute to what the authors have identified as the spinal bones of a contemporary feminist pedagogy which are crisis, political strategy, responsibility, precarity, and care.

The importance of affects for the book is directly or indirectly related in all the chapters for two primary reasons. The first, as will be further explained later, is that care is one of the most important tools for our envisioned political strategy. We consider care as an intra-action that needs to be present in every feminist alliance as a strategic device helping feminist researchers and activists to practice generosity as part of our own development. According to Mahlknecht (Chapter 7), affects are appropriated by capitalism in order to use and abuse researchers, students, and all the actors partaking in contemporary society. Thus, reinforcing the politics of care explained by Conesa Carpintero (Chapter 3) serves as our material and discursive resource to fight contemporary social injustices. The second, already introduced by Mahlknecht's approach (Chapter 7), shows how affects are "a central aspect of contemporary culture and society", so they need to be approached "as a generic subject of study" (Mahlknecht, Chapter 7). If reconsidered in this way affects can be articulated as "the breaking apart from the way they have gradually become a socially accepted means of oppression and the empowerment of the very act of questioning them" (Harris Sánchez and Sánchez Espinosa, Chapter 8).

In addition, the editors of this volume consider affects to be (in)visible forces that materially relate different discourses of oppression that, when conceptualized within this pedagogical framework, can help to disrupt hierarchies of power. In this volume we are interested in the classroom because from primary school (as in Alexandra Cheira, Chapter 9) to postgraduate school and beyond, the classroom is one platform that enables political agitation and the learning and co-creating of knowledge. One of these invisible affective forces is the affect that relates teachers and students, and this book asks how bringing up the tension between teacher and students (already explored in other volumes of this series, e.g. "Teaching with Feminist Materialisms") might decentralize the role of the teacher and the position of the students as something other than containers of theory (as stated by Rosa Costa and Iris Mendel, Chapter 5).

Mahlknecht (Chapter 7) argues that education offers tools and methods to provoke "good" feelings and to channel "bad" feelings, a strategy that is also followed, though it is conceptualized differently, by Colman and Stapleton (Chapter 6). They conceive the classroom as a "safe space" and a "test laboratory" insomuch as teachers, together with students, co-create the type of knowledge that is being enhanced in the classroom. Focusing on students' feelings allows the creation of safe spaces in the classroom so that students can express their opinion freely and teachers can promote the generic skill of critical thinking without producing affective vulnerabilities in the classroom. Yet, in another vein, Harris Sánchez and Sánchez Espinosa in Chapter 8 focus on a relational approach to Ahmed's concept of happiness in order to reconstruct "knowledges from different positions and the role played in this process by a politic of social responsibility". Likewise, offering a multidimensional approach via three interviews with art therapy teachers, Harris Sánchez and Sánchez Espinosa (Chapter 8) look for an ethical gesture towards the other that implies an affective approach to the boundaries created within the classroom.

Bearing in mind how gender pedagogies need to be theorized in creative and innovative ways in order to engage with the complexity of the contemporary crisis (as stated above), some other chapters provide the analysis of feminist collectives (as in Verònica Gisbert Gracia, in Chapter 11) which could be considered exemplary for a classroom on social movements. Another example that can be used in the classroom that would decentralize the roles of teachers and students is Jessie Bustillos' analysis of self-presentation in social networking sites (Chapter 10). She describes how a student in the UK uses technology to resist surveillance of her gender identity, defining response-ability (Haraway, 2008; Barad, 2010) through social-networking sites by learning about sexuality, homophobia, and sexism in ways unavailable to her at school.

Regarding the position of the student, Colman and Stapleton (Chapter 6) offer a movement towards an appeal to the student's potentiality for consciousness of the political conditions of the screen media site; through the examination of the situation, the inhabitants of the screen, and their mediation the pedagogic screen narrative enables students to take up a responsive analysis in the first instance. Depending on the type and style of screen media experienced, the classroom can then diffract this reading into as many different possible positions as are conceivable within the medium's contextual and technological frameworks. This argues for the management of students' silences and opinions, which coincides with Alexandra Cheira's plea in Chapter 9 on deconstructing stereotypes (also in Esther Sánchez-Pardo, Chapter 4) to create safer spaces in which different opinions can be discussed. For instance, Cheira offers a reflection upon romantic ideas of relationships between Portuguese teens and shows how this can prompt a gendered type of dating violence against which she fights through a feminist elaboration of wonder tales in her classroom.

The political strategy that engages with the toolbox that is presented in this volume as a feminist pedagogy implies that "thinking-with, interrelationality, solidarity, and comparative cross-cultural analysis of power and oppression come to be major categories of analysis in any feminist-informed curriculum for today, in our current times of crisis" (Sánchez-Pardo, Chapter 4). Or, from the point of view of social movements, this political strategy has to do with women's alliances (as Verònica Gisbert Gracia, in Chapter 11), or with lived social relations (as Bustillo, in Chapter 11). Using Costa and Mendel's words (Chapter 5) we understand crisis as a "congestion of ongoing social contradictions, as contested processes that allow for new forms of domination as well as for new forms of critique and resistance". This is not a nostalgic or glorifying move towards a distant past (or in their words, a "golden past" of democracy or science, let alone of gender relations). It is rather the pursuit of relations instead of separations, entanglements between past, presents, and imagined futures, relations capable of breaking through crises with tools of care and of fighting precarity with feminist responsibility. In Conesa Carpintero's words, we would like to see the book as offering "the potential to engage with the connections between the exclusionary neoliberal scientific model and the well-being of academics and science itself, promoting the necessary debate around time and care, to create resistances and spaces that sustain life collectively in local and broader senses" (Chapter 3).

This book is conceptualized as a conglomerate of perspectives offering the reader many points of view and reflection to be used in classrooms with undergraduate and postgraduate students that move beyond their research topics. Contextualizing the chapters through time and space, disciplinary background, differing positions within and outside the academy, and differing – at times even contradictory – feminist stances, we endeavor to enact gender pedagogies able to respond to contemporary political crises. We invite our readers to engage with us in the adventurous enterprise of being a feminist researcher and to reinvent this book by putting it into practice, thanks to the suggested assignments that our contributors have kindly offered in order to present tentative curricula for gender pedagogical strategies. With this, we aim at fighting the precarity installed by the contemporary neoliberalism which "defines our existences, although always in articulation with social and political implications which redistribute unequal and differentiated strategies of *precarity* that are at once a material and a perceptual issue" (Gisbert Gracia, Chapter 11). Understanding teaching and learning as a precarious movement, these contributors depart from the school as a political site to encourage reflection upon the differences between realities and stereotypes.

To conclude, the editors of *Teaching Gender: Feminist Pedagogy and Responsibility in Times of Political Crisis* would like to thank ATGENDER, the European Association for Gender Research, Education and Documentation for their help during the process of editing and publishing this volume, as well as their confidence in us and their willingness when choosing this important topic. Thanks are especially due to Dasa Duhacek, Sara de Jong, Giovanna Vingelli, Adriano J. Habed, and Sveva Magaraggia for their invaluable help assisting with the process of making this book. Also, to the publisher, Routledge, many thanks for believing in our project from the beginning and for publishing this "Teaching with Gender" series for ATGENDER. Additionally, we would also like to thank Thomas Spitzer-Hanks for his labor as assistant editor during the first round of reviews, relieving our managerial tasks but also offering very valuable comments to improve the content of our book. We would like to thank the contributors of the book for their amazing chapters and their generosity with deadlines, suggestions, and many other parts of the process. Their promptness has been extremely helpful in carrying out this project. And, dear reader, please: help us to rework the contributions here in light of a different and hopeful future with social justice and responsible understanding.

Notes

1 www.nytimes.com/2016/05/30/world/europe/migrants-deaths-mediterranean-libya-italy.html?_r=0 (accessed October 9, 2016).
2 www.dailymail.co.uk/news/article-3703186/Dying-new-start-West-20-migrants-day-killed-crossing-Med-3-000-lives-lost-year-250-000-complete-trip.html (accessed October 9, 2016).
3 www.greenpeace.org/international/en/news/features/concrete-stranglehold/ (accessed October 9, 2016).

References

Barad, Karen, 2007. *Meeting the Universe Halfway: Quantum Physics and the Entanglement of Matter and Meaning*. Durham, NC: Duke University Press.

Barad, Karen, 2010. "Quantum Entanglements and Hauntological Relations of Inheritance: Dis/continuities, SpaceTime Enfoldings, and Justice-to-Come". *Derrida Today*, 3 (2), 240–68.

Butler, Judith and Athena Athanasiou, 2013. *Dispossession: The Performative in the Political: Conversations with Athena Athanasiou*. Cambridge: Polity Press.

Grosz, Elisabeth, 2005. *Time Travels: Feminism, Nature, Power*. Durham, NC: Duke University Press.

Haraway, Donna, 1988. "Situated Knowledges: The Science Question of Feminism and the Privilege of Partial Persepctive". *Feminist Sudies*, 14 (3), 575–99.

Haraway, Donna, 2008. *When Species Meet*. Minneapolis: University of Minnesota Press.

Haraway, Donna, 2016. *Staying with the Trouble: Making Kin in the Chthulucene*. Durham, NC: Duke University Press.

Hickey-Moody, Anna, 2016. "Affect as Method: Feelings, Aesthetics and Affective Pedagogy". In: Rebecca Coleman and Jessica Ringrose, eds, *Deleuze and Research Methodologies*. Edinburgh: Edinburgh University Press, 79–95.

Hinton, Peta and Pat Treusch, eds, 2015. *Teaching with Feminist Materialisms: Teaching with Gender. European Women's Studies in International and Interdisciplinary Classrooms*. Utrecht: ATGENDER.

hooks, bell, 1994. *Teaching to Transgress: Education as the Practice of Freedom*. London: Routledge.

Lykke, Nina, 2010. "Introduction". In: Nina Lykke, ed., *Feminist Studies: A Guide to Intersectional Theory, Methodology and Writing*. New York: Routledge, i–xii.

1

SHARING VULNERABILITIES

Searching for "unruly edges" in times of the neoliberal academy

Monika Rogowska-Stangret

Neoliberalism is one of the labels used to describe key factors that shape the contemporary world, its relations and institutions, its power structures and modes of subjectification (Foucault 2008 [2004]). Apart from Michel Foucault's work, which traced the points of emergence of the contemporaneity or the genealogies of a present situation through historical analysis, the humanities reveal many insightful analyses and studies of what neoliberalism stands for. The transformations that constitute the present moment are many, and they are approached from different perspectives that accentuate its various aspects: capitalism, "liquid times" and uncertainty (Bauman 2007), "control societies" (Deleuze 1995 [1990]: 177–82), "risk society" (Beck 1992 [1986]), or the "society of the spectacle" (Debord 2000 [1967]) among others. Those investigations coincide with reflections on the ways universities have transformed in the past two decades along neoliberal lines (Reading 1996, Slaughter and Leslie 1997, Pocklington and Tupper 2002, Côté and Allahar 2007, 2011, Nussbaum 2010, Collini 2012). Importantly, the debates concerning the crises of the universities are held from various standpoints, and the recognitions are all but homogeneous; to exemplify the intensity of those discussions let me mention Sara Ahmed's criticism (2015) of an article by Terry Eagleton published in the *Chronicle of Higher Education* (2015).

Today's academy, diagnosed as product-oriented, fast, competitive, and as imposing growing demands on individuals, is at the center of attention for the increasing number of scholars approaching it critically. More and more academics engage in discussions concerning life at the academy *per se* and do not restrict themselves to the narrow area of their expertise. In consequence, a movement devoted to introducing changes in a "slow academy" vein is emerging (Slow Science Manifesto (http://slow-science.org/), Berg and Seeber 2016). If the image of the "ivory tower" as a symbol of scientists' disengagement with practicality and reality was ever true, it was shattered in the mid-twentieth century by engaged intellectuals such as Jean Paul Sartre, Simon de Beauvoir, and Albert Camus. The crises that led to World War 2 and intensified afterward, especially socio-economic inequalities and divisions, proved that one of the key roles of an intellectual is to face reality and to treat theory as a "box of tools" (Deleuze and Foucault 1977: 208) with which one can meet the challenges of the surrounding world and unpack the power relations subtending them. In the neoliberal academy, though, using theory for practical aims reached its own limits and became paradoxical, due to the fact that it lost its critical dimension (Berg and Seeber 2016). What can be heard in the voices criticizing the neoliberal academy today is that science has become all too useful, too handy, too practice-and-product-oriented and as a paradoxical result, too distanced from the material conditions of knowledge production and too unconcerned about the material effects such useful science has on society and especially on subjects living the academic life (this is a point of criticism mentioned by "slow professors" and the slow science movement). Academics are flooded with self-help books that offer ways to succeed in learning how to manage one's time in a better and more effective manner, but they are not encouraged to problematize how this affects their lives, health, intimacy, relations, or bodies and how it influences education, democracy, and society (Berg and Seeber 2016, chapter 1).

On the one hand, neoliberalism (also at the academy) promotes individualism through advocating for new neoliberal virtues such as productivity, efficiency, and competition: "[t]ime management does not take into full account the changes to the university system: rather it focuses on the individual, often in a punitive manner (my habits need to be pushed into shape)" (Berg and Seeber 2016: 25). In response, academics offer solutions that are based on rethinking the potentials of collectivity (Berg and Seeber 2016, chapter 4, Mountz et al. 2015, Cielemecka and Rogowska-Stangret 2015). On the other hand, as Foucault points out, one of the tasks of engaged and critical thinkers is to trace modes of individuation, the ways in which power turns beings into individual subjects and in response "[w]e have to promote new forms of subjectivity through the refusal of this kind of individuality which has been imposed on us for several centuries" (Foucault 1983: 216). The slow scholarship movement also addresses the problem of how individuals are constituted as individuals, and the advice they offer on how to handle the accelerated academy as an individual (Berg and Seeber 2016, Mountz et al. 2015: 1249–53) is thought to stress the individual's role in systematic change, but also might be understood as efforts to alter modes of subjectification, because what is at stake is a radical change (this need for change is accentuated in different texts written from "slow" standpoints). What is lacking from the above-mentioned perspectives and what this chapter hopes to address is a more developed approach to the individual, a more advanced elaboration of how one is turned into a subject and what is elided from this process: what *does* matter in/about an individual and what *does not*. I aim at looking into how an individual might not only be a factor boosting neoliberalism in the academy, but also at describing approaches to subjectivity that might introduce ways to capture the subject that embrace its potential for resistance to neoliberalism. To achieve that I will look into the main points of criticism of the neoliberal academy with the aim to search for "unruly edges" (Tsing 2012) of individualization, zones where individualization reveals its seams and stitches and uncovers relationality as its *conditio sine qua non*. "Unruly edges" here are practiced as in Anna Tsing's essay, where she uses them to scrutinize "the changing practices of being human" (Tsing 2012: 145). To embrace these transformations I would like to offer a return to an ethics of the self as problematized by Michel Foucault (through his elaboration on the care of the self: Foucault 1988 [1984]), bearing in mind the question phrased by Judith Butler: "Under what conditions does self-poiesis become a relational category?" (Butler and Athanasiou 2013: 67). To answer this question, I will introduce the concept of sharing vulnerabilities, which derives its inspiration from the idea of "shared concerns" as described by Michael Hornblow in his essay entitled *A Sahara in the Head – The Problem of Landing* (2015) and from a feminist ethics of care.

Living a bodily academic life

In his lectures at the Collège de France, Foucault recognized a new right established in the nineteenth century: "the right to make live and to let die" that complemented the older right "to take life or let live" (Foucault 2003: 241). This shift demonstrates the change that occurred with respect to power's focus. The right "to take life or let live" was mainly concentrated on the issue of whether one deserves to live or not, and on *what* kind of activities may lead to death; otherwise one's way of life was outside power's interest, whereas "the right to make live and to let die" voices its concern chiefly about *how* subjects live and how much they can endure before they are "let die". Thus, "the right to make live and to let die" opens up the question of how this life is to be lived, and centers the notion of endurance. How much can we endure? How much can we bear? When and under what conditions does life become unbearable, unlivable, intolerable? Therefore, this shift marks the transition from "what" one does to "how" one does it. The change occurs with respect to what is perceived as the main object in power relations analysis, and the question of endurance proves to be one of pivotal importance for those living an academic life.

Testimonies of scholars prove that academics endure a lot just to be able to stay in the realm of academy (see Conesa Carpintero, Chapter 3). Moreover, they both and at the same time actively shape and maintain the conditions that inhibit their well-being, and are passively formed by institutional, organizational, and cultural demands, the tasks they are faced or flooded with, and the time pressures they are subjected to. They are capable of treading a fine line between staying active in the academy in wellness as in illness. To a large extent the state of being unwell is erased from the bigger picture of neoliberal research and higher education institutions, and thus material conditions of knowledge production are wiped out and considered less important than the goals and aims of these institutions. That is why Rosalind Gill stresses the need to "break the silence" and reveal the "hidden injuries of the neoliberal university" (2009: 228–44). Her conversations with colleagues and friends working in the academy uncover a grey sphere of illness (see Conesa Carpintero, Chapter 3) and suffering underlying official academic relations. Gill indicates problems such as: the lack of stability and the uncertainty of work at the academy, unpaid work, the 24/7 ideal of non-stop work, shame accompanying failures (like having one's text rejected by journal editors/reviewers or not being granted funding), and as a result of all of these, health issues, psychosomatic ailments, depression, and anxiety. Oftentimes it is not even problematized, partly because it is held to be normal. The sticky, stinking bodily dross is consequently wiped out as a necessary side effect.

This takes me back to the powerful keynote lecture presented by Nikki Sullivan at the conference *Open Embodiments: Locating Somatechnics in Tucson* entitled: *Somatechnics of Swallowing* (2015) and the potent mechanisms and dynamisms of physiology. The question of how much we can endure is here transformed into: how much can we swallow? The act of swallowing is depicted as a somatechnic that combines the natural gag reflex with the cultural ability to unlearn it: the more we swallow, the less we experience the gag reflex. Therefore, the political response would be to win the gag reflex back and to learn from the bodily impulses and instincts in order to form a visceral politics. On the other hand, Elizabeth Wilson points out that "the gag reflex itself may be attenuated" (Wilson 2004: 79); that is to say, the individual is not only forming the neoliberal system ideologically, but they are also attuning to it organically. Ideally, both swallowing/binging and vomiting would be performed smoothly without even the trace of gag reflex, so how can we win back the gag reflex if it can be erased to such a large extent? One possible answer to this question would be to simultaneously think organically, culturally, and psychologically. This may not seem a revelation, but given the scale of organic adjustments to the neoliberal academy and the bodily transformations individuals are subjected to, it might be a challenge to look into zones of organic attunements – into the literal "how" of "make live". What kind of organic life is possible? How does one define organically one's limits or one's "thresholds of sustainability" (Braidotti 2006: 5), taking into account the fact that psyche, culture, and biology are collaborating to such a large extent? Where are those limits, if the gag reflex is not enough?

To emphasize the organic aspects of life at the academy is also to come back to Foucauldian "make live and let die": to the questions of how to live, what a liveable life is, and how to endure the growing demands of the academy. Who will sustain "accelerated timeliness" (Mountz et al. 2015: 1237)? Who will fail, being organically incapable of increasing their speed? Not being able to keep up with what's called "fast science" makes one organically unfit to perform academic work. As Rose stressed in her essay *Slowly ~ writing into the Anthropocene*: "the culture of audit and surveillance is transforming us into zombies" (Rose 2013: 5). Rose's zombies are quite literal: they are placed precisely on the border between life and death, they batten on the living to derive their powers from them, and they are doing their job without sleep.

Sleeplessness, constant activity, the impossibility to be passive, inert, or idle are the key characteristics of neoliberal universities that serve as the ground for demands imposed on and by academics. The need for sleep, rest, not to mention the wish to laze around are turned into inadequacies, shameful flaws of character. "Would not less sleep allow more chance for 'living life to the fullest'?" (Crary 2013: 14). To sleep less and fuel relentless activity means to attune one's speed to the intensity and pace of neoliberal transformations, and to excite the ever growing appetite and unquenchable desires to achieve more, to make the most of one's zombie-like life. This attunement happens in multiple dimensions: organic, psychological, cultural, social, and demonstrates how far neoliberalism reaches, how extensive and in-depth it gets. But where to search for an ally if this body of ours (together with our psyche, plans, intents, wishes, dreams) is organically attuning to a neoliberal tempo?

One of the possible solutions might be to care – for oneself and for others – and to notice with care the signs of bodily unsettlement, the traces of imposing on the body the need to harmonize with a neoliberal pace and to abandon the body's gag reflex: "Self-care becomes warfare. This kind of self-care is not about one's own happiness. It is about finding ways to exist in a world that is diminishing" (Ahmed 2014). I understand the "diminishing world" as the world that speeds up to the extent that it is no longer possible to grasp differences, and this results in the fact that some do not have to insist that they matter, whereas others "have to insist they matter to matter" (Ahmed 2014). The recognition of the accelerated world and the divisions it tries to hide (including organic differences that are to be understood individually, and as such are normalized or treated as the side effects with which one should come to terms) is the first step to understanding care as preparing the space and time for response-ability/responsibility.

Response-inability and the crises of responsibility

The problem of responsibility in the "accelerated timeliness" of the neoliberal academy has from my perspective at least two major facets. First of all, the question arises: how do the neoliberal academy and fast science contribute to the life of future generations? Second, given the semantic nuances introduced by Donna Haraway and Karen Barad in transforming responsibility into response-ability, the issue of response – its definition and the conditions of its possibility – comes to the fore. Who is able to respond and – in particular – will future generations be able to respond? So in a way these two questions might be combined into one: who is invited to take part in a dialogue about the condition of the academy and the world in which it flourishes, and who is included in the sphere where the response might be given and heard? As Deborah Rose puts it: "[D]ialogue is a form of ethical practice amongst subjects (human and nonhuman)" (Rose 2013: 7). The problem of responsibility is precisely about the ethics of making a dialogue possible across spaces and times.

Isabelle Stengers, in her inaugural lecture at Vrije Universiteit, Brussels, calls for another science – slow science. She stresses the fact of her feeling "ashamed before those young people entering university with the hope of getting a better understanding of the world we live in. … Can we claim that what we are proposing them meets, or even vaguely meets, this situation?" (Stengers 2011: 5). To meet the futurity in the present is im/possible, the future is that which is to come, but has not yet emerged. However, to adequately recognize the situation we live in now might encourage awareness of the present situation, multilayered and ripe with times, speeds, im/possibilities, and intensities of life. It is accompanied by the effort to "activate the possible and not … describe the probable" (Stengers 2011: 1). With this Stengers is attempting to prepare a sphere of response-ability – to make it possible for students to respond to the ever changing world and to stop the zone of response-inability that is proliferating in times of academic neoliberalism. The same attempts are seen in the work of Karen Barad as she stresses the need to think science and justice, facts and values together to "practice science responsibly" (Barad 2012: 15), to face the commitment of young people to engage in science with the aim of making the world a better place to live and with the need to recognize how science affects the world.

To open up the space and time for response-ability means to put response-inability *in ability* and to think through the question of ability and inability in terms of agency on the one hand and, on the other, in terms of the very nature of response. Reconceptualizations of agency and response in new materialist scholarship by thinkers like Karen Barad, Elizabeth Grosz, or Brian Massumi destabilize hierarchical power structures, grasp the dispersed net of agency, and posit a notion of response beyond an anthropocentric paradigm. Barad specifies: "agency is for me not a matter of something somebody has but it's a doing, it's the very possibilities for reworking and opening up new possibilities, for reconfiguring the apparatuses of bodily reproduction" (Barad 2012: 17). Along these lines, ability becomes not an inner feature that enables or hinders action but an activity of searching for the possibilities to act under given circumstances. Thus, the question is not "can I not act?", but instead *how* to act. The task here would be to create conditions that encourage dialogue as a key ethical concept and to fight paralyzing and unjust circumstances. Response-inability resembles numbness in psychological terms, that is, a situation where one is convinced one is unable to undertake action, whereas in fact, this felt or experienced inability is caused by the collaboration of a constellation of heterogeneous factors overshadowing the possible and blocking movement.

Notably, response-ability (and putting response-inability *in ability*) should be grasped organically in order to give its *response* to how one attunes organically to a neoliberal pace and tempo. Thinking response-ability without taking into account its organic aspects might mean giving an inadequate response to neoliberalism, while an adequate response is successful because it manages to respond to the fact that neoliberalism becomes-with-bodies: organically, psychologically, culturally, socially, technologically, and simultaneously influences them by taking into consideration this complex interlacement of factors. To respond to this manifold phenomenon one needs to think response organically, biologically, socially, ethically, and politically.

Response, thought organically, combines organic reaction and organic interpretation. As Grosz reminds us: "[A]ll biological reactions require a mode of interpretation" (Grosz 2011: 238) and quotes Jakob von Uexküll: "[E]ven the simple reflex of blinking at the approach by a foreign body to the eye is no mere progression of a chain of physical causes and effects, but rather, a simplified functional circle, which begins with perception and ends with effect" (Uexküll 2010: 147). Massumi, analyzing animal play, also shifts response beyond human and consciousness-oriented conceptualizations as he observes that instinctive reactions are not automatic, they carry with them the potential to respond to changing environmental conditions, and thus the ability to improvise and invent. They embrace "a margin of maneuver" (Massumi 2014: 13) which opens up space for spontaneity, creativeness, and – indeed – response. This perspective might help us to put response-inability *in ability*. Linked analogically to the agency that is doing and "reconfiguring the apparatuses of bodily reproduction" (Barad 2012: 17), response is linked to action based on our organic, psychological, cultural, and social interpretation (indeed a reconfiguration) of the world.

Thought organically, response-ability challenges the process of individuation by providing an account of response-abilities as a multitude, as a swarm of re/actions that reconfigure the world on macro and micro scales. In this way the individual is "pushed to the extreme", revealing its seams and "unruly edges" in the sense that it uncovers the plethora of response-abilities, re/actions, re/interpretations, and re/configurations that sparkle at the – always provisional – borders of an individual. In ethical terms it is also important that response-ability is captured here beyond the anthropocentric paradigm, which means mobilizing human-non-human dialogue and relation.

Ethics of the self as a relationality

Response-ability as a form of dialogue or relation and – organically thought – as a factor reorganizing the individual, is an attempt to approach the neoliberal crises of the academy ethically. As such it reveals simultaneously the "unruly edges" of individuation, and therefore reworks one of the key concepts attached to the neoliberal framework. The ethics of the self that I am arguing for here is a struggle to address these issues.

By asking "Under what conditions does self-poiesis become a relational category?" (Butler and Athanasiou 2013: 67), Judith Butler is trying precisely to work out the way leading to grasping an individual, who creates and forms oneself, who cares for oneself, as a relational entity. This also introduces relationality to the ethics of the self and increases the motivation to think through the importance and role of relations in a process of individualization. To think individualization ethically and relationally is also a response I offer in this text to the neoliberal academy. In order to disarm the painful repercussions of neoliberal individualization one may be willing to look into how the self is produced – or better put – out of what it emerges. Self-poiesis – as demonstrated above in the elaboration on response-ability – is the relational category *per se*. It means that there are no conditions that "add" the relational aspect to the self, since it is relational from the start (as we have seen in the example of organic response). With reference to grasping relationality and the entangled character of the self, I argue here for an ethics of the self that consists of four tasks to be thought through, four acts of unpacking the self to be experimented with, or to put it differently: four attempts to search for the "unruly edges" of the self that will reveal its relational character. All those tasks, or – if you will – steps of self-unpacking are interconnected, one will not happen without all others.

First of all, consider unpacking the notion of the identity of the self. This task was probably initiated by Sigmund Freud (e.g. Freud 1923), whose notion of unconsciousness offered the concept of the self as non-transparent, not autonomous and dependent on hidden affects, emotions, and states. Thus, Freud presented the self as evolving around a central strangeness, as later developed by Julia Kristeva in *Strangers to Ourselves* (1991). To some extent this approach coincides with posthumanist tendencies that aim to manifest the human dependency on non-human, more than human, or beyond-human factors and present "human" as entangled with more-than-human words (see for example: Haraway 2003, Grosz 2004, Butler 2009, Alaimo 2010, Tsing 2012).

Second, I suggest unpacking the self with reference to how it might be normalized and classified. Ervin Goffman (1986) demonstrated that stigmatization and normalization act through exclusion and that what is classified as excluded from the image of a desirable body, self, or member of a group stays in the actual bodies, selves, or groups' members and causes various affective, psychological, and social effects. As Goffman states, we seem never to fulfil our own norms. Normalization therefore shows that we are imposing rigid structures on the self, but in fact the self eludes them. This again attests to the "unruly edges" of the self as a "boundary project": "boundaries shift from within; boundaries are very tricky. What boundaries provisionally contain remains generative, productive of meanings and bodies" (Haraway 1991: 201). "Self" might also be unpacked in terms of epistemological categories, following the works of Iris van der Tuin. How does the individual produce knowledge, right ways of knowing, a knowing subject, or canons of thought, and what kind of epistemological frames emerge there? To answer these questions, consider unpacking the normative power of classifications, because as van der Tuin notes, "a classification is not a neutral mediator but is thoroughly entangled with the work that it does" (van der Tuin 2015: 19). Revealing the classifixations, to use van der Tuin's term (van der Tuin 2015: 19–38), helps us understand the complex genealogies of the dynamics of today's theoretical approach and also the political load of classifixation-oriented thinking (thus hierarchical, dualistic, establishing categories opposing one another). It also demonstrates the knowing self as constantly challenging classifixations and canons.

Thirdly, unpacking the self happens through situating oneself in time and space, and thus through asking about one's own complex genealogies. Why do I believe in what I believe in? What are the roots of my worldview? Why am I inclined to this rather than that theoretical apparatus? How many entangled factors percolate through what I consider my identity? What is my class, ethnic, historical, geographical background?

Last but not least, I consider recognizing the complex entanglements of social, political, economic, and environmental factors and how one's decisions and actions impact the world as being important for self-unpacking. The example of such an investigation is provided by Stacy Alaimo and her introduction of a concept of transcorporeality:

> [M]atters of environmental concern and wonder are always "here", as well as "there", simultaneously local and global, personal and political, practical and philosophical. Although trans-corporeality as the transit between body and environment is exceedingly local, tracing a toxic substance from production to consumption often reveals global networks of social injustice, lax regulations, and environmental degradation.
>
> *(Alaimo 2010: 15)*

All the above-mentioned tasks reveal the complex constellations of relations that form what is considered "self". Moreover, they provide an image of the self whose borders are tentative and volatile. Relations between consciousness and unconsciousness, between what is hidden and what is uncovered, between human and more-than-human, between a mode of thinking and an act of normalizing, between theory and politics: the self emerges from those very relations as a mosaic of heterogeneous factors, as a zone of proximities, contacts, and disruptions, as a sphere of cacophony, as an assembly of multitudes "on the razor edge of non/being" (Barad 2012: 13).

This particular ethics of the self would not only aim at recognizing the complexity of entanglements and dependencies involved in the process of subject formation, but also at enabling the space and time for a dialogue – approaching relations ethically and with care. As Deborah Bird Rose puts it: "Dialogue is a form of ethical practice amongst subjects (human and nonhuman). … dialogue begins where one is, and thus is always situated; … dialogue is open, … the outcome is not known in advance" (Rose 2013: 7). Dialogue, response-ability organically enacted in our bodies, the self that is a stranger from within, the self that proliferates on its borders, the self that might be traced back and forward to reveal its relations with the past, present, and future – all this attests to the fact that the self is anything but fixed and sharp, and that it is – by its very nature – dialogical.

Bringing differences into an open dialogue is central to the ethics of the self also in terms of response-ability. This is precisely what boosts the possibilities to respond and react – outside of an anthropocentric paradigm – and what traces the possibilities of relations among human and beyond-human factors that interpret one another and respond accordingly.

Shared concerns – shared vulnerabilities

The emerging self (that which appears tentatively as a result of the four steps of self-unpacking mentioned above), perceived as a site of relations that are included in a dialogue, and hence in an ethical relationship, offers a way to reconsider subversiveness and radicality as a political stance along the lines of care. Victoria Lawson asks: "Instead of radical geography, how about caring geography?" (2009: 210) and the authors of "For Slow Scholarship: A Feminist Politics of Resistance through Collective Action in the Neoliberal University" shift this proposal to argue for slow scholarship as "cultivating caring academic cultures and processes" and "bringing attention to *how* we work and interact with one another" (Mountz et al. 2015: 1238).

As Michael Hornblow observes: "To play the subversive academic is still to adopt the guise of being for and against, to recognize and be recognized by the university" (Hornblow 2015: 232). The subversiveness of such a position is embedded in a critical approach that, as some have pointed out, "has run out of steam" (Barad 2012: 14). The need to consider care instead of radicality or, at least, together with it, is heard throughout feminist research – Karen Barad, Maria Puig de la Bellacasa, and other feminist researchers mentioned above are just a few examples of this recent shift or re-turn (as the ethics of care has an established tradition in feminist scholarship from the publication of the important book by Carol Gilligan, *In Different Voice: Psychological Theory and Women's Development*, in 1982). Care also addresses what is both within and beyond the academy, and thus it transgresses "the guise of being for and against, to recognize and be recognized by the university" and directs itself to the "unruly edges", to the precarious situatednesses on the borders of the academy that bifurcate with miscellaneousness. From the perspective introduced in this chapter, caring is enabled by the fact that selves share the conditions of the emergence of the "self". As Barad claims, "ongoing reconfigurings of the world are iteratively remaking 'me' " (Barad 2012: 23), and this establishes a common ground for every "me", for every self. The relations out of which the self emerges also form shared circumstances for remaking selves. The importance of relationality as a key term to think through the self is also visible in discussions that stress the need to undertake collective actions, to introduce changes together – changes that are not limited to the area of the neoliberal university but apply globally: "the time is ripe for radical change not just in our universities, but in creating solidarity among these different sectors and struggles across the globe" (Mountz et al. 2015: 1249). This collectivity stems from the self, reconsidered as an entanglement, as constellation, situatedness, and transcorporeality. The remaking of the self (as always already collective) offers what I reckon is a light of hope for rearranging the neoliberal university.

One gleam of hope would be to share concerns in the process of teaching–learning at the academy. As Hornblow suggests in developing his idea of shared concerns: "Where study becomes a lived endeavor, pedagogical encounters always affect and are affected by converging fields of practice, already diverging into the beyond where a field of forces feels the weight of the outside" (2015: 235). To share concerns would thus mean to keep the connections with the outside alive and to keep one's courage and passion for engaging with the outside awakened.

The second gleam of hope I see for the future would be to share vulnerabilities, thus not only uncovering the hidden injuries as suggested by Gill (2009), but also recognizing the fact that the injuries one experiences in the neoliberal academy, including bodily injuries and ailments, are the results of bodily plasticity, bodily responsiveness, and the organic capacity to comply with numerous incentives. The relationality implied in this bodily response-ability is responsible for both the eagerness and ease with which one enters into neoliberal relations (regardless of the harmful influence it might have) and the need to keep shared bodily vulnerabilities open, in a dialogue with no predetermined result and with awareness towards the here and there – local and global. Seeing individuality as unpacked selfhood, with tentative borders and in relations of sharing vulnerabilities, embraces the promise of the ethics of the self as sketched in this article: an ethics that enables caring for the relations out of which the self emerges, caring for the shared vulnerabilities.

Suggested assignment

Let me conclude with questions that, from the perspective of the ethics of the self here described, are worth rethinking and that were posed in this chapter:

*   How do we define "thresholds of sustainability" organically, given the collaboration of the body with the neoliberal academy?
*   What kind of visceral politics may be possible on the ground of organically rethought "thresholds of sustainability"?
*   What constitutes the "self" – consciously and unconsciously, in the background and in the foreground, and what kinds of factor are entangled within the self, permeate the self, and penetrate it?
*   How do we redefine response beyond an anthropocentric paradigm, thus activating the ability to respond and interpret in the more-than-human world?
*   How do we stay connected to the zone of shared concerns and shared vulnerabilities?

References

Ahmed, S. (2014), Selfcare as Warfare, http://feministkilljoys.com/2014/08/25/selfcare-as-warfare/.

Ahmed, S. (2015), Against Students, *New Inquiry*, June 29, http://thenewinquiry.com/essays/against-students/.

Alaimo, S. (2010), *Bodily Natures: Science, Environment, and the Material Self*, Indiana University Press, Bloomington.

Barad, K. (2012), Intra-active Entanglements: An Interview with Karen Barad by Malou Juelskjaer and Nete Schwennesen, *Kvinder, Køn & Forskning*, 1–2: 10–23.

Bauman, Z. (2007), *Liquid Times: Living in an Age of Uncertainty*, Polity Press, Cambridge.

Beck, U. (1992 [1986]), *Risk Society: Towards a New Modernity*, transl. by M. Ritter, Sage, Los Angeles.

Berg, M. and B. K. Seeber (2016), *The Slow Professor: Challenging the Culture of Speed in the Academy*, University of Toronto Press, Toronto.

Braidotti, R. (2006), The Ethics of Becoming Imperceptible, in: *Deleuze and Philosophy*, ed. by Constantin Boundas, Edinburgh University Press, Edinburgh: 133–59.

Butler, J. (2009), *Frames of War: When Is Life Grievable*, Verso, New York.

Butler, J. and A. Athanasiou (2013), *Dispossession: The Performative in the Political*, Polity Press, Cambridge.

Cielemecka, O. and M. Rogowska-Stangret (2015), Stigmergy as a Collective Research Practice, in: *Imagine There Were No Humanities ... Transdisciplinary Perspectives*, ed. by I. Ackermann, K. Chruszczewska, E. R. Janion, Á. Máté, and N. Obukowicz, Wydawnictwo DiG, Warsaw: 51–8.

Collini, S. (2012), *What Are Universities For?* Penguin, London.

Côté, J. E. and A. L. Allahar (2007), *Ivory Tower Blues: A University System in Crises*, University of Toronto Press, Toronto.

Côté, J. E. and A. L. Allahar (2011), *Lowering Higher Education: The Rise of Corporate Universities and the Fall of Liberal Education*, University of Toronto Press, Toronto.

Crary, J. (2013), *24/7: Late Capitalism and the Ends of Sleep*, Verso, London.

Debord, G. (2000 [1967]), *The Society of the Spectacle*, Black & Red, Kalamazoo, MI.

Deleuze, G. (1995 [1990]), *Negotiations 1972–1990*, transl. by M. Joughin, Columbia University Press: New York.

Deleuze, G. and M. Foucault (1977), Intellectuals and Power: A Conversation between Michel Foucault and Gilles Deleuze, in: M. Foucault, *Language, Counter-Memory, Practice: Selected Essays and Interviews*, ed. by Donald F. Bouchard. Cornell University Press, Ithaca, NY: 205–17.

Eagleton, T. (2015), The Slow Death of the University, *Chronicle of Higher Education*, April 6, www.chronicle.com/article/The-Slow-Death-of-the/228991/#disqus_thread.

Foucault, M. (1983), The Subject and Power, in: H. L. Dreyfus and P. Rabinow, *Michel Foucault: Beyond Structuralism and Hermeneutics*, University of Chicago Press, Chicago: 208–26.

Foucault, M. (1988 [1984]), *The Care of the Self. Volume 3 of The History of Sexuality*, transl. by R. Hurley, Vintage Books, Random House: New York.

Foucault, M. (2003), Society Must Be Defended. *Lectures at the Collège de France 1975–76*, ed. by M. Bertani, A. Fontana, transl. by D. Macey, Picador, Palgrave Macmillan, New York.

Foucault, M. (2008 [2004]), The Birth of Biopolitics. *Lectures at the Collège de France 1978–79*, ed. by M. Senellart, transl. by G. Burchell, Picador, Palgrave Macmillan, New York.

Freud, S. (1923), *The Ego and the Id*, many editions.

Gill, R. (2009), Breaking the Silence: The Hidden Injuries of Neo-liberal Academia, in: *Secrecy and Silence in the Research Process: Feminist Reflections*, ed. R. Flood and R. Gill, Routledge, London.

Gilligan, C. (1982), *In Different Voice: Psychological Theory and Women's Development*, many editions.

Goffman, E. (1986), *Stigma: Notes on the Management of Spoiled Identity*, Touchstone, New York.

Grosz, E. (2004), *The Nick of Time: Politics, Evolution, and the Untimely*, Duke University Press, Durham, NC.

Grosz, E. (2011), *Becoming Undone: Darwinian Reflections on Life, Politics, and Art*, Duke University Press, Durham, NC.

Haraway, D. (1991), *Situated Knowledges: The Science Question in Feminism and the Privilege of Partial Perspective*, in: D. Haraway, *Simians, Cyborgs, and Women: The Reinvention of Nature*, Free Association Books, London: 183–201.

Haraway, D. (2003), *The Companion Species Manifesto: Dogs, People, and Significant Otherness*, Prickly Paradigm Press, Chicago.

Hornblow, M. (2015), A Sahara in the Head: The Problem of Landing, *Inflexions*, 8, http://inflexions.org/radicalpedagogy/main.html#Hornblow.

Kristeva, J. (1991), *Strangers to Ourselves*, transl. by L. S. Roudiez, Columbia University Press, New York.

Lawson, V. (2009), Instead of Radical Geography, How about Caring Geography? *Antipode*, 41 (1): 210–13.

Massumi, B. (2014), *What Animals Teach Us about Politics*, Duke University Press, Durham, NC.

Mountz, A., A. Bonds, B. Mansfield et al. (2015), For Slow Scholarship: A Feminist Politics of Resistance through Collective Action in the Neoliberal University, *ACME, International E-journal for Critical Geographies*, 14 (4): 1235–59.

Nussbaum, M. C. (2010), *Not for Profit: Why Democracy Needs the Humanities*, Princeton University Press, Princeton, NJ.

Pocklington, T. C. and A. Tupper (2002), *No Place to Learn: Why Universities Aren't Working*, University of British Columbia Press, Vancouver.

Reading, B. (1996), *The University in Ruins*, Harvard University Press, Cambridge, MA.

Rose, D. (2013), Slowly ~ Writing into the Anthropocene, *TEXT* Special Issue 20: Writing Creates Ecology: Ecology Creates Writing, ed. by Martin Harrison, Deborah Bird Rose, Lorraine Shannon, and Kim Satchell, October 2013, www.textjournal.com.au/speciss/issue20/content.htm.

Slaughter, S. and L. L. Leslie (1997), *Academic Capitalism: Politics, Policies, and the Entrepreneurial University*, Johns Hopkins University Press, Baltimore, MD.

Stengers, I. (2011), Another Science Is Possible! A Plea for Slow Science, http://we.vub.ac.be/aphy/sites/default/files/stengers2011_pleaslowscience.pdf.

Sullivan, N. (2015), Somatechnics of Swallowing, keynote lecture at the conference Open Embodiments: Locating Somatechnics in Tucson, University of Arizona, Tucson, April 15–18.

Tsing, A. (2012), Unruly Edges: Mushrooms as Companion Species, *Environmental Humanities*, 1: 141–54.

van der Tuin, I. (2015), Classifixation in Feminist Theory, in: *Generational Feminism: New Materialist Introduction to a Generative Approach*, Lexington Books, Lanham, MD: 19–38.

von Uexküll, J. (2010), A Theory of Meaning, in: J. von Uexküll, *A Foray into the Worlds of Animals and Humans*, transl. by J. D. O'Neil, University of Minnesota Press, Minneapolis.

Wilson, E. (2004), Gut Feminism, Differences, *Journal of Feminist Cultural Studies* 15 (3): 66–94.

2

KNOWMADIC KNOWLEDGE PRODUCTION IN TIMES OF CRISIS

Olga Cielemecka and Beatriz Revelles-Benavente

Introduction

What does it mean to be a feminist researcher and teacher in times of neoliberal academic and capitalist acceleration? An initial answer might be to note that neoliberalism is "haunting" academia in multiple and mysterious ways that materialize knowledge into marketable commodities (Readings 1997). Athena Athanasiou defines this situation as a global phenomenon that sustains higher education via "a conception of knowledge as property, commodity, and a measurable commercial asset that needs to be immediately available to the managerial agendas of global business elites" (Athanasiou in: Butler and Athanasiou 2013, p 188). Even though more and more attempts to subvert this model are coming from many different areas of knowledge production, a certain state of crisis is denounced by academics, students, and mass media in general. We understand this crisis as one which concerns work security and labour conditions, the precariousness of both students and a large portion of academics, and a crisis of knowledge production in its being reduced to a commercial good available for the market. On the other hand, following Athena Athanasiou, we see the rhetoric of crisis, often used by politicians and authorities, as a powerful tool to design and remodel the university in a neoliberal fashion, renouncing the state's responsibility to support the university as it is no longer seen as a common good.

In this chapter we are interested in posing questions about the kind of knowledge and the kinds of relationalities that are being produced and reproduced in contemporary academia, given what we identify as the conditions upon which it hinges: the "knowmadism" of the cognitive work force and its precarity. Researchers' dancing with instability, which has become a condition of life and work for today's knowledge-production workers, and what seems to be an ocean of insecurities facing those workers, might seem frightening (to say the least); however, it is not the first time that feminism has faced society's relentlessness. Having an effect on contemporary times requires one first step, which is situating ourselves as Donna Haraway (1988) advised us many years ago. Thus we begin where we stand. The authors of this chapter are feminist academics, postdoc researchers, Eastern/ Southern European female bodies, precariously and peculiarly situated in the amorphous zone which stretches between, on the one hand, an academic positionality which is supposed to denote prestige, comfort, and disinterested intellectual passion and, on the other, a nomadic, anxious subjectivity of a present-day vulnerable cognitarian (Berardi 2005). We use our autobiographies and experiences as part of our "situated knowledges" approach, and briefly present the situation of higher education in our countries of origin. Departing from our own situatedness – a situatedness which is constituted by a paradoxical affective entanglement of empowerment and precariousness, privilege and *peripheralization* – we wish to look into the ways in which we can practice academia differently, both passionately and compassionately. Starting from our own backyard, we want to question the institutions and trouble the discourses and requirements they push forward in order to seek modes in which we can teach one another – in communities composed by students, researchers, teachers, and staff – to create and share knowledge, as well as to recognize the multiplicity of ways in which knowledge makes us.

Some of the questions that are pressing us as feminist researchers are: how can we recalibrate teaching/learning/sharing/producing knowledge practices from politically engaged and situated feminist positions? How can we enroot academic praxes in feminist values? And what are these feminist values to begin with? How can we reimagine our roles and responsibilities towards our students, colleagues, and epistemological communities? In the present chapter we offer a series of figures through which we would like to inquire into the multifaceted reality of feminist pedagogical and research experience in contemporary academia. Likewise, our objective here is to analyse and understand the reality of feminist researchers, especially those occupying intermediate job positions (between pre-doctoral and fixed positions), as well as offering strategies to produce acts of resistance to the rigid normativity present in the distribution of power, funding, and knowledge created at universities. We use Donna Haraway's concept of a "menagerie of figurations" to present a series of its ironic constituents: a melancholic accomplice, a cruelly optimistic failure, a slow academic, and an ir/responsible feminist. Each of them incarnates a set of coping strategies, positions, and realities emblematic of current-day academic work. The first section of the chapter diagnoses the situation of the university nowadays and identifies the characteristics of the crisis of the university. The following sections present a metaphorical cartography that is used as a guideline in order to detect how a feminist researcher can, individually and collectively, partake in shifting normativity through fluidity and the bending of categories. We look into the phenomena of complying, failing, and "slowing down" as different aspects of working in the academy. By tackling these aspects, we intend to shift their meaning in order to accomplish our political goals as feminist researchers. We link these aspects of academic work with questions of self-care, responsibility, and community. Finally, we elaborate a figuration of the "ir/responsible feminist researcher" or in other words, an academic engaged in the process of teaching and learning for a co-creation of material knowledge, knowledge engaged with/for society. We put forward the idea of ir/responsibility as an alternative to individualistic strategies of work in today's academia. We choose to write down the word "ir/responsibility" with a slash because it can thus reference both responsibility, i.e. various academic, administrative, scholarly responsibilities, and the sense of responsibility we feel towards our students, communities, institutions, and society, but also because it allows us to explore the subversive potentials of irresponsible acts.

Thinking through/with contemporary times: precarity and knowledge (re)production

There already exists a robust body of critically oriented work which looks at the conditions of knowledge production and at organizational practices in the contemporary academy (Williams 2012). The restructuring of the neoliberal university encompasses a plethora of processes including the reduction of state funding, the raising of tuition fees, increased dependence on contingent labour and external funding, and corporatization, with its metric-based accounting regimes and principles of productivity, efficiency, and high performance or "excellence" as guiding rules, all these ideas being transplanted into the university culture from the corporate world and modelled on its organization (Butler and Athanasiou 2013). "This restructuring", the authors of a collectively proposed manifesto *For Slow Scholarship* (further explored by Ester Conesa Carpintero in Chapter 3) tell us, "mirrors that of the global economy, a primary goal of which is to reduce the power of labor" (Mountz et al. 2015).

The crisis of the university takes many forms, and it is geographically and institutionally contextual, which means that it differs from country to country (at times even regionally) and from private to public. That is why we have decided to include our countries of origin in order to situate our argument more clearly. In the context of Poland, higher education is free and considered a common good. For decades it has functioned as a powerful mechanism to flatten class hierarchies. However, in recent years, voices calling for the elitization of university teaching have become more and more prominent, emerging as a response to the process of the devaluation of university diplomas and the reform of PhD programmes (a result of the acceptance of the Bologna scheme and its implementation in 2005). While students are being blamed for their increased sense of entitlement and their lack of engagement or even capacity to study for higher education, new generations of academics face significant deprivation. As a result of the reform PhD candidates are now thrown into a hybrid state between student and researcher, not fully considered either members of the student or academic research communities. In the aftermath of the neoliberal reorganization of university education, graduate programmes became a third cycle of study, imposing the readiness for life-long learning, flexibility, and constant mobility as necessary components of life and work. Here neoliberal individualization and the necessity to adapt ("publish or perish", "get a grant or leave") meet shrinking opportunities to finance one's research: both stipends and teaching assistant positions have become scarce and extremely hard to obtain. As an academic career entails more and more job insecurity and less financial gratification, it also becomes progressively more feminized (Michalak 2013). What is more, in the context of a conservative society such as the Polish one, and the ongoing backlash against feminism it is undergoing, feminist researchers face significant difficulties in carrying on their work (Grabowska 2013). Again, for many of us, the choice lies between, on the one hand, fighting for both symbolic (by which we mean a right to take up space within the academia) and material survival and, on the other hand, knowmadism[1] – a state of permanent impermanence tied to becoming a migrant cognitive work force.

In Spain, unlike in Poland, higher education has not been considered a common good, nor has it been free. Nevertheless, the Spanish government has always tried to dedicate part of the financial system to the granting of scholarships for those who have a lower income. Increasing the amount of money dedicated to these kinds of scholarship has always depended on the government in power (left-leaning governments offering more scholarships and having lower requirements for obtaining them, while right-leaning governments act in the opposite way). However, at the present time, the normalization of the discourse of "economic crisis" has worsened this situation. According to Athanasiou, "The current governmentality of 'crisis' is enacted by means of the production and management of truth. … 'Crisis' becomes a perennial state of exception that turns into a rule and common sense and thus renders critical thinking and acting redundant, irrational, and ultimately unpatriotic" (Butler and Athanasiou 2013, p 149). This is particularly interesting in the case of the managerial practices characteristic of the Spanish system. Taking into account the fact that the number of defended doctoral theses has increased by 40 percent during the economic crisis (Economic Crisis Increases Doctoral Thesis, 2015), we would like to contrast this with the number of postdoctoral contracts granted by public scholarships in Spain. In 2016, the Spanish programme Ramon y Cajal received 2,300 applications and their success rate was 8 percent (Data on Success Rate in Spanish Scholarships, 2016), without mentioning the distribution between humanities, social sciences, and natural sciences. This step is between a PhD and a fixed position, since it is one of the most prestigious scholarships in Spain, and it has significant consequences for those who want to pursue an academic career because, even if the number of doctors has increased, the number of postdoctoral fellowships available to them has decreased. Therefore, following an academic career inside the Spanish public system becomes an exceptional situation that allows a general discourse created around a false concept of common sense: following an academic career is almost impossible in Spain, which is why it is highly recommended to travel elsewhere for work. These pressures are further strengthened by the discourse already mentioned that refers to the knowmadic researcher, and the discourse of "excellence" that permeates the international career of any researcher. One illustration of this situation would be the declaration made by the Secretary of State in 2012: "In Spain, we have an excess of scientists" (Pascual 2012).

From our situated experience, as both of us are currently occupying non-permanent postdoc positions in Spain and Sweden, it seems to us that working conditions in the contemporary academy produce a peculiar state of what we have called "knowmadism" and precarity. Our take on "knowmadism" goes beyond what Moravec (2013) identifies as a new society and education and includes embodied experiences and personal stories of moving between places, universities, countries, and continents in search of research projects, job opportunities, professional networks, and in pursuit of "excellence". A knowmadic position – a concept which brings to mind nomadic figurations offered by Gilles Deleuze and Félix Guattari (1987) and by Rosi Braidotti (2011) – is a position of being peculiarly privileged by being granted a position from which to speak in order to create and re-create knowledge, but at the same time grants a position that bizarrely displaces and painfully uproots knowmadic subjects, both as migrant workers and as people working primarily in and with non-native languages (we could call this linguistic nomadism). On this account we find it essential to take a closer look at the affective-material conditions of knowledge (re)production within a "precarious" framework. "Precarity" can refer to a newly emerging social class whose work conditions, by choice or necessity, are characterized by a lack of predictability and security (Standing 2011), or to Judith Butler's (2004) concept of "precariousness of life" as an existential condition of vulnerability. Going beyond these approaches, we explore precarity in the hope of showing that, at times, it could also be seen as a site for empowerment and transformation. We thus follow Anna Lowenhaupt Tsing (2015, p 20) as she writes:

> Precarity *is* the condition of our times – or, to put it another way, what if our time is ripe for sensing precarity? … Precarity is the condition of

being vulnerable to others. Unpredictable encounters transform us; we are not in control, even of ourselves. Unable to rely on a stable structure of community, we are thrown into shifting assemblages, which remake us as well as the others. We can't rely on status quo; everything is in flux, including inability to survive. Thinking through precarity changes social analyses. A precarious world is a world without teleology. Indeterminacy, the unplanned nature of time, is frightening, but thinking through precarity makes it evident that indeterminacy also makes life possible.

Therefore, we need to pursue a differing kind of non-linear movement transversal to every sphere of life: political, academic, economic, etc. We need to pursue relationality to collectively co-create certain spaces able to resist normative, fragmenting, and nomadic isolation. The argument we present holds that knowledge production in times of crisis – be it produced by teaching practices or otherwise – requires respond-able acts (Haraway 2008, Barad 2010), a practice of responding and being responsible, to others as well as to ourselves (other authors following this argument in this volume are Monika Rogowska-Stangret, Chapter 1 and Ester Conesa Carpintero, Chapter 3).

Suggested assignment

- Go to GENERA's project webpage: http://genera-uoc.com/en/. There you will find information regarding women's situation in the Spanish academy. According to the report that you can find on that webpage, more women abandon scientific careers than do men (among many other interesting facts that can be found). Taking the GENERA project as an example, we would like to invite our students to reflect upon these questions: Can you think of a similar project in your country? If so, could you contrast them both (GENERA and your country), using similarities and differences regarding methodologies and figures?

Menageries of figuration and the subversive power of laughter

Even though the contemporary situation has not been defined as very promising for early career feminist researchers, we would like to move forward into what we consider feminist practices of making life more liveable. That is to say, we would like to discuss our political strategies or "toolbox" in order to practise resistance with/in this "university crisis" as identified in the introduction. In order to do this, we engage with Donna Haraway's concept of figuration. As Haraway explains, a figuration is where "sign and flesh are profoundly tied together" (1992, p 86). A figuration helps to explore the changing conditions of life, pointing to a need for new projects and understandings of the surrounding reality; it is about "resetting the stage for possible pasts and futures" (p 86). It is a mode of theory that works against "the more 'normal' rhetoric of systematic critical analysis [which] seem only to repeat and sustain our entrapment in the stories of the established order" (p 86). Ours is a menagerie of figurations (Haraway 2000, pp. 135–8) – to borrow once again from Haraway – whose aim is to contribute to what Butler and Athanasiou have identified as the "continuous political work of engagement" (2013, p 154) in order to find "proximity and reciprocity that demands a political analysis involved with modes of longing and be-longing in order to reconfigure sociality from a stance of left critical engagement" (p 154). In this chapter, we would like to propose this menagerie of figurations as a political strategy in order to resist the crisis. That is to say, we will explain different figurations (in the following sections) rooted in our own situated experiences, and describe what we are learning from other feminist thinkers and researchers.

A menagerie of figurations is different from a classification or taxonomy, concepts which feminist thinkers (e.g. van der Tuin 2015) have been wary of for decades in their work of exposing the patriarchal and imperialist bias which underlies them, denouncing the violence inherent to them, and mocking their pseudo-scientific veneer (Haraway 1991). But a menagerie of figurations is also different from a metaphor or a set of metaphors. Our menagerie is not pure, nor is it comprehensive, and it is not supposed to be. It hopes to tap into the subversive power of laughter – one which shakes the foundations of our thinking, as Foucault would have it. Hélène Cixous (1976) and Judith Butler (1999) taught us that laughter can be a tool for feminist politics. Donna Haraway showed us how to have fun as we style ourselves into tricksters and cyborgs. Through this menagerie we wish to learn how to laugh at our predicament and at ourselves. This is thus a collection of figures: they feature different ways of reacting to the pressing neoliberal conditions that hegemonic university governance structures are imposing on feminist researchers. We propose to define a melancholic accomplice, a cruelly optimistic failure, and a slow academic as the figures which lead us towards an ir/responsible feminist. The phrase "ir/responsible feminist" itself points to ways of creating connections and intergenerational alliances, ways of weaving academic communities together which generate and share knowledge.

Suggested assignment

* Think of a collective action organized at your university, one which you know of or were a part of. What were the arguments of the protesters?

Whose interests were represented? What kind of affinities emerged or could have emerged from it?

The melancholic accomplice, or, on being a good girl

Nikki Sullivan, in her 2015 lecture delivered at the *Somatechnics* conference at the University of Arizona (Sullivan 2015), suggested the "somatechnics of swallowing" as a diagnostic tool to talk about the contemporary conditions of work in academia (this can be further explored in Rogowska-Stangret, Chapter 1). We draw on Sullivan's idea as we portray the first figure on a map of the academic landscape: a melancholic accomplice. For a melancholic accomplice is the one who "swallows" – accepting what is unfair or hard to take, keeping quiet about it, pretending that it is all fine. Teaching, publishing, supervision, administration, reviews, applications, audits, and reports – she juggles all these tasks even if it is at the expense of her own well-being and the quality of her work. In a patriarchal system, trying to be a good girl, a valedictorian who can manage it all often seems like the only way to get validated. An accomplice suffers from the work-related ills of academic life: fatigue, insomnia, life/work imbalance, irritability, anxiety, guilt, and burn-out, but also she complies with them. An accomplice is the one who can relate to this joke: "The great thing about academia is the flexibility. You can work whatever 80 hours a week you want!"[2] At the same time, being an accomplice makes her sick to her stomach. In doing this she maintains and solidifies the status quo, while at the same time questioning it through the exhaustion of her own bodily capabilities: through the protest of her gut.

What kind of pedagogic relationship can a melancholic accomplice engender? Trying to meet the neoliberal expectations of productivity by proving that she can always perform to the highest standards, hiding the failures and the tiredness, flexing her muscles "Rosie the Riveter"-style to show that she is fine is a highly individualistic strategy which can only take her (and us) so far. In the long run, it impedes connection between students and fellow faculty/staff and reproduces what an anonymous academic called in a blog entry "a culture of acceptance" (Academic Anonymous Higher Education Blog Series 2014), in which exhaustion becomes an accepted and expected standard.

Is failure a way out?

The not-well-being of a melancholic accomplice makes us think of "failure" as an intrinsic part of being in academia, for students and researchers alike. Failure becomes institutionalized in order to produce those who deserve the position and those who do not deserve it. Not so long ago an academic CV of "failures" went viral (Haushofer, date unknown). Despite the enthusiasm around this coming-out as a failure, we could not shake off the impression that the "CV of failures" somehow taps into the fact that even in the art of failing, some of us are better than others, and that at the end of the day it is about how my failures turn out to be better than yours. This however only proves how nuanced the notion of "failure" is; especially if we treat it as a political concept and one which is closely linked to privilege or to a lack thereof.

What is it that keeps us going despite rejections, vain attempts, exhaustion, and frustrations? Perhaps the driving force behind it is what Lauren Berlant in her 2011 book called *cruel optimism*: a shaky promise of getting a good job once we have a degree in hand or of having a successful academic career in the future. In Berlant's own words: "A relation of cruel optimism exists when something you desire is actually an obstacle to your flourishing" (2011, p 1). There is however another way of understanding failure to which we wish to point. Jack Halberstam writes that "under certain circumstances failing, losing, forgetting, unmaking, undoing, unbecoming, not knowing may in fact offer more creative, more surprising ways of being in the world" (2011, p 2). Following this claim, we suggest that "being a failure" may be seen as a crucial device for resisting and rebelling against the forms of exploitation and relationality which we are expected to reproduce under the neoliberal paradigm. A "failure" here stands as a figure of unlearning: unlearning the ways in which things are supposed to be, the business-as-usual part of our work, the biases, the hierarchies and the canons, and the taken-for-granted. It is also about disrupting the relationship between productivity and excellence, and between frustration and rejection; it is about resistance to the pressing neoliberal demand to produce more. An affirmative, accepting reading of failure and the ability to laugh at our failures can help grasp a positive moment within our academic practices in what seems to be the unpromising moments of frustration, tiredness, boredom, and even unprofessionalism. A figuration of failure encompasses ambivalent elements: expectations, ambitions and aspirations, neoliberal politics, professionalism, excellence, academic standards, but also acceptance, understanding, bodily needs, self-care, and sympathy. What would it mean if we allowed ourselves and others to fail? Would it open possibilities of empowerment and solidarity? Can we imagine that happening?

While pointing to failure as a practice of resistance, we also see the limits of this discourse. The embodiment of failing does not materialize as a relationality but rather leads to isolation and shame which then eats us up from the inside. Reworking these affects should be an important part of feminist academic praxes, through care directed at ourselves and others, and through building and strengthening communities and networks which can help accept and overcome failures. In the idea of the ir/responsible feminist we come back to these ideas, as we show a necessity for taking risks (which means risking failure) in order to build new feminist affinities from within our research and pedagogical practices.

Slow academic: one possibility?

In recent years, there have been more and more voices calling for a different, more sustainable metabolism of academic work. A "slow academic" comes into being as an embodied response to material conditions of knowledge production in today's academy, becoming the next figuration to be added to our menagerie. Inspired by the "slow food" movement, which opposes fast, low-quality food culture on aesthetic and ethical grounds, the movement for slow science (Slow Science Academy 2010, Stengers 2011, Bird Rose 2013, Mountz et al. 2015) seeks alternatives to the acceleration of the current-day academia with its fast-paced scholarship, calling instead for a slow-down in order to think and digest, share, explore, and relish. Deborah Bird Rose writes: "Slow is a movement toward quality over quantity, toward connection rather than fragmentation, and toward ethical mutualities rather than self-interest alone. In relation to scholarship, slow is a movement toward thought and attention" (2013, p 6). In a similar tone Maggie Berg and Barbara K. Seeber in their *Slow Professor Manifesto* "advocate deliberation over acceleration. We need time to think, and so do our students. Time for reflection and open-ended inquiry is not a luxury but is crucial to what we do" (2016, p x). The Slow Science Academy's slogan sums up these approaches quite well when they write: "*Bear with us, while we think*" (2010).

While slow academics speak in unison when advocating freedom to take time, they vary in responding to the question of how to do that. Problematically, many of the answers they provide focus on individual strategies, such as turning off your email, "just saying no" (Pyke 2011, pp. 85–7), or even a two-speed research: a strategic "fast" research track which secures funding renewal and a slower, more mindful, quality-oriented one. In this we see the slow scholarship movement displaying a tendency to slip into a reparative mechanism conducive to the perpetuation of the neoliberal paradigm. This is precisely where a feminist intervention is necessary: to oppose "slowing down" as a strategy to be more productive with "slowing down" as a path towards a collectively conceived critical resistance. Being a feminist is not about being comfortable, but about acting as a trickster and a killjoy; instead of taking it easy, we see our role as vehemently disturbing the status quo.

Suggested assignment

- Our last assignment has to do with the "Slow Science Manifesto". Please read the Manifesto at http://slow-science.org. Could you think of how this manifesto would apply, depending on different positions of privilege within academic structures? What are the promises and traps of "slowing down"? Could you think of strategies for slowing down which could be used in everyday life and research practice?

An ir/responsible feminist

The emergent calls for slow academia encourage us to offer yet another figure of doing university differently, namely, that of an "ir/responsible feminist". This figuration opens up the following questions: for what or whom are we responsible in our teaching and research praxes? What is the subversive potential of irresponsibility? To what or whom should we respond or refuse to respond? The ir/responsibility of feminist pedagogy and scholarship, as we envision them, rests in blurring the boundary between the private, the public, and the theoretical. An ir/responsible feminist moves between and confuses her roles and capacities – as a teacher, mentor, evaluator, friend, feminist comrade, companion, and activist. This idea of ir/responsibility is further informed by the concept of *response*-ability as it is theorized by Karen Barad. According to Barad, *response*-ability means "to respond, and be responsible, to take responsibility", it "is by necessity an asymmetrical relation/doing, an enactment, a matter of *différance*, of *intra-action*, in which no one/no thing is given in advance or ever remains the same" (2010, p 264). It includes taking into account and being accountable towards the other and their needs, but also towards ourselves. Thus it takes up the idea of care as much as it does the idea of self-care. This "response-ability" should not, however, be confused with "responsibilization" understood as "the appeal to personal responsibility as a flight from social responsibility in the discourses of neoliberal corporate purposes, struggles, and responsibilities, only individual risks, private concerns, and self-interests" (Butler and Athanasiou 2013, p 105). Quite the opposite, it is also about being unresponsive to the dominant power regimes, neoliberal requirements, and hierarchies in a refusal to listen to them and reproduce them in our praxes.

The figure of the "ir/responsible" researcher is also in dialogue with Donna Haraway's plea to become "respond-able" (2008, pp. 19–27, *passim*), that is, to care and practice respect. Following Haraway, we discern the task of feminist researchers' respond-ability in their capacity to take the risk to act from within a particular "situatedness", embracing partiality of perspective, supporting local struggles, giving up hegemonic positions granted to us in our capacities as evaluators, supervisors, or university instructors, and sharing privilege. For a feminist researcher this entails engaging with a specific phenomenon and looking for differing engagements to solve it. That is to say, moving away from abstract structures and, instead, looking for local instances of realities. Far from falling back into the universalizing and objectifying gesture of a "God Trick" (Haraway 1988), what Haraway is suggesting is to move forward to political agitations in a specific context, taking a micropolitical approach to our contemporary society by entangling with it instead of distancing from it. We denounce the discourse which normalizes crisis, treating it as an excuse to cut funds and withdraw financial support from the humanities. This discourse, we claim, serves as a device which homogenizes the kind of knowledge being produced, in other words becoming a certain "God Trick", as Donna Haraway would have it.

Ir/responsibility is a permanent movement in which locality and globality conflate, traversing generations, disciplines, and discourses in order to pursue feminist political goals. A feminist researcher we envision may at times be "cruelly optimistic", but first and foremost she is hopeful, as in Felicity Colman's manifesto, understanding "hope as a device signalling the transversal rupture to the operations of global capitalism, and providing a collective moment for appreciating historical materialism and for taking stock of political positions" (Colman 2010, p 388). In the course of figuring out and reconfiguring our menagerie, we point to generosity, response-ability, care, and affirmation as the feminist values which we wish to embrace and promote in our feminist knowledge (re)production practices. It is in these values that we see ways of overcoming the logics of scarcity – the paucity of resources such as university positions and funds, and the cut-throat competitiveness and jealousy which it gives rise to – and we object to these logics as they are destructive of our teaching/learning communities, thwarting their growth and stalling their members' creativity.

"Exteriority within": ir/responsible feminism in academic practices

We would like to further complexify the traditional terms of academic responsibilities in favour of a feminist "ir/responsibility" through the idea of being "in" and "out" of the traditional academy. This movement of "in/out" (Hemmings et al. 2015) dislocates traditional configurations of space and time because it not only entails working in and out of the academy, but also in and out of the traditional scientific canon, in and out of traditional research funding schemes, and even in and out of our traditional theories. Ir/responsibility involves putting oneself at risk as one reduces distance (distance between instructors and students, between ourselves and what we teach, between academia and a larger social reality) while also making connections possible. In a similar vein, Clare Hemmings suggested pursuing this movement of "in/out" of the academy in the roundtable discussion "Feminist Toolkit for Survival of Young Researchers" (2015). We consciously aim at confusing academic roles as educators, evaluators, mentors, authors, etc., by reclaiming spaces of co-creation and collaboration. This means engaging with the emotional state of being comrades and pursuing generosity by looking for these spaces *in*, *out*, and *in-between*. Ir/responsibility rests in becoming "porous" researchers and compassionate companions for our students and fellow scholars. We urge the subversion of normative common sense by opening new spaces not only in the academy, but also in scientific journals, conferences, the streets, etc. This builds upon a risk already well acknowledged by many feminist researchers: being left out of the system. However, that is why we also persist, staying "in", because we need to keep on tricking the academic system from within. As Butler claims, "we urgently need to recover and reclaim the uncommodifiable unconditionality of the university, although it is worth remembering that universities have always been places of power … So there is also a question about what exactly is to be reclaimed here" (in Butler and Athanasiou 2013, p 189).

Taking into account that we can only respond to specificities in order to avoid the before mentioned absolutist position of a "God Trick", what we pursue here is a position "in/out of the academy" and an "exteriority within" to encounter those borderlands in which acts of resistance become materialized. By acting from the "exteriority within" the norm, we are able to engage with the academic system while creating interventions in this very system in order to disrupt it in an iterative way, a way which would open spaces for forming and developing critical interventions. This is what John and Jill Schostak define as radical research: "raising questions that make the powerful feel uncomfortable, even threatened. … this political dimension (that) suggests the possible overthrow of previously stable ways of knowing, thinking, believing, acting" (2008, p 1; see also: Revelles-Benavente, forthcoming). This is an "ir/responsible" process insofar as we need to adjust our projects to a norm in a first stage, and then subvert that norm in the second stage in order to create our own patterns. In order to understand what this would mean for feminist pedagogy and research, let us reflect a bit more upon what Barad means by "exteriority within". In her words (Barad 2007, pp. 176–7),

> Agential separability presents an alternative to these unsatisfactory oppositions [exteriority vs. interiority]. It rejects the geometries of absolute exteriority or absolute interiority and opens up a much larger space that is more appropriately thought of as a dynamic and ever-changing topology. More specifically, *agential separability* is a matter of *exteriority within phenomena*.

Therefore, if we follow this premise, we find that situating feminist pedagogies and research within the phenomena that we explore in this chapter, i.e. changes in knowledge production paradigms largely conditioned by know-madism and the precarity of cognitive labour, frees our framework from opposition to the system we are engaging with, but by means of diffraction rather than reflection. That is to say, knowing the outcome of the current situation is impossible. The only thing that we are certain about are regular patterns and structures in force that are constructing it, and therefore we channel our acts of resistance into particular situations. Nevertheless, we do not yet know what the outcome of incorporating these practices into the academic system will be. This entails breaking with logics of direct causes and direct effects, and instead looking for intra-actions between these different engagements. Thus, at the limits, at the porous border, at the "in/out", we can locate our responsibility, not our responsibilization, fostering our hope for better conditions of life for future researchers, without any guarantees.

Conclusion

With this chapter, we wanted to identify those alliances that go beyond identities, recognitions, and generations. Departing from our own backyard as early-stage feminist researchers, and learning from our colleagues who taught us about the type of hope needed, we have summarized the currents that move in and out of what a traditional researcher is. We also wanted to engage with differing practices to resist and "re-exist". That is, we wished to rethink how to resist mercantilized ways of teaching and the production of homogenized knowledges that hierarchize not only the kind of knowledge that we produce, but also the very conditions of life. Nevertheless, we also want to "re-exist" them, that is, to reinvent them, to go beyond them by engaging with, by diffracting, by being in and out of the academy.

"To put oneself at risk, risk oneself (which is never one or self), to open oneself up to indeterminacy" (Barad 2010, p 264), "porosity" and ir/responsibility, while being prerequisites to teaching and to learning from others, amounts to a capacity to be limitless, to generously engage with everyone in a horizontal way, in a willingness to transform the very processes of teaching, peer reviewing, mentoring, and evaluating and the economies which currently underpin these. By offering the idea of ir/responsibility we tried to envision compassionate companionship and precipitate other possible ways of pursuing feminist affinities. We believe that in changing the dominant patterns of relating to one another and dominant ways of doing things in academia, we can open up political resistances against a system that wants to silence critical thinking and creative knowledge.

Acknowledgement

Some research has been carried out thanks to the Spanish project funded by the Ministerio of Economía y Competitividad of the Spanish government, also funded by the European Union. It is framed within the GENERA project (FEM2013-48225-C3-1-R), "Promoting a more inclusive and competitive knowledge economy", conducted by Dr. Ana María González Ramos.

Notes

1 We develop the concept of "knowmadism" independently from John Moravec and his concept of "knowmad society" (see: Moravec 2013). Moravec defines a know-mad as "a creative, imaginative, and innovative person who can work with almost anybody, anytime, and anywhere. Industrial society is giving way to knowledge

and innovation work. Whereas industrialization required people to settle in one place to perform a very specific role or function, the jobs associated with knowledge and information workers have become much less specific in regard to task and place" (Moravec 2013: 79).

2 This and many similar memes/jokes can be found in this digital community, which mocks the contemporary situation in academia based upon the facts described in this chapter. To see these examples and many others visit: http://academicssay. tumblr.com.

References

Academic Anonymous Higher Education Blog Series, 2014. "There is a culture of acceptance around mental health issues in academia", 1 March. Available from: www. theguardian.com/higher-education-network/blog/2014/mar/01/mental-health-issue-phd-research-university [Accessed 1 September 2015].

Barad, Karen, 2007. *Meeting the Universe Halfway: Quantum Physics and the Entanglement of Matter and Meaning*. Durham, NC: Duke University Press.

Barad, Karen, 2010. "Quantum Entanglements and Hauntological Relations of Inheritance: Dis/continuities, SpaceTime Enfoldings, and Justice-to-Come". *Derrida Today*, 3 (2), 240–68.

Berardi, Franco (Bifo), 2005. "What Does Cognitariat Mean?" *Cultural Studies Review*, 11 (2), 57–63.

Berg, Maggie and Barbara K. Seeber, 2016. *The Slow Professor: Challenging the Culture of Speed in the Academy*. Toronto: University of Toronto Press.

Berlant, Lauren, 2011. *Cruel Optimism*. Durham, NC: Duke University Press.

Bird Rose, Deborah, 2013. "Slowly ~ writing into the Anthropocene". *TEXT* Special Issue 20: Writing Creates Ecology and Ecology Creates Writing, eds. Martin Harrison, Deborah Bird Rose, Lorraine Shannon, and Kim Satchell. Available from: www.textjournal.com.au/speciss/issue20/Rose.pdf [Accessed 7 July 2016].

Braidotti, Rosi, 2011. *Nomadic Subjects: Embodiment and Sexual Difference in Contemporary Feminist Theory*. New York: Columbia University Press.

Butler, Judith, 1999. *Gender Trouble: Feminism and the Subversion of Identity*. New York: Routledge Press.

Butler, Judith, 2004. *Precarious Life: The Powers of Mourning and Violence*. London: Verso.

Butler, Judith and Athena Athanasiou, 2013. *Dispossession: The Performative in the Political: Conversations with Athena Athanasiou*. Cambridge: Polity Press.

Cixous, Hélène, 1976. "The Laugh of the Medusa". Transl. K. Cohen and P. Cohen. *Signs*, 1 (4), 875–93.

Colman, Felicity, 2010. "Notes on the Feminist Manifesto: The Strategic Use of Hope". *Journal for Cultural Research*, 14 (4), 375–92.

Data on Success Rate in Spanish Scholarships, 2016. Blog, 20 June. Available from: https://juandelaciencia.wordpress.com/2016/06/20/algunos-datos-y-estadisticas-de-los-jdc-y-ryc/#more-1770 [Accessed 23 June 2016].

Deleuze, Gilles and Félix Guattari, 1987. *A Thousand Plateaus*. Transl. B. Massumi. Minneapolis: University of Minnesota Press.

Economic Crisis Increases Doctoral Thesis, 2015. Press article, 5 June. Available from: www.20minutos.es/noticia/2481236/0/tesis-doctorales/aumentan-desde-inicio/crisis-economica/ [Accessed 23 June 2016].

Grabowska, Magdalena, 2013. *Between Gender Studies and Gender Ideology. Gender Education in Poland*. Warsaw: Heinrich Boell Stiftung. Available from: https://pl.boell.org/sites/default/files/downloads/Magda_Grabowska_gender_education.pdf [Accessed 6 September 2016].

Halberstam, Judith/Jack, 2011. *Queer Art of Failure*. Durham, NC: Duke University Press.

Haraway, Donna, 1988. "Situated Knowledges: The Science Question in Feminism". *Feminist Studies*, 14 (3), 575–99.

Haraway, Donna, 1991. "A Cyborg Manifesto: Science, Technology, and Socialist-Feminism". In: D. Haraway, *Simians, Cyborgs, and Women: The Reinvention of Nature*. New York: Routledge, 149–81.

Haraway, Donna, 1992. "*Ecce Homo*, Ain't (Aren't) I a Woman, and Inappropriate/d Others: The Human in a Post-Humanist Landscape". In: Judith Butler and Joan Wallach Scott, eds, *Feminists Theorize the Political*. New York: Routledge, 81–101.

Haraway, Donna, 2000. *How Like a Leaf: An Interview with Thyrza Nichols Goodeve*. New York: Routledge, 135–8.

Haraway, Donna, 2008. *When Species Meet*. Minneapolis: University of Minnesota Press.

Haushofer, Johannes, date unknown. CV of Failures. Available from: www.princeton.edu/haushofer/Johannes_Haushofer_CV_of_Failures.pdf [Accessed 1 June 2016].

Hemmings, Clare, Mia Liinason, and Katrine Smiet, 2015. "Survival Kit for Young Researchers: Getting Funded, Getting Published". Roundtable discussion in *9th Feminist European Research Conference: Sex and Capital*, 5 June, University of Lapland University of Lapland, Rovaniemi, Finland.

Michalak, Dominika, 2013. "Studia doktoranckie w Polsce – łatwo zacząć, trudniej skończyć". 11 March. Available from: https://noweotwarcie.org/tag/ uniwersytet/ [Accessed 6 June 2016].

Moravec, John, 2013. "Knowmad Society: The 'New' Work and Education". *On the Horizon*, 21 (2), 79–83.

Mountz, Alison, Anne Bonds, Becky Mansfield et al., 2015. "For Slow Scholarship: A Feminist Politics of Resistance through Collective Action in the Neoliberal University". *ACME: An International E-Journal for Critical Geographies*. Available from: www.academia.edu/12192676/For_Slow_Scholarship_A_Feminist_Politics_of_Resistance_through_Collective_Action_in_the_Neoliberal_University [Accessed 1 March 2016].

Pascual, Alfredo, 2012. "La secretaría de: ía de Estado de Investigación: 'En España sobran científicos'". Press article, 7 June. Available from: www.elconfidencial.com/sociedad/2012-06-07/la-secretaria-de-estado-de-investigacion-en-espana-sobran-cientificos_253768/ [Accessed 1 March 2016].

Pyke, Karen, 2011. "Service and Gender Inequity among Faculty". *Political Science and Politics*, 44 (1), 85–7.

Readings, Bill, 1997. *The University in Ruins*. Cambridge, MA: Harvard University Press.

Revelles-Benavente, Beatriz, forthcoming. "Affecting Feminist Pedagogies: Performing Critical Thinking in the Relation between Social Networking Sites and Contemporary Literature". In: Edyta Just and Wera Grahn, eds, *Adventurous Encounters*. Newcastle: Cambridge Scholars Publishing.

Schostak, John and Jill Schostak, 2008. *Radical Research: Designing, Developing and Writing Research to Make a Difference*. London: Routledge.

Slow Science Academy, 2010. "Slow Science Manifesto". Available from: http://slow-science.org/slow-science-manifesto.pdf [Accessed 1 June 2016].

Standing, Guy, 2011. *The Precariat: The New Dangerous Class*. London: Bloomsbury Academic.

Stengers, Isabelle, 2011. "Another Science Is Possible! A Plea for Slow Science". A public lecture delivered at Faculté de Philosophie et Lettres, Université Libre de Bruxelles, 13 December. Available from: https://threerottenpotatoes.files.wordpress.com/2011/06/stengers2011_pleaslowscience.pdf [Accessed 1 January 2016].

Sullivan, Nikki, 2015. "The *Somatechnics* of Swallowing", lecture delivered at the *Somatechnics: Open Embodiments: Locating Somatechnics in Tucson* conference, 17 April, University of Arizona, Tucson.

Tsing, Anna Lowenhaupt, 2015. *The Mushroom at the End of the World: On the Possibility of Life in Capitalist Ruins*. Princeton, NJ: Princeton University Press.

Tuin, Iris van der, 2015. *Generational Feminism: New Materialist Introduction to a Generative Approach*. London: Lexington.

Williams, Jeffrey J., 2012. "Deconstructing Academe: The Birth of Critical University Studies". *Chronicle of Higher Education*, 19 February. Available from: http://chronicle.com/article/An-Emerging-Field-Deconstructs/130791/ [Accessed 1 April 2016].

3

(NO) TIME FOR CARE AND RESPONSIBILITY

From neoliberal practices in academia to collective responsibility in times of crisis

Ester Conesa Carpintero

Introduction

In recent years, new managerial practices enacted jointly with cutbacks have affected the environment of collegiality, the well-being of academics, and their time and capacity to engage with social problems. Thus, it is important to pose the following question: Who is able to respond? Who is able to take on responsibility? The aim of this chapter is to delineate a possible answer to these questions by exploring the effects of the neoliberal academy from a gender perspective, and to delve into the ethics of care as a potential approach to analyse and find applications to address this phenomena.

Firstly, this will require us to discuss new managerial practices and the rise of austerity politics in Western countries, with specific attention to the Spanish context and to the effects of these political practices on the well-being of academics. Secondly, I reflect on the intersection of these practices and their effects with gender, talking then about gendered embodied effects, especially in relation to time and care issues. A parallel with women's health is made, reflecting on one common illness among women nowadays, fibromyalgia, helping us to connect the macro and the micro level and to promote politicization.

Afterwards, I expand on the questions raised about the politics of responsibility (who is able to be responsible) in the academic context, but also in a broader sense. To approach these questions I use Tronto's concept of an *ethics of care* (regarding *attentiveness*, *responsibility*, and *privileged irresponsibility*) to reflect on the delicate ethical position of academics around time, care, and availability to respond.

I finally end with a critical approach to the initiatives that aim to challenge the new managerialism in academia and its accelerated pace. The

Slow Science movement, "La Désexcellence", the Accelerated Academy, and Feminist Slow Scholarship will be outlined as potential tools to approach the politics of responsibility, taking into account care and time. A summary and conclusions about the appropriation of the concept of care as a political notion are developed at the end of the chapter.

New managerialism and austerity in academia: effects on academics' well-being

The introduction of the new managerialism in academic institutions has produced important changes affecting academic careers and experiences. Following Rosemary Deem, new managerialism "refers both to ideologies [sic] about the application of techniques, values and practices derived from the private sector of the economy to the management of organisations concerned with the provision of public services, and to the actual use [sic] of those techniques and practices in publicly funded organisations".[1] In universities and other scientific institutions, new managerial practices were implemented in the mid-1990s, and became more widespread during the 2000s in Western countries, and have caused academics to place more focus on research (and output), high-impact publications, patents, more internationalization and transference, and providing and managing external funding.[2] The weight and responsibility in the provision of resources is more and more placed on individuals that have to manage their own revenue that, in turn, is directly related to their research output and publications. Another important feature of these practices is that academic outcomes are regulated by external measurement and evaluation through audits – agencies of quality assessment – that "may be largely finance-driven".[3] At the same time, this means "more subtle self- and peer-regulation" based on individual performance, as Deem notes.[4]

In parallel, or perhaps as part of the same neoliberal drift,[5] austerity politics have affected universities and research centres in many countries through cutbacks in funding. For example, in the case of Spanish universities, the budget was reduced to 1.388 million euros from 2010 to 2013, which has meant a loss of 3,500 teachers.[6] Universities have thus tended to have a greater teaching workload for fewer personnel, altering in turn the quality of the education received. This teaching load is often carried by people in lower positions with precarious contracts, and this might constitute "one source of gender inequality", because in many cases these positions are more likely to be held by women. In Spanish public universities the percentage of women filling these lower positions during the 2013–14 course was 43 percent. However, the stable and more highly paid positions, which are held by civil servants, are 35.4 percent occupied by women. Regarding full-professor positions women comprise only 20.7 percent.[7] Recently, what has constituted a major preoccupation for many Spanish academics is that no new stable vacancies are being opened due to crisis cutbacks and *rationalization*,[8] creating a bottleneck situation with many people waiting for an assignment. This context contributes to creating hostile academic environments characterized by competition and discomfort. Moreover, the precariousness of these lowest positions tends to hinder research development and promotion opportunities.

Thus, the shift on the demands of academic careers "in times of crisis" implies an intensification of the workload in a highly competitive environment while academics are also suffering the effects of precariousness. Social relations and individuals are being damaged by this climate and by the recurrent challenges of meeting intensified expectations of achievement, accompanied by losses such as the sense of collegiality and love for scholarship, as Morley or Baker highlight.[9] The long-hours culture has been extended with academics experiencing a lack of time in their lives, as has been acknowledged by many researchers.[10]

Some of these studies point at the damage thus done to the well-being of academics, forming bodies in their psychic-physical dimension as bodies that experience anxiety, exhaustion, feelings of precariousness, guilt, obesity, or back problems, as Shahjahan and Walker both report in studies based in the United States.[11] Morley's findings relate "numerous stories of occupational stress, illness, alienation, fear and resentment" under the audit culture in the English academy, and suggest that the distress, low morale, and fatigue she detected could be connected to what she calls the "micropolitics of quality".[12] Andrew Sparkes' paper gives a fictional autoethnographic account of how these embodied effects are generated through acts and thoughts that are part of daily academic life in the United Kingdom.[13] His account gives consistency to the description of the health dangers that great numbers of academics face as a consequence of the scientific system embedded by the managerial model of the audit culture. Moreover, recent surveys in the United Kingdom report a high increase of mental health problems among members of the academic community, surveys with astonishing results that need to be carefully interpreted.[14]

Rosalind Gill and Maggie O'Neill talk about fast academia in relation to the increasing pace of academic life regarding the intensification of work and its relationship with measurement and *marketization*, also stressing the physical and psychic consequences.[15] Following Hartmut Rosa's framework of "social acceleration dynamics",[16] Filip Vostal highlights that the temporal tension between the increasing workloads of academics and the relatively constant amount of available time "might have particularly misfortunate implications – for social environment, human relations, mental health and well-being".[17] In the final section of this chapter I will elaborate a bit more on his account of the "accelerated academy" but, for the moment, what can we learn about these academic dynamics in the Western world by thinking them in terms of gender? The following section focuses on the intersections between these pressures and gender issues that lead to a discussion of gendered embodied effects, women's health, and the problem of decontextualization.

Gendered embodied effects, women's health and depoliticization

Mountz et al. (2015) stress that "the effects of the neoliberal university are written on the body" – calling them embodied effects – and that they "are felt more by some bodies than others" following gendered, classed, raced, and other axes such as the ability-disability paradigm.[18] Women, for instance, show harmful embodied effects such as exhaustion and stress, as well as shame, guilt, and paralysis or mental health problems such as depression, anxiety, or isolation.[19] In their paper "Sleepless in Academia", Acker and Armenti focus on detrimental embodied effects mainly in those who were experiencing motherhood, but also in women experiencing other situations.[20] They note that these pressures and the concomitant deterioration of research trajectories lead women to experience internalized feelings of never being "good enough" or smart enough, accompanied by a stronger internalized need to follow the rules "because they have to prove themselves worthy".[21] Important factors such as care and time are gendered,[22] so women are forced to deal with clashing roles, having to juggle and to make hard decisions about social relations, care, and work in ways that often result in tension or guilt, as Ana M. González Ramos and Núria Vergès (2013) state.[23] Following Schulte, Mountz et al. (2015) say that "Globally, women are more likely than men to report chronic stress and the feeling that life is out of control because their time is "contaminated" by multiple and conflicting responsibilities".[24] From their own experiences – Mountz et al. (2015, p 1245) use as empirical data their own quotes in their paper – an interesting issue emerges: "it is partly my own fault for not learning the art of saying no",[25] which suggests an exploration of gendered issues around difficulties establishing limits and being always ready to give support, of caring for others, together with the so-called "stereotype threat".[26]

Academics tend to say that academic work is a "passion", but more women tend to talk about sacrifices and suffering regarding the impossible equilibrium in their work-life balance due to gendered roles, as Susana Vázquez and Mary Ann Elston's study points out. Vázquez and Elston give a stark demonstration of this idea in the words of a woman researcher who states "my life is gone", talking about the sacrifices she has made in order to pursue her successful career.[27] In a project with which I am connected, GENERA,[28] a woman who had to work very hard over two years said "I can erase those years", because during that time she had had no time for herself. She had to achieve more than men in similar circumstances, without credited authority in her leadership position until she achieved "objective" merit. Another woman, currently in her second postdoc position, said that her life is "an excel sheet" with respect to the difficulties of planning her life, conjugating the end of one grant and the beginning of another, the age of pregnancy, maternity leave, and the elaboration of publications. She also reported the increase of these difficulties when having to coincide with her partner's next career step – her partner is also a scientist – and her own future in science, which lacks continuity due to the scarcity of positions in the next tier – a tier that she considers is only reserved for "top researchers" – so she is now planning to abandon her research career. Other women in our study highlight the importance of holding stable positions so they are able to have external help such as paid care services, which are less affordable for those in lower positions. They also stress the importance and good fortune of having family support because they do not live far from their relatives and these relatives are available to help them; this begs the question of how women (and men) in lower positions and/or lacking family support are able to remain in academia, and it also raises this question: is "success" in one's academic work a question of individual merit? In a survey conducted by Heather Menzies and Janice Newson about time and stress in academia, the authors report higher rates in women than in men of "practically all the indicators of stress" (sleep deprivation, new allergies or food sensitivities, short-term memory loss, problems concentrating, stress in personal relationships, and isolation).[29]

We can find some connections between the damage that the neoliberal academy does to female academics and one of the most prevalent illnesses among women nowadays, fibromyalgia, which affects women disproportionately: 75 percent to 90 percent of fibromyalgia sufferers in Western countries are women.[30] This so-called "invisible illness" has created controversy in the medical community and has been redefined multiple times during the last century, but there is a general agreement around the symptomatology.[31] In a study where women with fibromyalgia were asked about the symptoms they experienced, they reported pain and fatigue (in 98 percent of the cases) and, among other symptoms, difficulty concentrating, loss of strength, and memory problems (from 92 to 90 percent of the cases), and feeling anxious and depression (87–86 percent).[32] While these are some of the most common symptoms of fibromyalgia, what is most significant, perhaps, is that when they were asked about the most important causes they believed produced the illness, they identified as the first three stress or worry (74 percent), overwork (55 percent), and accident or injury (55 percent).[33]

While we cannot display these connections without further research, we can be aware of and alert about them, especially taking into account the tendency to explicate these kinds of symptoms through essentializing explanations such as "these are women's issues". As Pujal and Mora (2015) say, there is an "epistemological concealment of the feminization of malaises"[34] and they consider that "The effect is that the labour malaises constructed as feminine diseases, finish to be considered, from the androcentric hegemonic perspective that assess the labour health, as an illegitimate malaises, dubious, alien", and which entails the pathologization and the medicalization of femininity.[35] Pujal and Mora also underline the importance of taking into account the role of broader social contexts such as "crisis" and the neoliberal drift in the health system, which have to be considered in an analysis of academic labour practices.

Nevertheless, these harmful effects on the well-being of both men and women are not problematized nor explained in relation to their context: they are neither related to new neoliberal organizational and economic approaches, nor are they related to gendered power relations;[36] instead they are depoliticized and individualized. As Gill (2009) and Sparkes (2007) say, academics tend to mask these harmful effects or think they are their own fault,[37] while scientific policies and institutions are not taking action, continuing to expect from individual academics a greater output with fewer resources.

Additionally, when it comes to mental health problems such as depression, anxiety, or other symptoms that make everyday life hard to handle, the stigma operates for both men and women but, again, these problems are more often considered to be "feminine" based on gender stereotypes.[38] For example, in men these embodied effects are often hidden due to the expectations of their gender role – in this case, not showing vulnerability – as the study carried out by Rosaleen O'Brien and her colleagues shows (2007).[39] Thus, not only do gendered power relations make it more difficult for women academics to do their work, but gender roles also essentialize and depoliticize their suffering. Moreover, these kinds of illness are mainly treated with antidepressants and anxiolytics that can create addictions and have side effects,[40] instead of being addressed as broader social problems. It seems that there is not a serious concern about the effects of the neoliberal academy, either in relation to gender, class, social status, or race.[41]

All in all, this might stir us up to think about the relationships among academics' work overload and work environment together with their bodily well-being, and their connections with health and gender, as well as the intersection of other inequalities. We would say that such an entanglement[42] suggests interdisciplinary connections between fields of knowledge. A wider and contextualizing "biopsychosocial" approach for the health-care system has been championed, at least since the Beijing Conference in 1995, as shown by this powerful definition of women's health: "Women's health involves their emotional, social and physical well-being and is determined by the social, political and economic context of their lives, as well as by biology".[43] This definition and point of departure provides a gender-sensitive and non-medicalizing perspective that challenges the bio-psycho-medical paradigm that pathologizes, psychologizes, and individualizes people, especially women.[44]

These harmful effects might imply exclusions in academia raising two specific questions: which bodies are able to pursue scientific careers? And regarding science policies and institutional practices: who cares? The next section will be focused on the care and responsibility that academia and academics are facing in this context.

Time, care, availability, and responsibility

With the managerial demands and austerity politics resulting in sickness and exclusion, we have no time to care for ourselves, to care for others (meaningful persons that already sustain us in a wider notion) and to care for the world. The responsibility to engage with a myriad of phenomena needs to be acquired by all members of society. But how can we be involved in social change if our lives are characterized by the fight against time, by our trying to improve our productivity in order not to be fired or by our trying to care for our closest meaningful persons or even for ourselves? How can we get involved in a devastating number of urgent issues, such as the refugee crisis or the infertility of the soil, with no *care time*?[45] With no stable positions, with the pressure not to be forgotten in the scientific universe, how can feminist politics engage with responsibility? As O'Neill (2014) points out, neoliberal changes in academia "reduce the possibilities for critical analysis amidst growing bureaucratisation and measurement", since time is what is most needed to create spaces for interpretation, reflection, and dialogue.[46] She emphasizes as well that these pressures interfere with the need to create mental space and symbolic abstract thought to confront the situation. Menzies and Newson (2008) also reflect on the time needed to think and for deep, reflective reading and in-depth conversations.[47] So, the time needed to care for the students, to engage with them in social issues, in and outside the classroom, or to transform the class into an *act of resistance*, as Beatriz Revelles (2015) notes,[48] is delicately pushed to its limit.

Responses to these questions might entail working with the concepts of *care*, *attentiveness*, *responsibility*, and *privileged irresponsibility* from the framework that Joan Tronto developed in 1993. In 1990, Berenice Fisher and Joan Tronto defined care in a very meaningful way:

> On the most general level, we suggest that caring be viewed as a species activity that includes everything that we do to maintain, continue, and repair our "world" so that we can live in it as well as possible [sic]. That world includes our bodies, our selves, and our environment, all of which we seek to interweave in a complex, life-sustaining web.[49]

Afterwards, Tronto (1993) elaborated an "ethic of care" that recognizes care as an integral concept that destabilizes the idea of autonomy (the self-made man) in order to better support ideas of interdependency and vulnerability, and that claims to displace care from the periphery (or private space) to the "centre of human life".[50] She displays care widely to operate with the concept analytically[51] and then develops an "ethic of care" in order to include it as a political and philosophical notion. For Tronto, this entails ethical elements[52] on which I focus.

The notion of *attentiveness* implies the recognition of a need to be cared about, and therefore, the recognition of others. Ignorance can be unintentional, but for Tronto, it might also be inattentiveness. Without falling into a normative vision of an ethic (or a morality),[53] what is interesting in Tronto's reflection is the idea of ignorance as a built-in social structure and as the attitude of being "not willing to listen": "That caring has been so obscured in our current accounts of society helps to explain how the process of inattentiveness operates", so we need caring to be more central in social and political life.[54] Regarding *responsibility*, Tronto (1993) explains that responsibility requires constant evaluation, and differs from *obligation* because the former is embedded in a set of implicit cultural practices that can become political and a matter of public debate, rather than formal rules or promises related to duties of the latter. Responsibility to care is "something that we did or did not do [that] has contributed to need for care, so we must care".[55] However, she argues for a "flexible notion of responsibility" taking into account its different meaning "depending upon one's perceived gender roles, and issues that arise out of class, family status, and culture, including cultural differences based on racial groupings".[56] As *privileged irresponsibility* Tronto understands that the privileged can "ignore hardships they do not face dividing up responsibilities";[57] she also explains this notion as the caring needs of some being "more valued" and being met more completely than those of others in relation to the distribution of power in society; this dynamic being how privilege works.[58] Care is socially constituted as the work of the least well members of a society, work done by groups traditionally excluded from the centres of power.

In the case we are concerned about, we might say that academics as agents are in a complex position, having no time and suffering the effects of institutional pressures on their bodies. This means that the ability to respond and to be responsible is limited. Those who implement managerial and austerity politics have remained *inattentive* when faced with the need for care. These politics, forged in global scientific competitiveness, do not recognize *others* (in this case academics) and their needs (their well-being). We can distinguish here two moments: first, the moment when these policies are going to be implemented (*to care about* the consequences of an action), and afterwards, the moment in which there should be an *assessment of its functioning*. Therefore, we could say that those in power positions lack *attentiveness* about their *responsibilities*, responsibilities that need to be in *constant evaluation*. They have remained *ignorant* (ignorance as "not willing to listen") of the critiques of the damages produced in the well-being of academics, as well as of the quality of research and teaching itself; not being *responsible* has become a matter of public debate, as we will see in the next section. Care as a political notion is defined culturally, but those who implement these policies are not outside the social problematic they have created; perhaps it is more precise to say that they are embedded in and reproduce neoliberal individualism that reinforces care as something private that is gendered, classed, and raced. Thus, being in a position of power, they perform *privileged irresponsibility*.

As Clarke and Knights (2015) point out, academics, in turn, also have to engage themselves with ethical subjectivities to counteract and resist individualist careering strategies and to deal with the duplicity of their roles.[59] This point is also made by Menzies and Newson (2008) who note that, on the one hand, academics are bringing these changes on themselves without awareness and under the effects of stress, but, on the other hand, academics also embrace a "series of seemingly innocuous individualized ad hoc survival strategies".[60]

Nevertheless, these claims can reinforce some harmful embodied effects by adding more pressures, creating guilt, discordant feelings, and other tensions that might lead to mental health problems. Moreover, the situation differs for those who are in lower, precarious positions marked by a lack of stability from the situation of those who work in stable positions, though every position suffers different kinds of pressures. This problematic might be better approached by raising a strong corpus of forces against this neoliberal drift, such as more research about it, but also more affective and political networks and better interpersonal support among academics. More awareness of the problems associated with neoliberal drift and coordinated action for solving them is also necessary. This is what *to care for* and *being cared for* might mean for *all* academics: to create space and time for care to foster the *availability of the processes of response and responsibility*. This can lead us to understand that care requires application in a broader and more emphatically political sense.

Thus, to care and to create spaces for responsibility is a shared matter. At this point, if those who design, implement, and assess these managerial policies do not respond and do not take on responsibilities, academics need to stop and ask what allows for the availability to respond, and question what the availability of a process of care and responsibility, intertwined with power relations, actually means. Having to respond and be responsible for *feminist politics in times of crisis* means to stop for a moment, think critically and create spaces of availability to engage with the problems that affect us as a community, as well as broader ones, acknowledging that some positions *can respond* more than others. Creating spaces of availability means to create time to organize and sustain life collectively in a broader sense – students, colleagues, vice-chancellors, policy-makers, citizens – and perhaps this is our greatest responsibility as academics in our different positions. Our sense of precariousness can make us turn to individualism to survive in this hostile environment, or it can lead us to collectively engage in order to create better scientific institutions, to care broadly in responsibility with other axes of exclusion, and to create time for care.

Suggested assignment

- In groups, think about and discuss the concept of responsibility, regarding power relations and the distribution of privilege in connection to local and to broader social issues (look for examples where you can find yourself involved). After that, think about and discuss the role of the notion of care in these examples.

Time to think and time for care: "slow science", or repoliticizing exclusionary practices of the neoliberal academy

The concept of "slow science" began with an essay written by Eugene Garfield in 1990 called "Fast science vs. slow science, or slow and steady wins the race".[61] This text draws on a claim for time and resources needed for science and its discoveries, as well as for the relationships and pressures of the media, public opinion, and the political, thus challenging ideas of the genius and of serendipity. Interestingly, Garfield was one of the founders of the Institute for Scientific Information, the Science Citation Index, and the Journal Citation Reports, among other citation databases.[62] The topic of slow science is revitalized by Lisa Alleva in 2006, who published a letter in *Nature*, basing her claims on the slow food movement and arguing that scholars need to "savour the rewards of slow science".[63] Alleva also argues for a "slow science" in order to address what she believes is damaging the basis of scientific enquiry, and in doing so she is perhaps the first to acknowledge the damages instability wreaks on the self of academics: "I may not be here in six months, twelve months, two years, but I am not going to work 100 hours a week to try to attain the elusive goals of my own grant, my own lab, perhaps even tenure".[64] A famous manifesto, published by German scientists in 2010 and called the Slow Science Manifesto, argued that science needs time to think, to read, and to fail.[65] However, the Slow Science Academy still argues in favour of the "ivory tower" model for "selected brains" and is thus situated in a disembodied and depoliticized account of the problem at hand.[66]

In 2011, Olivier P. Gosselain took the critiques related to the slow science concept and linked them with the notion of excellence, publishing an article in Uzance called "Slow science. La désexcellence".[67] He emphasizes the importance of community-building to create an honest science based on quality, one that challenges the discomfort brought by the politics of competition, productivity, and accountability, inspired by the free software movement. The same year, Isabelle Stengers gave an inaugural lecture at the Université Libre de Bruxelles, called "Another science is possible! A plea for slow science",[68] wherein she reflected on the responsibility of the roles of academics and referees, making a hard critique of the conditions of knowledge production nowadays and of the interconnections between knowledge itself and unsustainable progress.[69] Jean-François Lutz published a paper in *Nature* in 2012 that, in turn, claims that the quality of scientific research is deteriorating due to "duplicate publication, plagiarism, irreproducible results and fraud".[70] Scientists have no time to read the quantity of literature published in their field; on the contrary, more mature and slower writing would improve the advancement of knowledge. In the publish-or-perish culture, Lutz defends young researchers who have fewer opportunities to be considered and face greater pressure and competition than ever before.

Nevertheless, many authors have raised criticisms of the concept of slow science. Luke Martell suggests that slow science can be transformed into something somehow related to the middle class, and that it is important to look for the economic and social processes behind speediness, processes such as autonomy and power.[71] In his work on the "acceleration of the academy", Vostal recognizes that "academics are worn out, stressed and satisfaction-less victims lacking temporal agency",[72] although he notes that "slowness is barely recognised as an all-purpose principle".[73] He distinguishes between "constraining acceleration" as the negative effects of acceleration on "mental health and family" and "energizing acceleration" as a positive term integral to academic work-life. Thus, he concludes by arguing in favour of "unhasty time, which is not a slow time" and in favour of a politicization of time.[74] Mark Carrigan, together with Vostal, understands slow science as an initiative more related to those who can slow down the pace of their academic activity without acknowledging power relations and thus as drawing more on an individualistic drift. In contrast, they defend a position that focuses more on hierarchical and on power relations in the academy as they are related to "relevant variables such as age, gender, academic status, discipline, family situation, psychological disposition".[75] They are engaged with the Accelerated Academy initiative.[76]

However, a paper by some members of the Great Lakes Feminist Geography Collective, called "For slow scholarship: A feminist politics of resistance through collective action in the neoliberal university", offers an account of what slow scholarship might mean if informed by a feminist approach.[77] Their work, already cited in the second section of this chapter, is a condensed analysis – grounded in a collective autoethnography – of gendered and colonized time and care refracted through managerial orientations. Mountz et al. (2015) draw on the negative embodied effects on the health of (women) academics and claim for a feminist ethics of care, in order "to radically transform social reproduction" and centre it socially.[78] The authors acknowledge questions of privilege in the neoliberal academy for those who are not there "due to gendered, racialized, classed, heteronormative, and ableist structures and daily practices" in order to challenge elitist exclusions.[79] In sum, they argue in favour of encouraging scholars to fight collectively for a good (slow) model of scholarship by using a feminist politics of resistance, which would have the effect of improving the quality of research and teaching while disrupting the uneven power relations of academic life.

"The slow science", "la désexcellence", "accelerated academy", or "feminist slow scholarship" accounts differ from each other in their local context and approach. However, all might have the potential to engage with the connections between the exclusionary neoliberal scientific model and the well-being of academics and science itself, promoting the necessary debate around time and care to create resistance and space that sustain life collectively in the local and broader sense.[80]

Suggested assignment

- Try to imagine the creation of a slow science movement (or similar) in your university that takes into account the feminist notions of care and time. Work in groups to discuss what this would look like and ask yourselves which already existing groups would be stakeholders (e.g. associations of workers, associations to defend the public university, unions, professors, other universities, etc.).

Conclusions: repoliticizing the damages of the neoliberal academy

In this chapter I have outlined how neoliberal or "accelerated" managerial practices affect academics and their work, creating pressures and fostering more competition at an international level, promoting a long-hours culture and devaluing teaching, among other effects. Together with the austerity crisis context they also create precariousness, especially in the lowest positions of academic employment, and they reduce the possibility of advancement in a given career trajectory. The embodied effects of these managerial practices on academics have been pointed out regarding physical-psychological damages such as stress, exhaustion, eating disorders, back problems, or mental illness.

I have combined an analysis of these embodied effects with a focus on their intersection with gender. Gender operates as an aggravation, since time and care are gendered and affect specifically those (women) who have to manage conflicting roles that create tensions and suffering in their bodies, and this acts together with biased gender practice and discrimination well documented in research trajectories. Those gendered embodied effects, then, have been connected to some parallels with women's health, as it is socially shaped, and concretely with the example of fibromyalgia, a socially gendered illness. Connections with broad social and political measures have been outlined to link the macro level with the micro and thus to foster contextualization.

I then delved into Tronto's ethics of care, especially regarding her concepts of *attentiveness, responsibility,* and *privileged irresponsibility* in order to apply them to the problem of new managerial practices and their embodied effects. This has allowed me to note the potentially positive effects of including a feminist ethics of care in the analysis of and intervention in questions of responsibility.

I have also presented a critical review of the slow science initiatives – including "la désexcellence", the accelerated academy and slow feminist scholarship – as examples of what has been done to approach and intervene in the complex challenge posed by neoliberal drift in academia. The engagement in a feminist politics of resistance developed by the Great Lakes Feminist Geography Collective, drawing on ideas of collective responsibility and placing care in the centre of social life, becomes a very nuanced framework with which to continue working on this problematic.

Using the notion of care not as an idealized but as a political force that makes us understand that we all *maintain, continue,* and *repair* our world in a "complex, life-sustaining web"[81] can be a useful tool during challenging times characterized by a sense of the loss of politicization in academic culture, a sense that is "actually adverse to practices of (feminist) critical pedagogy", as Hanna Meissner (2015) states.[82] So, following the feminist motto that the *personal is political,*[83] I conclude by arguing that strategies to retake and repoliticize the situation, to place care in the centre of life,[84] and to create the availability for time to care and care for time constitute some of the feminist politics of resistance and responsibility useful for scholars facing this time of crisis.

Acknowledgement

This work is part of a thesis granted by the Ministerio de Economía y Competitividad of the Spanish government, also funded by the European Union. It is framed within the GENERA project (FEM2013-48225-C3-1-R), "Promoting a more inclusive and competitive knowledge economy", conducted by Dr. Ana María González Ramos.

Notes

1 Rosemary Deem, "Globalisation, new managerialism, academic capitalism and entrepreneurialism in universities: Is the local dimension still important?" *Comparative Education*, 37 (1), 7–20 (2001), 10.
2 Sheila Slaughter and Gary Rhoades, "The neo-liberal university", *New Labor Forum*, 6, 73–9 (2000). Retrieved from www.jstor.org/stable/40342886; Maureen Baker, "Career confidence and gendered expectations of academic promotion", *Journal of Sociology*, 46 (3), 317–34 (2010); Rosemary Deem and Jennifer T. Ozga, "Transforming post-compulsory education? Femocrats at work in the academy", *Women's Studies International Forum*, 23 (2), 153–66 (2000); Louise Morley, "The micropolitics of quality", *Critical Quarterly*, 47 (1–2), 83–95 (2005); Alison Mountz, Anne Bonds, Beckye Mansfield et al., "For slow

scholarship: A feminist politics of resistance through collective action in the neo-liberal university", *ACME, International E-Journal for Cultural Geographies*, 14 (4), 1235–59 (2015). Retrieved from http://ojs.unbc.ca/index.php/acme/article/view/1058.

3 Deem, "Globalisation, new managerialism": 11.

4 Ibid., 11.

5 As Rosemary Deem acknowledged in 2001, "The search for new sources of finance to replace declining government funding of higher education may have been one of the strong imperatives for adopting new managerialism in a number of Western economies", p 11, in "Globalisation, new managerialism".

6 Ivanna Vallespín and Elisa Silió, "Las universidades pierden 1.400 millones en tres años, *El País*, 6 March 2014. Retrieved from: http://sociedad.elpais.com/sociedad/2014/03/06/actualidad/1394132046_611684.html. This news is based on a report from the Comisiones Obreras Union that can be consulted here: www.fe.ccoo.es/cms/g/public/o/0/o138595.pdf (retrieved on 20 August 2016).

7 Ministerio de Educación, Cultura y Deporte, *Datos y cifras del sistema universitario español. Curso 2014/2015* (Secretaría General Técnica, 2015), 133. It can be consulted here: www.mecd.gob.es/dms/mecd/educacion-mecd/areas-educacion/universidades/estadisticas-informes/datos-cifras/Datos-y-Cifras-del-SUE-Curso-2014–2015.pdf (retrieved on 20 August 2016).

8 Lucía Gómez and Francisco Jódar, "Ética y política en la universidad española: la evaluación de la investigación como tecnología de la subjetividad", *Athenea Digital*, 13 (1), 81–98 (2013).

9 Morley, "The micropolitics of quality"; Baker, "Career confidence and gendered expectations": 325.

10 Sandra Acker and Carmen Armenti, "Sleepless in academia", *Gender and Education*, 16 (1), 3–24 (2004); Baker, "Career confidence and gendered expectations"; Deem and Ozga, "Transforming post-compulsory education?"; Morley, "The micropolitics of quality"; Mountz et al., "For slow scholarship"; Judith Walker, "Time as the fourth dimension in the globalization of higher education". *Journal of Higher Education*, 80 (5), 483–509 (2009). Retrieved from http://doi.org/10.1353/jhe.0.0061; Gómez and Jódar, "Ética y política en la universidad española"; Riyad A. Shahjahan, "Being 'lazy' and slowing down: Toward decolonizing time, our body, and pedagogy", *Educational Philosophy and Theory*, 47 (5), 488–501 (2015).

11 Shahjahan, "Being "lazy" and slowing down"; Walker, "Time as the fourth dimension".

12 Morley, "The micropolitics of quality", 86.

13 Andrew Sparkes, "Embodiment, academics, and the audit culture: A story seeking consideration", *Qualitative Research*, 7 (4), 521–50 (2007).

14 For example, from a total of 2,561 respondents the *Guardian* Survey of 2014 reports that 83 percent experienced anxiety, 75 percent depression, and 42 percent panic attacks during the time of working or studying in higher education. Two thirds of the respondents think these effects are a direct result of their university work. Retrieved from: http://static.guim.co.uk/ni/1399472932147/Mental-health-in-academia-s.pdf. See also the news about the survey in the *Guardian*: www.theguardian.com/higher-education-network/blog/2014/may/08/work-pressure-fuels-academic-mental-illness-guardian-study-health; The Times Higher Education University Workplace Survey, 2016: www.timeshighereducation.com/sites/default/files/best-university-workplace-survey-2016-results.pdf; and the University and College Union 2014 survey: www.ucu.org.uk/media/6908/UCU-survey-of-work-related-stress-2014–summary-of-findings-Nov-14/pdf/ucu_stresssurvey14_summary.pdf.

15 Rosalind Gill, "Breaking the silence: The hidden injuries of neo-liberal academia", in *Secrecy and Silence in the Research Process: Feminist Reflections*, ed. Flood, R.

and Gill, R. (London: Routledge, 2009); Maggie O'Neill, "The Slow University: time, work and well-being", *Forum Qualitative Sozialforschung/Forum: Qualitative Social Research*, 15 (3), 14 (2014). Retrieved from: www.qualitative-research.net/index.php/fqs/article/view/2226/3696, accessed 20 January 2017.

16 Rosa Hartmut, *Social Acceleration* (New York: Columbia University Press, 2013).
17 Filip F. Vostal, "Speed kills, speed thrills: Constraining and enabling accelerations in academic work-life", *Globalisation, Societies and Education*, 13 (3), 298 (2015).
18 Mountz et al., "For slow scholarship", 1245.
19 Acker and Armenti, "Sleepless in academia"; Mountz et al., "For slow scholarship".
20 Acker and Armenti, "Sleepless in academia".
21 Ibid., 20.
22 Mountz et al., "For slow scholarship".
23 Ana María González, "Inclusion of women in science: Long-term strategies for alone or with partners women", *GÉNEROS: Multidisciplinary Journal of Gender Studies*, 3, 459–82 (2014); Ana María González and Núria Vergés, "International mobility of women in S&T careers: Shaping plans for personal and professional purposes", *Gender, Place and Culture: A Journal of Feminist Geography*, 5, 613–29 (2013).
24 Mountz et al., "For slow scholarship", 1245 (on Brigid Schulte, *Overwhelmed: Work, Love and Play When No One Has the Time* (New York: Sarah Crichton Books, 2014).
25 Mountz et al., "For slow scholarship", 1245.
26 Steven J. Spencer, Claude M. Steele, and Diane M. Quinn, "Stereotype threat and women's math performance", *Journal of Experimental Social Psychology*, 35, 4–28 (1999). doi: 10.1006/jesp.1998.1373; Michael Inzlicht and Sonia K. Kang, "Stereotype threat spillover: How coping with threats to social identity affects aggression, eating, decision making, and attention", *Journal of Personality and Social Psychology*, 99 (3), 467–81 (2010).
27 Susana Vázquez and Mary Ann Elston, "Gender and academic career trajectories in Spain: From gendered passion to consecration in a *Sistema Endogámico*?", *Employee Relations*, 28 (6), 588–603 (2006), 595.
28 The GENERA project (FEM2013-48225-C3-1-R) is working on the gender biases in scientific institutions in the context of Spain, conducted by Ana M. González Ramos, leader of the project.
29 Heather Menzies and Janice Newson, "Time, stress and intellectual engagement in academic work: Exploring gender difference", *Gender, Work and Organization*, 15 (5), 504–22 (2008), 512.
30 Alexa K. Stuifbergen, Lorraine Phillips, Wayne Voelmeck, and Renee Browder, "Illness perceptions and related outcomes among women with fibromyalgia syndrome", *Women's Health Issues* 16, 353–60 (2006); Margot Pujal, Pilar Albertín, and Enrico Mora, "Discursos científicos sobre el dolor cronificado sin-causa-orgánica. Incorporando una mirada de género para resignificar-repolitizar el dolor", *Política y Sociedad*, 52 (3), 921–48 (2015).
31 Kristin K. Barker, "Listening to Lyrica: Contested illnesses and pharmaceutical determinism", *Social Science and Medicine* 73, 833–42 (2011); Frederick Wolfe and Brian Walitt, "Culture, science and the changing nature of fibromyalgia", *Nature Reviews Rheumatology*, 9, 751–5 (2013); Carme Valls-Llobet, *Mujeres, Salud y Poder* (Madrid: Cátedra, 2011).
32 Stuifbergen et al., "Illness perceptions and related outcomes", 356.
33 Ibid., 356. The next three are: altered immunity (46 percent), family problems or worries (44 percent), and "my emotional state (feeling down, lonely, anxious)" (43 percent).

34 Margot Pujal and Enrico Mora, "Subjectivity, health and gender: An approach to chronified pain through the Psychosocial Gender Diagnostic methodology / Subjetividad, salud y género: una aproximación al dolor cronificado mediante la metodología del Diagnóstico Psicosocial de Género", *Estudios de Psicología*, 35 (2), 212–38 (2014), 214, my translation.

35 Margot Pujal and Enrico Mora, "Dolor, trabajo y su diagnóstico psicosocial de género: un ejemplo", *Universitas Psychologica*, 12 (4), 1181–93 (2013), 1182, my translation; see also: Kristin K. Barker, *The Fibromyalgia Story: Medical Authority and Women's Worlds of Pain* (Philadelphia, PA: Temple University Press, 2005).

36 It is connected neither to race, class, ability, nor other axes of power relations, but this work is focused on gender.

37 Rosalind Gill, "Breaking the silence"; Andrew Sparkes, "Embodiment, Academics".

38 Barker, "Listening to Lyrica".

39 In a study of men affected by depression, O'Brien et al. (2007) highlight: "The majority believed that it was appropriate to remain silent and conceal their experience of mental illness in line with what they felt was expected of them as men", in Rosaleen O'Brien, J. Graham, and Kate Hung, "'Standing out from the herd': Men renegotiating masculinity in relation to their experience of illness", *International Journal of Men's Health*, 6 (3), 178–200 (2007), 190.

40 Mountz et al. "For Slow Scholarship: A Feminist Politics of Resistance through Collective Action in the Neoliberal University": 1246; Kristin K. Barker, "Listening to Lyrica: contested illnesses and pharmaceutical determinism", *Social Science and Medicine*, 73 (2011).

41 This excerpt from an article in the *Guardian* shows the intersection of different axes: "Finally, about gender equality. As a female lecturer from an ethnic minority, I am at the very bottom of the pecking order. I have not one, but two, glass ceilings to break. I am supposed to inspire and empower my female students, but here I am, a woman with a substantial publication record, all kinds of teaching qualifications and 13 years of experience, still begging for another fixed-term contract. My survival is decided by a system that cares neither about me, the lecturer, nor about you, my students." Retrieved from: www.theguardian.com/higher-education-network/2016/may/26/students-your-lecturers-are-on-strike-because-they-are-struggling-to-survive [accessed 26 May 2016].

42 Karen Barad, "Posthumanist Performativity: Toward an Understanding of How Matter Comes to Matter", *Signs: Journal of Women in Culture and Society*, 23, 3 (2003), 801–31.

43 Definition of the health section from the Platform for Action of the Fourth World Conference on Women of the United Nations, September 1995, Beijing, China, in Cecile M.T. Gijsbers Van Wijk, Katja P. Van Vliet, and Annemarie M. Kolk, "Gender perspectives and quality of care: Towards appropriate and adequate health care for women", *Social Sciences Medicine*, 43 (5), 707–20 (1996), 707.

44 Gijsbers Van Wijk et al., "Gender perspectives and quality of care"; Valls-Llobet, *Mujeres, Salud y Poder*; Pujal and Mora, "Subjectivity, health and gender".

45 María Puig de la Bellacasa, "Making time for soil: Technoscientific futurity and the pace of care", *Social Studies of Science*, 45 (5), 691–716 (2015).

46 O'Neill, "The slow university", 13.

47 Heather Menzies and Janice Newson, "Time, stress and intellectual engagement in academic work: Exploring gender difference", *Gender, Work and Organization*, 15 (5), 504–22 (2008). See also Heather Menzies and Janice Newson, "No time to think: Academics' life in the globally wired university", *Time and Society*, 16 (1), 83–98 (2007).

48 Beatriz Revelles, "Materializing feminist theory: The classroom as an act of resistance", in *Teaching with Feminist Materialisms*, ed. Peta Hinton and Pat Treusch (Utrecht: ATGENDER, 2015).

49 Joan Tronto, *Moral Boundaries: A Political Argument for an Ethic of Care* (New York: Routledge, 1993), 103, emphasis in original; see also Berenice Fisher and Joan Tronto, "Toward a feminist theory of care", in *Circles of Care: Work and Identity in Women's Lives*, ed. Emily Abel and Margaret Nelson (Albany, NY: State University of New York Press, 1991), 40.

50 Tronto, *Moral Boundaries*, 101.

51 For example, Tronto and Fisher have distinguished four phases of caring: *caring about* (acknowledging the existence of a need that should be met); *taking care of* (embracing some responsibility and deciding how to respond to it); *care-giving* (the act of giving care); and *care-receiving* (the object of care responding to the care received in order to know how adequately care has been provided). See Tronto, *Moral Boundaries*, 106–7.

52 The main four elements that arise from the displaying of care (see previous note) are *attentiveness*, *responsibility*, *competence*, and *responsiveness*. See Tronto, *Moral Boundaries*, 127–36.

53 Puig de la Bellacasa reflects upon this point, based also on Tronto, in: María Puig de la Bellacasa, "Nothing comes without its world: Thinking with care", *Sociological Review*, 60 (2), 197–215 (2012), 198–9.

54 Tronto, *Moral Boundaries*, 130.

55 Ibid., 131–2.

56 Ibid., 132–3.

57 Ibid., 121.

58 Ibid., 116, 146–7.

59 Caroline A. Clarke and David Knights, "Careering through academia: Securing identities or engaging ethical subjectivities?", *Human Relations*, 68 (12), 1865–88 (2015), 1883.

60 Menzies and Newson, "Time, Stress and Intellectual Engagement in Academic Work", 518.

61 Eugene Garfield, "Essays of an Information Scientist: Science Reviews, Journalism, Inventiveness and Other Essays", 14 (1991), 380. It can be found here: www.garfield.library.upenn.edu/essays/v14p380y1991.pdf.

62 Information retrieved from Wikipedia: https://en.wikipedia.org/wiki/Eugene_Garfield. You can also see a talk Garfield did at the International Congress on Peer Review and Biomedical Publication Chicago, 16 September 2005, www.psych.utoronto.ca/users/psy3001/files/JCR.pdf.

63 Lisa Alleva, "Taking time to savour the rewards of slow science", *Nature*, 443 (2006), 271. Retrieved from www.nature.com/nature/journal/v443/n7109/full/443271e.html.

64 Ibid., 271.

65 Slow Science Academy, "The slow science manifesto" (2010). Retrieved from: http://slow-science.org/slow-science-manifesto.pdf [Accessed 20 January 2017].

66 Ibid., 2. Against the "ivory tower" myth you can see a nuanced explanation in Yvonne Benschop and Margo Brouns, "Crumbling ivory towers: Academic organizing and its gender effects", *Gender, Work and Organization*, 10 (2), 194–212 (2003).

67 Olivier P. Gosselain, "Slow science. La desexcellence", *Uzance*, 1 (2011), 128–40. Retrieved from: https://www.academia.edu/4930403/Slow_Science_-_La_d%C3%A9sexcellence [Accessed 20 January 2017]. Gooselain and other academics wrote La Charte de la Désexcellence in 2014, retrieved from: http://lac.ulb.ac.be/LAC/charte_files/Charte_Desexcellence_1-1.pdf, which remarks on, among other things, the phenomena of precariousness, the standardization of evaluation, hypercompetition, as well as negative effects such as demotivation,

low self-esteem, and a diminishing quality of work. It also lists critical engagements regarding the teaching, research, administrative work, and what they call "service to the collectivity".

68 Isabelle Stengers, "Another science is possible! A plea for slow science", inaugural lecture Chair Willy Calewaert, 2011–12, Faculté de Philosophie et Lettres, Université Libre de Bruxelles, 13 December 2011. Retrieved from: https://three-rottenpotatoes.files.wordpress.com/2011/06/stengers2011_pleaslowscience.pdf [Accessed 20 January 2017].
69 This is further elaborated in Rogowska-Stangret (Chapter 1) and Cielemecka and Revelles-Benavente (Chapter 2).
70 Jean François Lutz, "Slow science", *Nature Chemistry*, 4 (8), 588–9 (2012), 588. Other authors such as John Horgan (2011) express similar thoughts, at http://blogs.scientificamerican.com/cross-check/the-slow-science-movement-must-be-crushed/.
71 Luke Martell, "The slow university: Inequality, power and alternatives", *Forum Qualitative Sozialforschung / Forum: Qualitative Social Research*, 15 (3), Art. 10 (2014), 13. Retrieved from: www.qualitative-research.net/index.php/fqs/article/view/2223/3693 [Accessed 20 January 2017].
72 Vostal, "Speed kills, speed thrills", 308.
73 Ibid., 309.
74 Filip Vostal, "Academic life in the fast lane: The experience of time and speed in British academia", *Time & Society*, 24 (1), 71–95 (2015), 90.
75 Mark Carrigan and Filip Vostal, "Not so fast! A critique of the Slow Professor", *University Affaires*, posted on 22 April 2016, at www.universityaffairs.ca/opinion/in-my-opinion/not-so-fast-a-critique-of-the-slow-professor/#comments. Carrigan and Vostal critique the interview with the authors of the new book *The Slow Professor* for a perceived individualization in the claim of slowness, but their post has raised controversy (see the comments section). See also M. Carrigan, "Life in the accelerated academy: Anxiety thrives, demands intensify and metrics hold the tangled web together", *Impact Blog, Accelerated Academy* (London School of Economics, 2015). Retrieved from: http://blogs.lse.ac.uk/impactofsocialsciences/2015/04/07/life-in-the-accelerated-academy-carrigan/.
76 Accelerated Academy first conference: http://accelerated.academy/; second conference: www.cwts.nl/news?article=n-q2v2c4.
77 Mountz et al., "For slow scholarship". It was downloaded 30,000 times on academia.edu and researchgate, according to: www.universityaffairs.ca/opinion/in-my-opinion/slow-scholarship-slow-scholarship/. In this article there is also a response in favour of the book *The Slow Professor*.
78 Ibid., 1246.
79 Ibid., 1240.
80 Other initiatives can be found regarding the defence of the public and democratic university, such as the recent report "The alternative white paper for higher education. In defence of public higher education: Knowledge for a successful society. A response to 'Success as a knowledge economy', BIS (2016)", ed. John Holmwood, Tom Hickey, Rachel Cohen, and Sean Wallis (Convention for Higher Education, May 2016) at: https://heconvention2.files.wordpress.com/2016/06/awp1.pdf.
81 Tronto, *Moral Boundaries*.
82 Hanna Meissner, "Opening spaces: The politics of feminist materialisms as challenge to the entrepreneurial university", in *Teaching with Feminist Materialisms*, ed. Peta Hinton and Pat Treusch (Utrecht: ATGENDER, 2015), 127.
83 Carol Hanisch, "The personal is political", *Notes from the Second Year*, ed. Shulie Firestone and Anne Koedt (Durham, NC: Duke University Press, 1969). Retrieved from: www.carolhanisch.org/CHwritings/PersonalisPol.pdf.
84 Tronto, *Moral Boundaries*; Amaia Pérez-Orozco, *Subversión feminista de la economía. Aportes para un debate sobre el conflicto capital-vida* (Madrid: Traficantes de sueños, 2014).

References

Acker, Sandra and Armenti, Carmen. "Sleepless in academia". *Gender and Education*, 16, 1 (2004): 3–24. Retrieved from http://doi.org/10.1080/0954025032000170309.

Alleva, Lisa. "Taking time to savour the rewards of slow science". *Nature*, 443 (2006): 271. Retrieved from www.nature.com/nature/journal/v443/n7109/full/443271e.html.

Baker, Maureen. "Career confidence and gendered expectations of academic promotion". *Journal of Sociology*, 46, 3 (2010): 317–34. Retrieved from http://doi.org/10.1177/1440783310371402.

Barad, Karen. "Posthumanist performativity: Toward an understanding of how matter comes to matter". *Signs: Journal of Women in Culture and Society*, 23, 3 (2003): 801–31.

Barker, Kristin K. *The Fibromyalgia Story: Medical Authority and Women Worlds of Pain*. Philadelphia, PA: Temple University Press, 2005.

Barker, Kristin K. "Listening to Lyrica: Contested illnesses and pharmaceutical determinism". *Social Science and Medicine*, 73 (2011): 833–42.

Carrigan, Mark. "Life in the Accelerated Academy: Anxiety thrives, demands intensify and metrics hold the tangled web together". Impact Blog, Accelerated Academy. London: London School of Economics, 2015. Retrieved from http://blogs.lse.ac.uk/impactofsocialsciences/2015/04/07/life-in-the-accelerated-academy-carrigan/.

Carrigan, Mark and Vostal, Filip. "Not so fast! A critique of the Slow Professor". *University Affaires*, posted 22 April 2016. Retrieved from www.universityaffairs.ca/opinion/in-my-opinion/not-so-fast-a-critique-of-the-slow-professor/#comments.

Clarke, Caroline A. and Knights, David. "Careering through academia: Securing identities or engaging ethical subjectivities?" *Human Relations*, 68, 12 (2015): 1865–88.

Deem, Rosemary. "Globalisation, new managerialism, academic capitalism and entrepreneurialism in universities: Is the local dimension still important?" *Comparative Education*, 37, 1 (2001): 7–20.

Deem, Rosemary and Ozga, Jennifer T. "Transforming post-compulsory education? Femocrats at work in the academy". *Women's Studies International Forum*, 23, 2 (2000): 153–66. Retrieved from http://doi.org/10.1016/S0277-5395(00)00070-4.

Fisher, Berenice and Tronto, Joan. "Toward a feminist theory of care", in *Circles of Care: Work and Identity in Women's Lives*, ed. Emily Abel and Margaret Nelson. Albany, NY: State University of New York Press, 1991.

Garfield, Eugene. "Essays of an information scientist: Science reviews". *Journalism Inventiveness and Other Essays*, 14 (1991): 380. Retrieved from www.garfield.library.upenn.edu/essays/v14p380y1991.pdf.

Gijsbers Van Wijk, Cecile M. T., Van Vliet, Katja P., and Kolk, Annemarie M. "Gender perspectives and quality of care: Towards appropriate and adequate health care for women". *Social Sciences and Medicine*, 43, 5 (1996): 707–20.

Gill, Rosalind. "Breaking the silence: The hidden injuries of neo-liberal academia", in *Secrecy and Silence in the Research Process: Feminist Reflections*, ed. R. Flood and R. Gill. London: Routledge, 2009.

Gómez, Lucía and Jódar, Francisco. "Ética y política en la universidad española: La evaluación de la investigación como tecnología de la subjetividad". *Athenea Digital*, 13, 1 (2013): 81–98.

González, Ana María. "Inclusion of women in science. Long-term strategies for alone or with partners' women". *GÉNEROS: Multidisciplinary Journal of Gender Studies*, 3 (2014): 459–82.

González, Ana María and Vergés, Núria, "International mobility of women in S&T careers: Shaping plans for personal and professional purposes". *Gender Place and Culture: A Journal of Feminist Geography*, 5 (2013): 613–29.

Gosselain, Olivier P. "Slow science. La desexcellence". *Uzance*, 1 (2011): 128–40. Retrieved from www.patrimoineculturel.cfwb.be/index.php?id=uzance1.

Hanisch, Carol. "The personal is political", *Notes from the Second Year*, ed. Shulie Firestone and Anne Koedt (Durham, NC: Duke University Press, 1969). Retrieved from www.carolhanisch.org/CHwritings/PersonalisPol.pdf.

Inzlicht, Michael and Kang, Sonia K. "Stereotype threat spillover: How coping with threats to social identity affects aggression, eating, decision making, and attention". *Journal of Personality and Social Psychology*, 99, 3 (2010): 467–81.

Lutz, Jean-François. "Slow science". *Nature Chemistry*, 4, 8 (2012): 588–9. Retrieved from http://doi.org/10.1038/nchem.1415.

Martell, Luke. "The slow university: Inequality, power and alternatives". *Forum Qualitative Sozialforschung / Forum: Qualitative Social Research*, 15, 3, Art. 10 (2014). Retrieved from http://nbn-resolving.de/urn:nbn:de:0114-fqs1403102.

Meissner, Hanna. "Opening spaces: The politics of feminist materialisms as challenge to the entrepreneurial university", in *Teaching with Feminist Materialisms*, ed., Peta Hinton and Pat Treusch, 123–40. Utrecht: ATGENDER, 2015.

Menzies, Heather and Newson, Janice. "No time to think. Academics' life in the globally wired university. *Time and Society*, 16, 1 (2007): 83–98.

Menzies, Heather and Newson, Janice. "Time, stress and intellectual engagement in academic work: Exploring gender difference". *Gender, Work and Organization*, 15, 5 (2008): 504–22.

Ministerio de Educación. "Cultura y Deporte, Datos y Cifras del sistema universitario español. Curso 2014/2015". Secretaría General Técnica, 2015.

Morley, Louise. "The micropolitics of quality". *Critical Quarterly*, 47, 1–2 (2005): 83–95.

Mountz, Alison, Bonds, Anne, Mansfield, Beckye, Loyd, Jenna, Hyndman, Jennifer, Walton-Roberts, Margaret, Basu, Ranu, Whitson, Risa, Hawkins, Roberta, Hamilton, Trina, and Curran, Winnifred. "For slow scholarship: A feminist politics of resistance through collective action in the neoliberal university". *ACME, International E-Journal for Cultural Geographies*, 14, 4 (2015): 1235–59. Retrieved from http://ojs.unbc.ca/index.php/acme/article/view/1058.

O'Brien, Rosaleen, Hart, Graham J., and Hung, Kate. "'Standing out from the herd': Men renegotiating masculinity in relation to their experience of illness". *International Journal of Men's Health*, 6, 3 (2007): 178–200.

O'Neill, Maggie. "The slow university: Time, work and well-being". *Forum Qualitative Sozialforschung / Forum: Qualitative Social Research*, 15, 3 (2014). Retrieved from www.qualitative-research.net/index.php/fqs/article/view/2226/3696.

Pérez Orozco, Amaia. *Subversión feminista de la economía. Apuntes para un debate sobre el conflicto capital-vida*. Madrid: Traficantes de sueños, 2014.

Puig de la Bellacasa, María. "Nothing comes without its world: Thinking with care". *Sociological Review*, 60, 2 (2012): 197–215.

Puig de la Bellacasa, María. "Making time for soil: Technoscientific futurity and the pace of care". *Social Studies of Science*, 45, 5 (2015): 691–716.

Pujal, Margot and Mora, Enrico. "Dolor, trabajo y su diagnóstico psicosocial de género: Un ejemplo". *Universitas Psychologica*, 12, 4 (2013): 1181–93.

Pujal, Margot and Mora, Enrico. "Subjectivity, health and gender: an approach to chronified pain through the Psychosocial Gender Diagnostic methodology / Subjetividad, salud y género: una aproximación al dolor cronificado mediante la metodología del Diagnóstico Psicosocial de Género". *Estudios de Psicología*, 35, 2 (2014): 212–38.

Pujal, Margot, Albertín, Pilar, and Mora, Enrico. "Discursos Científicos sobre el dolor cronificado sin-causa-orgánica. Incorporando una mirada de género para resignificar-repolitizar el dolor". *Política y Sociedad*, 52, 3 (2015): 921–48.

Revelles, Beatriz. "Materializing Feminist Theory: The Classroom as an Act of Resistance", in *Teaching with Feminist Materialisms*, ed. P. Hinton and P. Treusch, 53–65. Utrecht: ATGENDER, 2015.

Rosa, Hartmut. *Social Acceleration*. New York: Columbia University Press, 2013.

Schulte, Brigid. *Overwhelmed: Work, Love and Play When No One Has the Time*. New York: Sarah Crichton Books, 2014.

Shahjahan, Riyad A. "Being "Lazy" and Slowing Down: Toward Decolonizing Time, Our Body, and Pedagogy". *Educational Philosophy and Theory*, 47, 5 (2015): 488–501.

Slaugther, Sheila and Rhoades, Gary. "The Neo-liberal University". *New Labor Forum*, 6 (2000): 73–9.

Slow Science Academy. "The Slow Science Manifesto" (2010). Retrieved from http://slow-science.org/slow-science-manifesto.pdf.

Sparkes, Andrew. "Embodiment, Academics, and the Audit Culture: A Story Seeking Consideration". *Qualitative Research*, 7, 4 (2007): 521–50.

Spencer, Steven J., Steele, Claude M., and Quinn, Diane M. "Stereotype threat and women's math performance". *Journal of Experimental Social Psychology*, 35 (1999), 4–28.

Stengers, Isabelle. "Another Science Is Possible! A Plea for Slow Science", 13 December 2011, inaugural lecture Chair Willy Calewaert 2011–12. Faculté de Philosophie et Lettres, Université Libre de Bruxelles. Retrieved from http://we.vub.ac.be/aphy/sites/default/files/stengers2011_pleaslowscience.pdf.

Stuifbergen, Alexa K., Phillips, Lorraine, Voelmeck, Wayne, and Browder, Renee. "Illness Perceptions and Related Outcomes among Women with Fibromyalgia Syndrome". *Women's Health Issues*, 16 (2006): 353–60.

Tronto, Joan. *Moral Boundaries: A Political Argument for an Ethic of Care*. New York: Routledge, 1993.

Vallespín, Ivanna and Silió, Elisa. "Las universidades pierden 1.400 millones en tres años". *El País*, 6 March 2014. Retrieved from http://sociedad.elpais.com/sociedad/2014/03/06/actualidad/1394132046_611684.html.

Valls-Llobet, Carme. *Mujeres, salud y poder*. Madrid: Cátedra Feminismos, 2009.

Van den Brink, Marieke and Benschop, Yvonne. "Gender practices in the construction of academic excellence: Sheep with five legs", *Organization*, 19, (2012): 507–524.

Vázquez, Susana and Elston, Mary Ann. "Gender and Academic Career Trajectories in Spain: From Gendered Passion to Consecration in a Sistema Endogámico?" *Employee Relations*, 28, 6 (2006): 588–603.

Vostal, Filip. "Academic Life in the Fast Lane: The Experience of Time and Speed in British Academia". *Time and Society*, 24, 1 (2015): 71–95.

Vostal, Filip. "Speed Kills, Speed Thrills: Constraining and Enabling Accelerations in Academic Work-Life". *Globalisation, Societies and Education*, 13, 3 (2015): 295–314.

Walker, Judith. "Time as the Fourth Dimension in the Globalization of Higher Education". *Journal of Higher Education*, 80, 5 (2009): 483–509. Retrieved from http://doi.org/10.1353/jhe.0.0061.

Wolfe, Frederick and Walitt, Brian. "Culture, Science and the Changing Nature of Fibromyalgia". *Nature Reviews Rheumatology*, 9 (2013): 751–5.

4

"IT'S A HELL OF A RESPONSIBILITY TO BE YOURSELF"

Troubling the personal and the political in feminist pedagogy

Esther Sánchez-Pardo

Introduction

To paraphrase the feminists of the 1970s, this chapter brings together the personal and the political in the new scenario, the contemporary society. The personal keeps being political and, inasmuch as politics permeates all aspects of our lives, I would like to take up the issue of pedagogical cultures and the generic acts (the production of both gender and genre) that make them possible. In an effort to locate the personal, mostly within ethics on its way to engage with the political – and thus at the crux between responsibility toward others and autonomy – I would like to raise some of the central concerns of a feminist pedagogical practice by bringing together three interwoven and passionate knowledge-making sets of problems as addressed by major feminist theorists: from Donna Haraway's relational paradigm of "thinking/becoming-with", to bell hooks' engaged pedagogy in the classroom as a dialogical scene, and finally to Chandra T. Mohanty's solidarity model of the feminist intercultural encounter.

My title comes from Sylvia Plath's *Journals*[1] and reminds us of the heavy burden responsibility places in the hands of women, feminists, grassroots activists, and finally in the hands of educators, teachers, mentors, guardians, and mothers. Responsibility, as it has recently been argued, has hardly disappeared in a postmodern context.[2] By rethinking the self as always faced by the other and as always embedded within prior social structures, it is claimed we should be able to reconceive the conditions upon which responsibility is possible.[3] "In times of crisis", at a very uncertain moment when global social relations are strained and hemispheric connections show tensions that divide and dissociate rather than unite in larger collective projects, Judith Butler has argued, "we must recognize that ethics requires us to risk ourselves precisely at moments of unknowingness, when what forms us diverges from what lies before us, when our willingness to become undone in relation to others constitutes our chance of becoming human".[4] This subjective "undoing" is also a chance "to be addressed, claimed, bound to what is not me, but also to be moved, to be prompted to act, to address myself elsewhere, and so to vacate the 'self-sufficient I' as a kind of possession".[5] In light of an increased relativism and the postmodern discreditedness of essentialized humanity, there seems to be room for ethical inquiry which, ideally, will show us new paths toward a more just political reality.

An essay on the issue of teaching a feminist politics of responsibility in the midst of a humanitarian crisis of unprecedented proportions in a still highly polarized world – polarized in financial and confrontational terms (the global vs. local, north vs. south, west vs. east), in terms of the crisis of values and of beliefs, and in terms of the supposed clash of civilizations, of the end of history, of climate change, and of environmental damage of the planet – is a challenge for any feminist-informed curriculum. Ours is a crisis that hits East and West at this late stage of capitalism and within an ever extending market-driven neoliberalism. At this point in time, when market principles of supply and demand, privatization, decentralization, efficiency, and financial and personal self-sufficiency are rampant, how do we enact a politicized feminist pedagogy that grants space to all voices and identity locations within the university and society at large? Now that even educational institutions are increasingly structured around the market, in the midst of social attitudes hostile to progressive and egalitarian principles, how are we best to challenge systemic oppression if not with recourse to feminist critical pedagogy? This certainly raises the question of a more fundamental and already well-established relation: that of feminism and philosophical-ethical thought writ large. The subject of several important books and papers, this more general relationship (feminist pedagogy and ethics) hardly seems in need of documentation or further discussion, especially in the context of a book that takes as its primary subject a current and comparatively unexplored phase within this ongoing relation ("in times of crisis"). And yet, from another point of view, one wonders: has the issue of feminism and ethics even been broached? That is, has feminist theory ever adequately addressed the essential nature of this relation? The potential reasons for its endurance? The particular discursive configurations that result from feminist engagements with myriad unresolved conundrums in our times? Everywhere this relation, despite its materialization in countless acts, is often elided, as if its endurance somehow negates the need to determine exactly what is happening in feminism's more than two-centuries attraction to a body of canonical philosophical texts on morality and ethics, and their relations to politics, religion, and diverse cultural contexts[6] speaking to patriarchy.

In this chapter, I will focus on our relation with the workings of the peda-gogical encounter as a daily practice of responsibility. In this context, what the "practice of everyday life"[7] does for us is assert a thinking of the personal into the workings of every single theorization. It is precisely the numerous entangled habits – Bourdieu's habitus[8] – and commitments of everyday life that is at issue, as an inspirational force, behind the following thoughts.

Where, the personal?

> How long do I pretend to be all of us.
>
> *(Denise Riley[9])*

In this chapter I think of ethics as relationships to others (whether human, animal, ecological, or natural) rather than as morality or a code of con-duct. This definition comes from the work of Emmanuel Levinas. Otherness, which Levinas[10] also calls the Face (or, the Other, the infinite, and the irre-ducible mystery: that which confronts, that which is always beyond us), demands a "thinking-aboutness" which sets the stage for an ethical relation with the other.[11] As I understand it, the recognition of the radical mystery of Otherness (as infinity) suggests that there is something outside our own subjectivity worthy of being, and demanding to "become". This becoming is radically opposed to "colonizing": while becoming is a participation and an engagement with the other by means of emotional resonance, colonizing is an objectification of the other's subjectivity. True recognition of the other's otherness prevents the other from being colonized by the self.[12]

From this understanding of ethics, I will engage in an exploration of three pedagogical approaches that draw on relational models of knowledge pro-duction in the humanities – Donna Haraway's, bell hooks' and Chandra T. Mohanty's. These models, I argue, offer critical ways of rethinking an eth-ics of engagement, interpretation, and action in which practice and theory actively fuse to reconfigure new pedagogical landscapes.

Feminism in its late twentieth-century configurations has demanded responsible knowledge production. Responsibility, then and now, demands a display of response-ability – an ability to respond and account for one's investment, one's position in any theoretical or material production, an interest that refuses any simple distinction between public and private cat-egories, and works to craft new practices of receiving, listening, and attend-ing as crucial to the always relational knot of response-ability.[13] This chapter is deeply entangled with feminist ethics in thinking with the pedagogical, the personal, and the political.

On another front, we should also reflect upon the modes of accountabil-ity we are invited to by the intersections of feminism and critical pedagogy. How might the structural organization around knowledge, modelled by the-ory and praxis, be productively thought with the dialogic democratic ideals inflected by critical pedagogy? Thinking through feminism[14] brings these two together into a complex configuration within which an egalitarian educational climate does not require symmetrical relations of power, but instead calls for an awareness of the asymmetries that exist and for an investment in their visibility. This is an analysis that complicates the oppositional relationship between the hierarchical and the non-hierarchical and in which a self-reflexive hierarchy might be a more productive means of informing an ethical pedagogy and a politics of inclusiveness and care.

Engaging the political: a politics of inclusiveness

> Difference is that raw and powerful connection from which our personal power is forged.
>
> *(Audre Lorde[15])*

Political theorist Chantal Mouffe argues that it is precisely the necessity of an ongoing challenge to the different angles of identity that marks a radical feminist politics. This is due to Mouffe's conception of the social: to truly serve a democracy organized around the principles of liberty and equality, it is necessary to discard all notions of transparent, rational, self-conscious agents able to cohere into a homogeny of subject positions, in favour of a position from which one could "theorize the multiplicity of relations of subordination".[16] If each and every one of us is understood as simultaneously inhabiting subordinated and dominant social positions, we must therefore relate to ourselves as a multiplicity that is at odds with any theory of essentialism. For Mouffe the subject must be understood as contingent, precarious, and temporarily fixed at intersections of identification that are always relationally constituted. This has important consequences for how feminist political struggles are formulated: it shifts the terms of a debate organized around a struggle for recognition (what is/constitutes woman such that she can be recuperated and celebrated – woman's imagery/labour/worldview) and equality (in which a unity called "man" has rights that should be shared with a unity called "woman") to a discursive framework in which attention must be paid to located specificities of difference constructed through a plurality of discursive configurations: "The central issues become: how is 'woman' created as a category within different discourses? How is sexual difference made a pertinent distinction in social relations? And how are relations of subordination constructed through such a distinction?"[17] It is to an analysis of specific and differential constructions of subordination that we must shortly turn.

Feminists' concern with sociality and with the socio-historical conditions that may lead women to occupy a space in the public arena have proved instrumental in the development of feminist consciousness, and in the strategies and processes of empowerment to counter male domination in society. Consequently, the idea of power has played a crucial role in feminist struggles and theories up until now.[18] There is also an almost commonplace and central question that shows up in current discussions on politics, community, and grassroots feminism that has to do with the intricacies of the power-and-morality tandem, one that has major repercussions in the way the young feminist scholar reacts in times of crisis: are power and morality necessarily opposed? In other words, how does woman become responsive to a changing political milieu in which there seems not to be a way out of the "master-slave" morality?

The intertwining of power and morality, whereby the state appears as a necessary step in the evolution of the moral man, and in turn is needed to sustain and advance the freedom of man, was radically shattered by the nihilist views of Friedrich Nietzsche. For him, power and morality are intrinsically opposed. Morality was the slaves' manner of restraining the powerful and imposing their own will. Ultimately, for Nietsche morality is a constraining force preventing humanity from ever attaining its "highest potential and splendour"[19] at any point in the future of history, making the present "live at the expense of the future".[20] Nietzsche's main problem with morality is its stifling of creativity and constraining of what the "highest exemplars" of the species could achieve in order to ameliorate the existence of the majority. In his view, the concepts of power and morality are evidently opposed when it comes to producing something great for humanity.[21]

The antithesis between morality and power presented by Nietzsche could only be solved, in his view, with a counter-ideal that would eliminate, from its roots, the idea of morality as a whole, and allow for power to fall into the hands of the few rather than the many.[22] Confronting this, we need to ask ourselves a question: wouldn't the creative result of this wielding of authority be more active and visionary if it were a common impulse, emanating from humanity, from women and men, in unison? Surely, humanity's power as a collective is greater (with this cohesiveness dictated to a great extent by the structure that morality gives to human life), if all wills are united to advance and exercise their will-to-power, than any few great men could achieve on their own?

This polarization between slave and master class is archaic. In modernity, an increasing meritocracy is imposed as an order in the world. Hence, the primacy of aptitude and talent contribute to achieving humanity's will(s) as a whole. We can certainly observe how power and morality can work together to bring the most apt individuals – including women, racial, ethnic, and sexual minorities, among others – and to hold power over the areas they are best at and manage better. Along the line of feminist thinking, I do not believe that power and morality are necessarily opposed. It is evident that Nietzsche's conception, though extremely interesting in debunking assumptions about morality being natural to mankind, is intrinsically incompatible with a current, more inclusive definition of humanity.

The ideal presented by the German philosopher also disregards differences between individuals. His sorting out of people in *On the Genealogy of Morality* as belonging to either a master or a slave class ignores the fact that all human beings are fundamentally different. This would not happen in Nietzsche's very elitist view of human society, whereby any talent appearing amongst a "slave" class would drown in the subjugation by the "master" class. Nietzsche's willingness to attribute humanity's *épanouissement* to a small selection of great, powerful men at the expense of the subjugation of the majority displays a very limited understanding of humanity. Only in amassing the different talents and aptitudes of the entirety of humanity (not just of the *Übermensch*) can there be hope to contribute positive, creative gains to society as a whole, and only when power and morality are intertwined can this common progression to more freedom and equality be guaranteed.

This chapter has been an attempt to move away from Nietzschean "master-slave" morality. Feminist teachers, students, and activists need to create alternative values to overcome this dualism. Feminist teaching and pedagogy, in the current times of crisis, can certainly benefit from challenging normative morality and values, the Nietzschean "will to power", and move beyond this unresolved dialectic. A crucial part of feminism's mission at the moment is a search for new models of giving and sharing, a critical pedagogy that should be fruitful in dialogue and exchange.[23]

Suggested assignment

- In what ways can we foster a pedagogy that imparts the skills and dispositions of democratic citizenship instead of teaching subjects and methods suited for standardized academic knowledge?
- How can we promote skills to create the democratic or intercultural citizen? How can we contribute to meet the challenges of citizenship education around the world? Reflect upon the role of cross-cultural analysis.

Donna Haraway: relationality and thinking/becoming-with

The question of accountability interests me, first within reading practices, whether reading as a teacher, reading as a student, or most often, as a mixture of both. It is the university that gives rise to my concerns in this chapter, and the notion of accountability is one that comes from critically interrogating the structures of identification and desire that articulate our epistemophilic drives. Judith Butler explores ethical subjectivity and responsibility and shows us the close connection between ethics and politics, responsibility and critique. The foundational gesture she verbalizes as "giving an account of oneself" takes place in the midst of a confrontational political terrain, and in discussing Foucault's ethical turn and his reading of the notion of *parrhesia* (telling the truth about oneself), she argues we reach the point when ethics ceases to be credible unless it becomes critique.

Butler's account of this crucial scene of the "emergence" of the individual as an ethical subject, who comes into existence in response to someone else's query, takes the form of a narrative. This narrative is, in Butler's rendering of this scene of address, the prerequisite condition for any account of moral agency we might give.[24] It is in this way that "narrative capacity constitutes a precondition for giving an account of oneself and assuming responsibility for one's actions through that means".

Feminist scholars in the humanities have amply shown that theoretical knowledge is an "enabling practice". In this active area of research, I will explore ethical models of engagement in academic and educational settings, focusing on conditions that foster cultures of interest, engagement, and commitment. A crucial function of pedagogy is to mark the practice of thinking-with, not as a process of addition or incorporation, but as a relational practice through which debts are incurred along practices of attention and care – debts that mark the labour of mentorship, friendship, survival, and also the labour of a kind of social ethics to which this chapter addresses itself. What matters here is that a certain politics of what we call "visibility" be practised – that is, a situated and reflexive marking of space and time, of individuality and community. Thus, one of the central questions to be raised is this: how are we trained to engage with each other pedagogically? As far as we are aware that we know what we know always only contingently and partially, and only in relation to those around me, our "knowledge" is always a conversation.

How do we think "about" our daily exchanges and conversational practices? The multiple ways in which we think "with" our exchanges and conversational practices – be they written, spoken, or digitally mediated – matters. Current pedagogical theory asks: how and where does what we are entangled with matter in relations of debt and care? Pedagogical theory is attentive to the material aspects of our conversational practices (in the classroom, on the street, or mediated through text) as well as to an ethics of curiosity and care within these practices – an ethics of curiosity and care that has to do with a politics and ethics of situatedness. This chapter explores a pedagogical mode that many feminists bring up in their practices. How are we trained to engage with each other pedagogically? One should probably answer that we are trained in a new mode in which the traditional model "I don't know and I should" is replaced by "what I know is always dependent on others, on those around me, and it usually takes the form of a conversation". Donna Haraway's "companion species" model comes to mind:[25] a model of becoming-with and a symbiopoesis, rather than one of poesis *tout court*, a companion species model in which we are all constitutive of each other.[26]

Donna Haraway in her classic essay "Situated Knowledges" argues that there is no one truth to be uncovered, but instead that all knowledge is partial and linked to the contexts in which it is created – all knowledge is en-gendered.[27] Haraway wants to recuperate the terms of objectivity for a feminist political practice. The intersection of the personal and the political is recuperated from the realms of a poststructuralism writ large and returned to its specificity in and with feminism not only as a theoretical (material-discursive) but simultaneously as a material historical and activist movement. In this, a personal, engaged, relational model does not become an excuse to eschew disciplinary or contextual specificities. Rather, to turn to the personal is to be interested in how what we are attentive to shapes our world, to be interested in what not-knowing – what disciplinary, discursive, psychical, and situational displacements – can facilitate. In practical classroom terms, not knowing provides an opening, an opportunity to ask any sort of question, to address any kind of query. In propositional theoretical terms, to champion not knowing is to insist that the "best" kind of theorist is the one who is not naturalized into the system. I read in Haraway's work a call for a practice of invested engagement in a discourse practice, with the understanding that practices never occur outside of discourses and vice versa. Donna Haraway grounds us in a feminist attention to located-ness to which I want to attend. Meaning, for Haraway, emerges through an embedded dia-logic rather than a simply conceived discovery model. And in suggesting a dialogic model here, I am invoking one that is characterized by tension, conflict, and irreconcilable difference, both internal and external – that is, one that remains open to ambiguity, conflict, and paradox at every turn.

Feminism here wants to maintain a tension-between rather than collapse the personal and the political. Feminism is not a secure or stable ground but is rather one marked by irreconcilable differences that cannot be collapsed into a fixed identity. Instead, a dialogic imperative emerges in which self-consciousness is read as a process that is never finally fixed, but instead emerges relationally. In this model situatedness is what, in fact and in effect, resists the politics of closure. Situatedness argues for a "usable but not innocent doctrine of objectivity"[28] – one that is "embodied and therefore accountable".[29] Division and difference are constitutive here, and values are made of tensions and contradictions that are always on the move.

Suggested assignment

- Write a short essay about the classroom as a situated enclave.
- Reflect upon why "situatedness" is a concept that can be so fruitful in a pedagogical environment.

bell hooks: critical pedagogy and dialogic exchange

Commenting on her indebtedness to Brazilian educator Paolo Freire (1921–97) in her book *Teaching to Transgress* (1994), bell hooks proposes a notion of "engaged pedagogy" – pedagogy in which theory-making only occurs in a collective context.[30] In this collective context, her practice of critical thinking is organized around a "dialogic exchange" in which an openness to difference prevails.[31] Important for hooks' intervention in Freirean pedagogy is the historical specificity of the late twentieth-century American feminist classroom as a passionate space in which the notions of "seriousness" and "excitability", figures that were said to undo each other, could now be said instead to reinforce each other.

hooks describes the feminist classroom as a "space where pedagogical practices were interrogated" and "where students could raise critical questions about the pedagogical process" in a way that functioned as a "crucial challenge inviting the students to think seriously about pedagogy in relation to the practice of freedom".[32] Here freedom comes to stand for a tireless commitment to critical thinking, to the defamiliarizing or "making uninhabitable" of naturalized constructs. While elements that are valued under the banner of the personal are of central concern here, this turn to the personal in hooks' thought is not a valuation of the personal for the personal's sake. Rather, "linking confessional narrative to academic discussion [is done] so as to show how personal experience can illuminate and enhance our understanding of academic material".[33]

This critical pedagogy produces the classroom as a dialogic and negotiated scene of knowledge production over and above its role as a repository for the reproduction of institutionally sanctioned ideas. For hooks, this engaged pedagogical practice encourages a passion for critical thinking that must be organized around a spatially and temporally situated "dialogic exchange". hooks ties this commitment to her own pedagogical upbringing. Describing her early educational experience in the segregated southern US during the 1960s, hooks tells us that "school was the place of ecstasy – of pleasure and danger. To be changed by ideas was the pure pleasure", it was "to place oneself at risk, to enter the danger zone".[34] Here, attention to differences (to "put oneself at risk") is linked to an unruly excitement in which the pleasure in teaching and learning is asserted as "an act of resistance countering the overwhelming boredom, unrest and apathy that so often characterizes the classroom experience".[35] Teaching here is a fundamentally political act: "learning is a revolution ... [a counter-hegemonic act]".[36] In hooks' narrative, with the arrival of racial integration "knowledge was suddenly about information only. It had no relation to how one lived, behaved".[37] Teaching and learning were no longer political acts linked to the practice of freedom, but instead became reproductive of dominant ideology. It became about "the banking system" – and in this anecdote lies the crux of hooks' pedagogical project.[38]

For hooks this engaged pedagogical excitement, however, must not only be about ideas but must be linked to an interest in each other. What constitutes a classroom as a learning community is shared responsibility for the generation of excitement. In this, what excitement offers as a value is an "active participant" versus "passive consumer" model in which the radical/ critical feminist classroom becomes a participatory space for the sharing of knowledge, and in which what constitutes "participation" remains an important and open question.

Suggested assignment

- Out of your own experience, illustrate with examples ways in which you understand what bell hooks means by the phrase "learning is a revolution ... [a counter-hegemonic act]".[39] Elaborate on your specific classroom situation.

Chandra Mohanty: solidarity without borders

In her work, Chandra Mohanty has called for opening up borders within feminism by drawing on diverse sites of struggle and activism that are informed by transnational feminist practices. She aims at showing how women around the world may appreciate other women's status and achievements. Mohanty's project aims at reconnecting women worldwide through "solidarity" rather than sisterhood and addresses her critique of globalization, focusing on the strengths of anti-racist, anti-capitalist feminism. Feminism's constant complaints about the bitter realities of the exploitation of women and girls depriving them of education and of equal opportunities are foregrounded in Mohanty's work. She argues for a feminist theory and practice based on solidarity. In her view, solidarity must be "worked for, struggled toward – in history",[40] and holds that "positing solidarity rather than vague, supposed sisterhood as the basis for feminist practice provides an equitable relationship among different communities of women".[41] Mohanty works transversally and is practice-oriented rather than identity-oriented, foregrounding communities of women who have chosen to work and struggle together.

The trope of borders and border-crossing are crucial in her work. "Feminism without borders" derives from the admirable "Doctors without Borders" organization and their internationalist commitment. Mohanty goes personal in her discussion of her own experiences of borders and border-crossing, and of the meanings of self and home derived from these. In her reflection, she writes a political geography of her identity and explains how she moved from "being a part of the 'absent elite' and the majority in India, while being a minority and racialized 'other' in the US".[42]

In her essays devoted to feminist pedagogy, Mohanty denounces the commodification of the university, the precarious position of feminism within the curriculum, the tokenization of race as one of oppression's most powerful weapons, and the handling of diversity training to compensate for rampant inequality and minorities' limited access to public education. In her view, the university is crucial as a site where knowledge is not only produced, but also appropriated and contested. Mohanty's example allows for the dismantling of the dichotomy of theory/research versus activism through critical pedagogy in the classroom. Her project can be best pursued upon three major lines of action: critical pedagogy, anti-capitalist solidarity, and transnational feminist practices.

Suggested assignment

- Write about the tropes of borders and border-crossing in your own personal and learning experience.
- Reflect upon how to teach solidarity in the humanities classroom. Elaborate and illustrate with examples.

Haraway, Mohanty, hooks: the drive to educate

The questions posed in the opening lines of *When Species Meet* (2008), "Whom and what do I touch when I touch my dog?" and "How is 'becoming-with' a practice of becoming worldly?" both instantiate a particular mode of address.[43] The mode is one of a rigorous and insatiable curiosity that stems from the drive that pushes us "beyond" in daily life, it models an encounter that is deeply ingrained in what constitutes the situated, relational, embedded, and intertwined specificity of the "everyday" in a way that makes us aware that every single deed is one of response-ability. Responsibility now demands a display of response-ability – an ability to respond and to account for one's investment, interest, and position in any theoretico-material production. This interest refuses any simple distinction between public and private, active and passive, categories and works in order to craft effective practices of receiving, listening, and attending as essential to the always relational tangle of response-ability; in other words, how we *do*, *think about*, or even *think-with* our conversational practices – be they spoken, written, or gestured matters. How, where, and with what/who we are entangled, in relations of indebtedness and care, matters. Haraway's nuanced theories are attentive to the material worldings of our conversation practices (in the classroom, on the street, mediated through text, in our own heads) as well as to an ethics of curiosity and care within these practices – the aforementioned has little to do with being simply an "empathetic listener/spectator" and everything to do with a politics and ethics of situated worlding.

We can certainly connect Haraway's concerns with those of Chandra T. Mohanty in her views of a comparative feminist politics at this moment in history. After her major critique of Western feminism in her "Under Western Eyes" (1986), where she charted the location of feminist scholarship within a global, political, and economic framework dominated by the "First World", today, the hegemony of neoliberalism, the rise of fundamentalisms, the importance of the profoundly unequal "information highway", and increasing militarism[44] pose profound contradictions in the lives of women and men in most parts of the world.

In Mohanty's view, it is imperative to count upon anti-globalization pedagogies, and she suggests a comparative feminist studies or feminist solidarity model.[45] Based on the premise that the local and the global are not defined in terms of physical geography but exist simultaneously and constitute one another, Mohanty stresses the links, the relationships that are foregrounded, and these links are material, conceptual, contextual, and so on. In her view, the framework of the solidarity model always assumes a comparative focus and an analysis of the directionality of power.[46] Besides its focus on mutuality and common struggles, Mohanty's solidarity model also requires one "[T]o formulate questions about connection and disconnection between activist women's movements around the world".[47] Mohanty argues that feminist pedagogy should not only expose students to a particularized academic scholarship, but should also envision the possibility of activism and civic engagement outside the academy.

Throughout her career, bell hooks has argued for a progressive, holistic education and an engaged pedagogy. This places very strong demands upon educators in terms of commitment: "[T]eachers must be actively involved and committed to a process of self-actualization that promotes their own well-being if they are to teach in a manner that empowers students".[48] In her view, they also have to foster "communities of resistance" that help dismantle systemic gender, race, class, language, and religious oppressions.

Central to her engaged pedagogy – a combination of reflection and action, a praxis – is that one never speaks from the designated position of the "other", since this is a point of reference defined by the dominant paradigm of white patriarchy. Acknowledging the fact that all participants bring to the class experiential knowledge, hooks rules out any claims to an "authoritative" voice. Both teacher and students can collaboratively learn together in a non-hierarchical way, freeing the classroom from its potentially coercive power as an institutional location.

It is precisely hooks' idea of dialogic exchange that connects with Haraway's attention to conversational practices and to Mohanty's comparative cross-cultural analysis of power and solidarity and civic engagement model for pedagogical practice. Their many similarities – with such diverse origins and trajectories – testify to the common endeavour of the feminist pedagogical project that travels across a range of localities and practices. In hooks' envisioning of a promising and hopeful future,

> The classroom with all its limitations remains a location of possibility. In that field of possibility we have the opportunity to labour for freedom, to demand of ourselves and our comrades an openness of mind and heart that allows us to face reality even as we collectively imagine ways to move boundaries, to transgress.[49]

As we have intended to show, thinking-with, interrelationality, solidarity, and comparative cross-cultural analysis of power and oppression come to be major categories of analysis in any feminist-informed curriculum for today, in our current times of crisis.

Throughout this chapter we have discussed pedagogical approaches to education that are essentially rebellious and non-imitative, and that constitute the practice of teaching-learning as made up of acts of resistance, with resistance understood as an inescapable gesture of contestation and rejection. Who and how each participant in a pedagogical encounter "is" is in part a function of who and how the other is. Who and what I am is organized around a willingness to engage, try on, fit myself into different models of knowing, texts, styles of being, styles of writing, and to come to know myself as always on the look-out for what else I might come to know. All texts ask us to engage our epistemological curiosity through attention to detail. As Rosi Braidotti has argued, "Loyalty is ... required to the intensity of the affective forces that compose a text or a concept, so as to account for what a text – or a concept, or theory – can do, what it has done, how it has impacted upon one's self and others".[50] Taking interest and curiosity as our guides, we might ask: what do I not know here? To what am I *not* attending? To take something as an object of epistemological curiosity is thus to make it an object of inquiry, of search, and of research. Curiosity leads us through the inquisitive on the way to acquiring knowledge, and propels us in a movement of pedagogical quest that holds inquisitiveness as its highest attribute and a deontological ethics of care as its aim.[51] We have returned full circle to Sylvia Plath's personal and almost confessional concerns: "it's a hell of a responsibility to be [oneself]. It's much easier to be somebody else or nobody at all."[52] The feminist autograph, no longer mystified or usurped by a tradition that was never the province of women, circulates today side by side and, alternatively, through a myriad of other channels that, far from overshadowing it, enhance it, both creatively and intellectually. This feminist autograph, its testimony of resistance and struggle, remains in a joint pedagogical project where the personal and the political achieve full significance in the young feminist student and poet of today.

Notes

1 Sylvia Plath argues in her *Journals*: "Very few people do this any more. It's too risky. First of all, it's a hell of a responsibility to be yourself. It's much easier to be somebody else or nobody at all". Sylvia Plath, *The Unabridged Journals of Sylvia Plath* (New York: Anchor, 2000), 492.

2 For an important reflection on ethics in postmodernity see Zygmunt Bauman, *Postmodern Ethics* (London: Wiley-Blackwell, 1993); see also Richard Rorty, *An Ethics for Today* (New York: Columbia University Press, 2010); Nancy Fraser and Axel Honneth, *Redistribution or Recognition?* (London: Verso, 2003); and Alison Jaggar, *Living with Contradictions: Controversies in Feminist Social Ethics* (Boulder, CO: Westview Press, 1994).

3 Judith Butler, in *Giving an Account of Oneself* (New York: Fordham University Press, 2005) clarifies that poststructuralism cannot be equated with moral nihilism (21). In Butler's view the basis for morality begins with the self-exposure to others. The self comes into existence as a product of the responses of and to others that have conditioned and instantiated our self-identity. She argues, in line with Michel Foucault, that "The first-person perspective assumed by the ethical question, as well as the direct address to a 'you', are disoriented by this fundamental dependency of the ethical sphere on the social" (25).

4 Ibid., 136.

5 Ibid.

6 Anthropological research on morality has focused on cross-cultural variations among different groups: from tribal and territorial morality, to the morality that applies to friends and foreigners (in-groups and out-groups, in anthropological parlance) to geo-cultural areas and different historical periods. See Celia Green, *Letters from Exile: Observations on a Culture in Decline* (Oxford: Oxford Forum, 2004); Christopher Peterson and Martin E. P. Seligman, *Character Strengths and Virtues* (Oxford: Oxford University Press, 2004).

7 With "The Practice of Everyday Life", I allude to Michel de Certeau's *L'Invention du Quotidien, Vol. 1 Arts de faire* (Paris: Gallimard, 1980) which examines the ways in which people individualize mass culture, transforming objects and rituals in order to make them their own. De Certeau shifts attention from production to consumption and discusses the ways in which ordinary people can subvert the representations that institutions seek to impose upon them.

8 As is well known, Bourdieu's influential notion of "habitus" is understood as "A structuring structure which organizes practices and the perception of practices" (Pierre Bourdieu, *Distinction: A Social Critique of the Judgement of Taste* (Cambridge, MA: Harvard University Press, 1984), 170. Habitus consists of our thoughts, beliefs, interests, and our perception of the world around us as it comes from early socialization and the educational environment.

9 Denise Riley, *Selected Poems* (London: Reality Street, 2000).

10 Emmanuel Levinas, *Totality and Infinity: An Essay on Exteriority*. Trans. Alphonso Longis (Pittsburgh, PA: Duquesne University Press, 1969 [1961]).

11 Stephen Frosh and Lisa Baraitser, "Thinking, recognition and otherness", *Psychoanalytic Review* 90 (2003): 779.

12 On otherness within feminist discourse, see Elizabeth A. Grosz, *Volatile Bodies: Toward a Corporeal Feminism* (Bloomington: Indiana University Press, 1994); Tamsin Lorrain, *Deleuze and Guattari's Immanent Ethics* (Albany, NY: SUNY Press, 2011); and Elzbieta H. Oleski, *Intimate Citizenships: Gender, Sexualities, Politics* (London: Routledge, 2009).

13 See Chapters 1, 9, and 10 on response-ability in this volume.

14 In *Transformations: Thinking through Feminism* (London: Routledge, 2000), Sara Ahmed and her colleagues "think through" and beyond what feminism has achieved and how the various feminist movements understand themselves.

15 Audre Lorde, "The master's tools will never dismantle the master's house", in *Sister Outsider: Essays and Speeches*, 114–17 (Berkeley, CA: Crossing Press, 1984).

16 Chantal Mouffe, "Feminism, citizenship and radical democratic politics", in *Feminists Theorize the Political*, ed. Judith Butler and Joan W. Scott (London: Routledge, 1992), 372.

17 Ibid., 373.

18 See Judith Butler, *The Psychic Life of Power* (Stanford, CA: Stanford University Press, 1997), Amy Allen, *The Politics of Our Selves: Power, Autonomy and Gender in Contemporary Critical Theory* (New York: Columbia University Press, 2008), Susan Caputi, *Feminism and Power: The Need for Critical Theory* (Lanham, MD: Lexington Books, 2013), and Johanna Oksala, *Foucault on Freedom* (Cambridge: Cambridge University Press, 2005).

19 Friedrich Nietzsche, *On the Genealogy of Morality* (Cambridge: Cambridge University Press, 2007), 8.

20 Ibid., xvi.

21 Ibid., xxvii; Julian Young, *Nietzsche: A Philosophical Biography* (Cambridge: Cambridge University Press, 2010), 465.

22 Nietzsche, *On the Genealogy of Morality*, xiv; Young, *Nietzsche*, 459.

23 See Carmen Luke and Jennifer Gore (eds), *Feminisms and Critical Pedagogy* (New York: Routledge, 1992).

24 Butler, *Giving an Account of Oneself*, 12.

25 Donna Haraway, *The Companion Species Manifesto: Dogs, People, and Significant Otherness* (Chicago, IL: Prickly Paradigm Press, 2003); *When Species Meet* (Minnesota: University of Minnesota Press, 2008).

26 At this point I would like to emphasize that, in line with feminist pedagogy, my interests are focused at the level of process and practice, of attention and inquiry, of care and solidarity. Saying that I am interested in these issues is not to say I am interested in producing a series of answers or even alternatives for the queries that might arise. Rather, I am keen on pursuing a larger interest in the ethics of teaching and learning, and its conditions of possibility in our current educational environment.

27 Donna Haraway, "Situated knowledges: The science question in feminism as a site of discourse on the privilege of partial perspective", *Feminist Studies*, 14 (3), 575–99 (1988).

28 Donna Haraway, *Simians, Cyborgs, and Women: The Reinvention of Nature* (New York: Routledge, 1991), 189.

29 Ibid., 190.

30 bell hooks, *Teaching to Transgress: Education as the Practice of Freedom* (London: Routledge, 1994), 61. For a reflection on Freire and feminism, see Maya Nitis, "Feminist materialisms in class: Learning without masters", in *Teaching with Feminism Materialisms*, ed. Peta Hinton and Pat Treusch (Utrecht: ATGENDER, 2015), 111–22.

31 hooks, *Teaching to Transgress*, 214.

32 Ibid., 6.

33 Ibid., 21.

34 Ibid., 3.

35 Ibid., 10.

36 Ibid., 2.

37 Ibid.

38 This is an idea that hooks takes from Paolo Freire. When referring to the "banking system of education", Freire argues against knowledge as something

deposited, static, immobilized, and waiting as "truth" in the text to be uncovered and decoded. The "banking system of education" is organized around a conception of information as depositable and usable at some moment completely separated from the original scene of learning. This model offers a completely different idea of what, in fact, constitutes learning (Paolo Freire, *Teachers as Cultural Workers: Letters to Those Who Dare Teach* (Boulder, CO: Westview Press, 2005), 54).

39 Ibid.
40 Chandra Talpade Mohanty, *Feminism without Borders: Decolonizing Theory, Practicing Solidarity* (Durham, NC: Duke University Press, 2003), 116.
41 Ibid., 193.
42 Ibid., 131.
43 Haraway, *When Species Meet*, 3.
44 Mohanty, *Feminism without Borders*, 229.
45 Ibid., 238.
46 Ibid., 242.
47 Ibid., 243.
48 hooks, *Teaching to Transgress* (1994), 15.
49 Ibid., 207.
50 Rosi Braidotti, *The Posthuman* (London: Blackwell, 2013), 167.
51 Etymologically related, curious (origin: 1275–1325) careful, inquisitive, cure; curiosity (origin: 1350–1400) rel. to curious, and cure (origin: 1250–1300) to take care of; refer to the practice of teaching/learning as crucial elements of a feminist ethics of care.
52 Plath, *The Unabridged Journals*, 492.

References

Ahmed, Sara, Jane Kilby, Celia Lury, Maureen McNeil, and Beverley Skeggs, eds. *Transformations: Thinking through Feminism*. London: Routledge, 2000.

Allen, Amy. *The Politics of Our Selves: Power, Autonomy and Gender in Contemporary Critical Theory*. New York: Columbia University Press, 2008.

Bauman, Zygmunt. *Postmodern Ethics*. London: Wiley-Blackwell, 1993.

Bourdieu, Pierre. *Distinction: A Social Critique of the Judgement of Taste*. Cambridge, MA: Harvard University Press, 1984.

Braidotti, Rosi. *The Posthuman*. London: Blackwell, 2013.

Butler, Judith. *The Psychic Life of Power*. Stanford, CA: Stanford University Press, 1997.

Butler, Judith. *Giving an Account of Oneself*. New York: Fordham University Press, 2005.

Caputi, Susan. *Feminism and Power: The Need for Critical Theory*. Lanham, MD: Lexington Books, 2013.

De Certeau, Michel. *L'Invention du Quotidien, vol. 1 Arts de faire*. Paris: Gallimard, 1980.

Fraser, Nancy and Axel Honneth. *Redistribution or Recognition? A Political-Philosophical Exchange*. London: Verso, 2003.

Freire, Paolo. *Teachers as Cultural Workers: Letters to Those Who Dare Teach*. Boulder, CO: Westview Press, 2005.

Frosh, Stephen and Lisa Baraitser. "Thinking, recognition and otherness". *Psychoanalytic Review* 90 (2003): 771–89.

Green, Celia. *Letters from Exile: Observations on a Culture in Decline*. Oxford: Oxford Forum, 2004.

Grosz, Elizabeth A. *Volatile Bodies: Toward a Corporeal Feminism*. Bloomington: Indiana University Press, 1994.

Haraway, Donna. "Situated knowledges: The science question in feminism as a site of discourse on the privilege of partial perspective". *Feminist Studies* 14, 3 (1988): 575–99.

Haraway, Donna. *Simians, Cyborgs, and Women: The Reinvention of Nature*. New York: Routledge, 1991.

Haraway, Donna. *The Companion Species Manifesto: Dogs, People, and Significant Otherness*. Chicago, IL: Prickly Paradigm Press, 2003.

Haraway, Donna. *When Species Meet*. Minneapolis: University of Minnesota Press, 2008.

hooks, bell. *Teaching to Transgress: Education as the Practice of Freedom*. London: Routledge, 1994.

Jaggar, Alison M., ed. *Living with Contradictions: Controversies in Feminist Social Ethics*. Boulder, CO: Westview Press, 1994.

Levinas, Emmanuel. *Totality and Infinity: An Essay on Exteriority*. Trans. Alphonso Lingis. Pittsburgh, PA: Duquesne University Press, 1969 [1961].

Lorde, Audre. "The master's tools will never dismantle the master's house". In *Sister Outsider: Essays and Speeches*, 114–17. Berkeley, CA: Crossing Press, 1984.

Lorraine, Tamsin. *Deleuze and Guattari's Immanent Ethics*. Albany, NY: SUNY Press, 2011.

Luke, Carmen and Jennifer Gore, eds. *Feminisms and Critical Pedagogy*. New York: Routledge, 1992.

Mohanty, Chandra Talpade. *Feminism without Borders: Decolonizing Theory, Practicing Solidarity*. Durham, NC: Duke University Press, 2003.

Mouffe, Chantal. "Feminism, Citizenship and Radical Democratic Politics". In *Feminists Theorize the Political*, edited by Judith Butler and Joan W. Scott, 369–84. London: Routledge, 1992.

Nietzsche, Friedrich. *On the Genealogy of Morality*. Cambridge: Cambridge University Press, 2007.

Nitis, Maya. "Feminist Materialisms in Class: Learning without Masters". In *Teaching with Feminism Materialisms*, edited by Peta Hinton and Pat Treusch, 111–22. Utrecht: ATGENDER, 2015.

Oksala, Johanna. *Foucault on Freedom*. Cambridge: Cambridge University Press, 2005.

Oleski, Elzbieta H., ed. *Intimate Citizenships: Gender, Sexualities, Politics*. London: Routledge, 2009.

Peterson, Christopher and Martin E. P. Seligman. *Character Strengths and Virtues*. Oxford: Oxford University Press, 2004.

Plath, Sylvia. *The Unabridged Journals of Sylvia Plath*, edited by Karen V. Kukil. New York: Anchor, 2000.

Riley, Denise. *Selected Poems*. London: Reality Street, 2000.

Rorty, Richard. *An Ethics for Today: Finding Common Ground between Philosophy and Religion*. New York: Columbia University Press, 2010.

Young, Julian. *Nietzsche: A Philosophical Biography*. Cambridge: Cambridge University Press, 2010.

5

FEMINIST SCIENCE LITERACY AS A POLITICAL AND PEDAGOGICAL CHALLENGE

Insights from a high school research project

Rosa Costa and Iris Mendel

Science and science education have to be considered as socially situated political endeavours.[1] In the current social situation they seem particularly contested fields. While the neoliberal knowledge society relies on scientific knowledge for the stabilization and reproduction of the social order, an anti-science stance and anti-intellectualism is increasing with the rise of authoritarian ideas – in extreme right-wing, religious fundamentalist, and anti-feminist movements, but also in the so-called "centre" of society. Both neoliberal and reactionary conceptions of science are limited and problematic, foreclosing the possibilities of freedom and emancipation that critical science and science education may – despite justified critique (in particular postcolonial and feminist critique) – still have to offer. What might a feminist science literacy look like in this configuration?

In this chapter we discuss the prospects of a feminist science education in times of political crisis. By "political crisis" we mainly refer to the neoliberal individualization of social responsibility and the simultaneous revival of authoritarianism and nationalist collectivist thought. We focus on gendered aspects of this crisis, in particular the ideologies of gender put forward by post-feminism and anti-feminism. In using the term "crisis" we do not want to imply some imaginary "golden past" of democracy or science, let alone of gender relations; rather, we understand crisis as a congestion of ongoing social contradictions, as contested processes that allow for new forms of domination as well as for new forms of critique and resistance.[2] In this context, we look at current challenges for the critical teaching and learning of science, in particular the feminist critique of science.

In the following, we draw on our experiences and on the results of an ongoing research project called "Critical science literacy: Why science isn't simply true, what that has to do with you and how you can change it".[3]

During a period of six months we worked with 13 eleventh-grade high school students in Psychology and Philosophy, which is one subject in Austrian schools. The project's aim is to encourage a critical understanding of science as a powerful, social enterprise and to develop methods and materials for teaching and learning the feminist critique of science. A main focus lies on the knowledge of gender in everyday life that is informed by (pseudo-)scientific, biologistic theories. The project lasted for 22 months and concluded in July 2016. A schedule with the topics we dealt with at school can be found at the end of this chapter.

The project is part of the "Sparkling Science" research programme funded by the Austrian ministry of science, research, and economy, and has a citizen-science perspective; scientists are explicitly requested to reach out to schools and work "side by side with young people".[4] In our project, students were asked to participate in research by doing interviews, analysing popular media, or writing reflections. In addition to our own field notes and reflections on the teaching and learning process, we used this material to elaborate how feminist science literacy may be encouraged. Our understanding of feminist science literacy and education is crucially linked to social transformation and liberation in Paolo Freire's (1985) sense. Freire brings together the power to read and write with the power to change the world. We apply this idea to the power to "read" and "write" science, to produce critical knowledge about one's living conditions in order to be able to transform them.

One of our ambitions was therefore to link science with students' everyday lives and to motivate students to politically engage themselves in the project, but in order to encourage critical thinking and feminist science literacy, power relations at school and in society have to be considered. To better understand what was going on in the classroom, in this chapter we revisit the role of science education in the context of neoliberalism and the rise of authoritarianism, both of which simultaneously shape power relations at school, attitudes towards science, and the teaching/learning situation. Reflecting on our pedagogical work, we discuss the importance of an epistemology of positioning and responsibility that considers science in the context of domination *and* liberation. We argue that teaching and learning critical thinking is a precarious movement that needs to reflect the social and personal power relations involved. Referring to what bell hooks has called a "feminist classroom" (1989) we strive for a pedagogical attitude that is aware of power structures, takes responsibility for one's position, and is able to appreciate students and to handle conflict.

Criticizing science: taking context into account

With Antonio Gramsci (2003) we see the school as a political site where hegemonic understandings of politics, democracy, science, and gender may be promoted as well as challenged. At school certain "truths" – e.g., about human nature or gender – are learnt and "the making of scientific facts" takes place (Fleck 1980). However, the school is also a contested site, where "scientific truths" may be questioned and where critical science literacy may be developed. Despite much critical research in the field of science studies, many school curriculums still support what we call "the empiricist world-view". Derek Hodson, a Canadian researcher in science education, has found a strongly empiricist conception of science and scientists in school curriculums (science as value-free, exclusively Western, and modern activity done by experts possessing certain scientific attitudes, based on accurate observation and experiments, proceeding via induction, etc.) (Hodson 1999). While Hodson is referring to the Canadian context, a similar conception of science can be identified for the Austrian curriculum.

Of course the school is not only constituted by the curriculum, it also comprises the people there and what they do and think. Which understandings of science did we encounter at school? In our project, the students did interviews with each other and with some of their teachers to find out what science is for them. The interviews showed a much more ambivalent and sceptical understanding of science than the curricular empiricism identified by Hodson. For example, one student stated, "[Science is] a word people use to give more meaning to what they are saying". Another said, "Objectivity, but no human will ever obtain that … We can try to approach experiments and theories neutrally, but we would need to transcend our bodies, and even then I don't know if it is possible". A teacher remarked, "Science is not independent from history. … The history of science has also been one of coincidences, where we are getting to, which branch is studied intensely". We found that students' and teachers' everyday understanding of science offers a good starting point for a critical engagement with science.

Based on the feminist critique of science (e.g., Haraway 1991, Harding 2006, Singer 2005) we identify three critical perspectives which somewhat correspond with the statements above: the sociological perspective that looks at science as a field of power and social endeavour (see student 1); the epistemological perspective that perceives science as a field of knowledge and questions what knowledge is (see student 2); and the historical perspective that asks how science, knowledge, and society have changed over time (see teacher). These three perspectives informed our work with the students (see the schedule at the end of this chapter). Although we think that these perspectives, all of which show some critique of empiricism, are central for the development of a feminist science literacy, in a reductionist understanding they easily lead to a problematic relativism or give away science altogether. In our view, feminist science literacy needs to simultaneously hold on to the liberating aspects of science and criticize the role of science in legitimating and producing social inequalities (e.g., Mendel 2015).

Anti-science stances seem to be increasingly visible, and pose new challenges for science education (Faulstich and Trumann 2016). One response to science's present legitimation and credibility problems in the knowledge society are efforts to "bring science back to the people", e.g., through science popularization and communication programmes, or to "involve the people in science", e.g., in citizen science, or to educate people – as in science education. However, the very foundations of science, its institutional logic of competition and exclusion, its history of dominance and violence, and its "epistemologies of ignorance" (Sullivan and Tuana 2007) are left intact in these approaches.

Our project is situated within the neoliberal logic of the knowledge society and we have found ourselves again and again faced by the Enlightenment narrative of education and science solving all kinds of problems. However, our optimistic perspective on critical science education has been altered. We now see education not necessarily as part of the "solution" but as part of the problem in a neoliberal knowledge society, for the increasing attention to science education in a knowledge society is less about a critical engagement with science and more in favour of exploitation and adjustment. Exploitation, in that cognitive capitalism relies on knowledge, science, and technologies and the importance of immaterial labour gains, i.e. information work, communication work, creative work; and adjustment, in that knowledge plays a key role in the governance of people. In particular, discourses of the human sciences (like psychology, medicine, and pedagogy) produce knowledge about what is normal and desirable and control the needs and wants of individuals. That is, they assist in producing certain subjects – subjects who individually, voluntarily, and independently participate in relations of domination – but who also develop practices of resistance. Foucault (2006) has elaborated this perspective on power and has called this form of governing people "governmentality", with individuals responsible for their "decisions" based on "knowledge". Knowledge and learning therefore can be considered central forms of governance in the neoliberal knowledge society, and thus questions of science education gain in importance.

A critical science education does not simply question the role of science and pedagogy in neoliberalism, but also authoritarian and reactionary conceptions of science and society most prevalent in extreme right-wing, religious-fundamentalist, and anti-feminist movements. Extreme right-wing thought cannot simply be located at the social margins; rather, ideas and norms like the naturalness of social inequalities, a reactionary scepticism of modernity and progress, and contradictory or arbitrary references to science resonate with the social "mainstream". Opacity and the misconception of social reality are central elements of authoritarian mindsets, and therefore educating students about social relations may be an important approach, though not a sufficient one by itself. It is also important to ask about the social and personal function of right-wing notions such as gender stereotypes and conceptions of "normality" in order to open up ways of alternative thinking (Rajal and Schiedel 2016: 94). This points not only to the need for critical social theory, but also for personal engagement on the side of teachers and students – the challenges for critical science education are by no means modest.

Thus, while our initial objective was to question empiricist notions of science and to popularize the feminist critique of science, our work with students showed that issues of science, school, and pedagogy are complex. We found that in our political and pedagogical ambition to encourage something like feminist science literacy we had to take into account the different power relations involved, as we will point out in the following.

Suggested assignment

• In pairs, conduct interviews with each other about science. Possible questions: what is science for you? What role does science play in your everyday life? How can science be oppressive/liberating? Can you give examples from your own life? You can also find other questions that seem interesting to you.

Teaching methods: powerful practices

The simultaneous existence of neoliberalism and authoritarianism also shapes everyday life in Austrian schools. Authoritarian disciplinary practices are still present, as discussions with our students showed. Students get yelled at, democratic participation is rare, and lecture-style instruction is a common teaching method. Critical pedagogy criticizes not only obvious grievances like authoritarianism and a lack of democratic student participation, but also asks methodological questions about how teaching takes place. For instance, Freire (1973) refers to the educational system as a "banking model" that perceives students as passive containers of information instead of subjects of critical thinking. One of the most important scholars in science education, John Dewey (1929), shaped the approaches of "learning by doing" and "project teaching", and linked his pedagogical considerations to the democratization of society. Feminists showed how a hidden curriculum is in place that indirectly teaches students socially expected behaviour. Especially lecture-style lessons privilege students with the "right" habitus: as research indicates, white, male, upper-class students tend to speak more freely in class (Onnen 2015: 95). Project teaching and small-group work are also some of the feminist answers to promoting greater gender equality in student achievement.

In the neoliberal knowledge society, some of these ideas have been absorbed as the "new learning culture", one which points more to the interests of cognitive capitalism and neoliberal governmentality than to efforts of democratization. Pedagogical ideas like involving the students in curricular decisions or focusing on creativity and teamwork are welcome forms of self-improvement, and workforce requirements in the knowledge society. These teaching methods may have an emancipatory impetus, but having been appropriated by neoliberal logic, they make it harder to identify existing power relationships and potential ways of resistance. While the classic lecture format allows students to wander off in their thoughts, which is an important way of resistance in a forced-learning environment like school, new teaching and learning methods demand more active involvement from the students. Also, open protest in teacher-centred instruction is directed toward the teacher, whereas resistance in group work often disadvantages fellow students.

In our work with students we have profited immensely from bell hooks' reflections on teaching, and we are inspired by her idea that "the classroom should be an exciting place" (hooks 1994: 7). We realized, however, that *our* desire for the students to be enthusiastic and to engage themselves in the project in a very personal way was deeply presumptuous and invasive. We started to understand the students' lack of engagement as a way of resistance against our project – one that was imposed on them. When we offered the students our interpretation of their behaviour as an act of resistance,[5] a lively discussion started about their critique of the school system and strategies of withstanding and protesting the hierarchical organization and unwanted requirements they were confronted with every day. The discussion with the students also showed that authoritarian structures are still in place, but accompanied by new forms of governance in the neoliberal knowledge society such as individual responsibility. Altogether the students' feedback on our teaching methods was ambivalent – while some enjoyed the group work and playful approaches, others were more sceptical.

Teaching methods certainly do influence class dynamics and learning processes in school, but they are cosmetic tools for hiding power relations if problems like hierarchy, force, pressure, disrespect, and indifference are not addressed. A project like ours does not change the fact that students have little to say about what and how they want to learn – or do research about, even though the students' active involvement in the research is explicitly requested in this project format. If participation is taken seriously, the students would have to take part in the development of the whole project, the research questions, its objectives, and its results. But *we* designed the project and assigned the students a particular role in it.

Participation runs the risk of becoming an empty buzzword in neoliberal governmentality. On the one hand, there are more and more citizen participation opportunities like referendums, public forums, or science participation projects. On the other hand, a general disillusionment with politics and a sense of powerlessness in important decisions concerning the economy or science is rising (Jörke 2011). The neoliberal absorption of participation

FIGURE 5.1 Students playing a game

FIGURE 5.2 Group discussion

may thus inhibit protest[6] and conceal authoritarian power relations that are still in place, or even support them.

Feminist science education: challenging anti-feminism and post-feminism

Of course, methods cannot be separated from content. One main objective of feminist science literacy is to question gender ideologies prevalent in society and present in the students' everyday life, i.e. their daily conversations, popular media, school books, etc. We particularly tackled biologistic conceptions of gender that can be found in both right-wing authoritarian and neoliberal thought, although they are articulated differently in each case.

The perception of the social order as natural, e.g., heterosexual gender relations, is key to extreme right-wing and anti-feminist world views. This biologistic thinking is often based on pseudo-scientific references to sociobiology or ethology advancing social-Darwinist ideas (Götz 2014: 55f). Anti-feminism brings together different political groups from extreme right-wing movements to Catholic and conservative actors, and is also taken up by the "mainstream". Therefore, anti-feminist stances towards science vary from anti-science attitudes to embracing simplistic empiricist notions of science as a pure and apolitical endeavour. The more "mainstream" part of

FIGURE 5.3 Students presenting a group work on gender stereotypes

anti-feminism disqualifies feminism and gender research precisely based on "science" by dismissing gender studies as "unscientific" and "ideological" (Mayer and Sauer forthcoming). Feminist science literacy, then, requires an epistemological conception of science that is able to challenge biologistic conceptions of gender even in their most elaborate scientific versions, while understanding science as an always social and political endeavour. Feminist epistemologies offer such conceptions by bringing together objectivity, situatedness, and critical positioning.

We raised epistemological questions with the students through discussion of the history of science, which allowed us to question the connections between history, myths, and facts, and between science and power. Reading the feminist historian Londa Schiebinger (1993)[7] on the naming of mammals and the modern division of gender generated a discussion on categories that proved to be useful when we questioned the biological existence of two fixed sexes. This was an interesting point in the project. For a long time we had been astonished by the anti-sexist consensus in the class, which corresponds with the post-feminist rhetoric of equality and the disacknowledgement of discrimination that one encounters very often when working with young people (Jantz and Rauw 2001). According to Angela McRobbie (2009), post-feminism is a common form of anti-feminism in the neoliberal society. It is not openly opposed to feminist ideas like gender equality, but rather embraces them as being realized. Pointing to individual women's successes in politics, education, and the labour market as well as to liberations in sexuality, post-feminism disposes of feminism as something out of date that nobody needs anymore. Thus the neoliberal modernization of gender relations hides power relations and structural inequalities in a rhetoric of individual choice and responsibility, ultimately attributing them to natural sex differences. Correspondingly, in our work with the students we found a belief in a natural gender order beneath the anti-discriminatory surface.

Like the critique of a blunt anti-feminism, an engagement with post-feminism therefore requires a discussion of biologistic assumptions about gender. Feminist research on the history of sex hormones (Oudshoorn 1990) or in neuroscience (Höppner and Schmitz 2014) opened the door to reassess biological explanations of gender differences. We also created playful methods of deconstruction to show some absurdities of evolutionary psychology. For example, we invented a game called "Make your own theory" in which students had to explain certain gender stereotypes like colour preferences by constructing their own theories referring to evolution. Sometimes we would include existing theories and ask students to guess which is the "scientific" one. This turned out to be a real challenge since the students' theories were not only creative and funny, but sometimes matched the "real" ones.

The role of the media in constructing scientific facts about gender and spreading biologistic gender theories and gender stereotypes was another topic we dealt with. In particular, the relationships between stereotypes and reality was hard for students to grasp. We turned to feminist social psychological experiments (Fine 2010) to discuss how gender stereotypes like "men/boys are better in maths" are part of social reality and (unconsciously) influence people's perception and behaviour. We emphasized the importance of research design and showed how minor changes in research setting can manipulate results and erase gender differences. Aware of the social aspects of science we had been dealing with, the students criticized this social-psychological approach as not profound enough because it is still based on what they had learned to identify as "myths of science". On the one hand, we interpret this as a valid critique of empiricism, but on the other hand, it may be a questionable overachievement that leads to a relativistic critique of science and may support problematic anti-science stances. We realized that it is easy to provoke outrage about the sexist aspects of science, but much harder to encourage a dialectic view of science as both oppressive and potentially emancipatory.

Suggested assignment

- Evolutionary psychology tries to explain social behaviour with reference to the Stone Age and to concepts like "man the hunter and woman the gatherer". Although there is much scientific and feminist critique of evolution psychology as pseudo-science and of the gender ideologies involved (e.g., Rose and Rose 2001, Ruck 2014), the explanation of sex differences by the so-called evolutionary tasks of mankind is widespread in popular media as well as in sociobiological research.

  In this game the task is to construct theories about gender differences by referring to the Stone Age and the hunter-gatherer theory. In small groups the students have to invent a convincing explanation of a popular gender stereotype. The instructor may add an existing (pseudo-)scientific theory (for inspiration you can look into Pease and Pease 2000). All theories are written on a sheet of paper and then randomly read aloud. Every group has to decide which is the most convincing theory. In order to raise the excitement you can give points for each explanation that gets picked and elect a winner at the end.

  Example: Why do girls prefer pink? Because women were gatherers and their brain is therefore constructed to be attracted to red because berries are always red (a similar theory can actually be found in Hurlbert and Ling 2007). Or: Because women were responsible for a comfortable atmosphere in the caves and therefore drew pictures on the cave walls with their menstrual blood, which turns pink when dry (a theory that was invented by a group of the students in our class).

Taking responsibility for one's position: feminist epistemology and pedagogy

The deconstruction of empiricism opens up a space for a reactionary criticism of science if it is not tied to an epistemology that links knowledge production, positioning, and responsibility. The feminist critique of science provides perspectives on science that neither do away with science nor understand science as absolute, neutral, and inherently progressive endeavour. Empiricism and relativism both relieve subjects from responsibility, as Donna Haraway (1988, p 584) points out:

> Relativism is a way of being nowhere while claiming to be everywhere equally. The "equality" of positioning is a denial of responsibility and critical inquiry. Relativism is the perfect mirror twin of totalization in the ideologies of objectivity; both deny the stakes in location, embodiment, and partial perspective; both make it impossible to see well.

As an alternative, Haraway proposes an understanding of objectivity that requires reflective and responsible positioning and is based on "shared conversations".

FIGURE 5.4 Changing the setting

FIGURE 5.5 Creating a different atmosphere

As in feminist epistemologies, positioning and responsibility are central issues in feminist pedagogy. One of the core questions when teaching critical thinking is how much political positioning is appropriate on the part of the instructor. There are concerns that taking a political stance in the classroom influences students' opinions, implying that it is possible to absent oneself from one's position while teaching. The same objection as to empiricist epistemologies applies here: there is no neutral standpoint. Declaring one's position makes it transparent and open to discussion. Especially in inherently hierarchical pedagogical contexts, it is important to encounter students and their opposing views with appreciation and respect, which is not the same as accepting every opinion or action. Otherwise teachers impose their way of thinking as the only right one, and may even provoke the students to take an opposite standpoint just for the sake of it. Making room for different positions – as in our case towards gender conceptions – allows students to engage with them and develop their own, which is the point of critical thinking.

Our positioning also became relevant with regard to the different and sometimes contradictory roles we had in the classroom: as researchers we needed to produce a certain scientific "output"; as educators we had to teach basic skills and materials (because the students would later be tested on the subject); as political persons we wanted to engage the students in discussions and critical thinking about science. Tensions between these different logics and demands emerged from time to time not only in our discomfort, but also in the students' resistance and silence. We responded with transparency and disclosed our thoughts and analysis to the students. Our opening up proved to be a constructive strategy and was rewarded with increased engagement by the students. As bell hooks writes about the power of "sharing personal experience" and its effects on building a learning community and establishing a feminist classroom: "By making ourselves vulnerable we show our students that they can take risks, that they can be vulnerable, that they can have confidence that their thoughts, their ideas will be given appropriate consideration and respect" (hooks 2010: 57).

Instead of following our first impulse to blame the difficulties on the students, we acknowledged our own insecurity and looked at the structures that created a silenced classroom. This meant not only analysing the power relations in school and in our project, but also taking into consideration the political and social conditions of learning. A learning environment that makes transformation possible must be one of trust and mutual respect. Thus we had to change the regular school setting in order to create an atmosphere that allowed us and the students to really engage ourselves. For example, we rescheduled the weekly classes to a few longer units and provided food and drinks. But we think what really made the difference was our reflective and open interaction with the students. A relationship based on recognition and appreciation is central for feminist teaching. Our students proved this insight of critical pedagogy in their reflections of the project: "The amicable basis that Rosa and Iris established at the beginning made the lessons 'easier'. You had the feeling that friends were telling you a story and therefore it was easy for me to listen".

Of course, critical pedagogy is about something else than being liked by the students. bell hooks points out that "the feminist classroom is and should be a place where there is a sense of struggle" (hooks 1989: 51). The acknowledgement of the students as equals does not mean that actual power relations are denied, but that serious consideration is given to different positions and the power hierarchies involved. Instead of shutting down the students' resistance in an authoritarian, silencing manner the challenge is to face critical questions. At one point the students refused to do a group discussion and it was not easy to accept that we had "failed" at this point. We experienced a crisis in our teaching/learning that the feminist social scientist Frigga Haug (2003) considers central for any learning process: with reference to critical psychologist Klaus Holzkamp, Haug understands learning as a way of processing conflicts. This implies the necessity of giving up a secure position in favour of something new, which may lead to uncertainty. Learning – and teaching – are precarious movements that demand taking risks. Not only on the political level as stated above, but also on the pedagogical level, crisis thus opens up possibilities for social and personal transformation.

In our case we eventually used the conflict that arose in the classroom "as a catalyst for new thinking" (hooks 1994: 113) and gained many insights from it. The students' protest illustrated some of the fundamental issues with our project: how much participation is possible in a pre-designed school project? Is dissent still welcome when it comes in reactionary, anti-feminist ways? And how can you teach the emancipatory aspects of science and the critique of science at the same time?

Teaching feminism *and* feminist teaching

Any conception of feminist science literacy has to be contextualized within present social relations and must embrace science and education as both liberating and oppressing. The concurrence of neoliberal and authoritarian ideologies shapes conceptions of science and pedagogy and the functioning of power. Feminist science literacy is therefore confronted with complex and sometimes contradictory challenges. The feminist critique of science offers valuable tools to question the naturalization of gender relations prevalent in authoritarian anti-feminism and neoliberal post-feminism. It also presents alternatives to the empiricist and relativist conceptions of science, and holds on to science as a potentially emancipatory endeavour. However, *teaching feminism* – the critique of the naturalization of gender relations and the critique of hegemonic conceptions of knowledge – is not enough. We also need *feminist teaching*, and we strive to put into practice the notions of positioning and responsibility developed by feminist epistemologies and pedagogies – trying again and again to create what bell hooks has called a "feminist classroom" (hooks 1994).

A feminist classroom is a place of conflict, but also of appreciation. As Haug (2003) pointed out, learning is about uncertainty, about questioning experiences and making new ones. Learning, especially about social relations, means transgressing boundaries and confronting (internalized) structures of dominance and oppression. Feminist teaching has to establish a room where this is possible, where students and teachers dare to leave well-known paths.

In our final session at school we reflected on the project together with the students and talked about the learning process and the conflicts that had previously arisen. Again trusting in transparency, we told the students most of the insights we had developed throughout the project. The developed trust between us, the naming of power relations, and our specific role as outsiders in the school system allowed the students to talk freely about their everyday struggles. The students complained about authoritarian teachers, told us about their strategies of resistance and concluded: "Democracy doesn't exist at our school". It became clear that biologistic gender theories were not so much their concern, but the non-existence of democracy at their school awakened their enthusiasm. Feminist pedagogy can provide a space for politicizing personal

1 What is science?

- Science in everyday life
- Interviews: understandings of science in school
- Science in popular culture
- History of the Scientific Revolution
- Modern scientific paradigm: empiricism

2 Science and society

- Science and politics (Sandra Harding)
- History of science: Organizing nature and the gender order (Londa Schiebinger)
- Scientific sexism & biologization
- Categories and stereotypes: What is gender?
- Everyday theories and scientific theories

3 Scientific theories of gender

- Critical perspectives on scientific theories of gender
- Socio-psychological experiments on stereotypes (Cordelia Fine)
- Evolutionary psychology: Make your own theory
- Methods: Discourse analysis
- Research assignment: Scientific theories of gender in the media (4 groups analyze different media: article, TV show, science show, textbooks)

4 Feminist critique of science meets biological theories of gender

- Presentation of the analyses of different media
- Biologization of gender
- Feminist critique of neuroscience (Grit Höppner/ Sigrid Schmitz)
- History of sex hormones (Nelly Oudshoorn)
- Discussion: Is gender a biological fact?
- Making of scientific facts (Ludwik Fleck, Karin Knorr-Cetina)

5 Critical Science Literacy

- Philosophical conversation: What is knowledge?
- Interviews: Critical science literacy
- Written reflection
- Discussion: Resistance and power in school

FIGURE 5.6 Schedule of our work with the students

experiences and for transformation. We found our own ideas about feminist science literacy changed, pointing to new questions. Whereas we had started by using the school as a space to talk about science and gender, we ended with feminist science education as a way to open up questions about school and democracy.

Suggested assignment

- Have you ever experienced a feminist classroom? What constituted it? How did learning and teaching take place? How were power relations reflected? How did everybody – you, the teacher, the other students, contribute to it? What emotions did you have and what emotions were present in class?

Notes

1 For a discussion that puts science education in a social context and shows that it always comprises both possibilities of liberation and adjustment, see Costa and Mendel (2016).
2 For a feminist discussion of different conceptions of crisis see Dück (2014).
3 A description of the project can be found here: www.sparklingscience.at/en/projects/show.html?–typo3_neos_nodetypes-page%5Bid%5D=760.
4 More information on the research programme can be found here: www.sparkling-science.at/en.
5 On a new materialist reading of the classroom as an act of resistance see Revelles-Benavente (2015).
6 This tendency is well documented in the case of the citizen protest against the new train station in Stuttgart, Germany (Wagner 2013).
7 We adapted all feminist science texts we used in class to facilitate student comprehension. This teaching material (in German) will be available online soon.

References

Costa, Rosa and Mendel, Iris (2016). Zwischen Anpassung und Widerstand. Critical Science Literacy in der Wissensgesellschaft. In: Magazin erwachsenenbildung.at, 28. Vienna. Online: http://erwachsenenbildung.at/magazin/archiv.php?mid=9928 (15/09/16).

Dewey, John (1929). *Democracy and Education*. New York: Macmillan Company.

Dück, Julia (2014). Krise und Geschlecht. Überlegungen zu einem feministisch-materialistischen Krisenverständnis. In: *Prokla*, 174, pp. 53–70.

Faulstich, Peter and Trumann, Jana (2016). Wissenschaftsvermittlung, Popularisierung und kollektive Wissensproduktion. In: Magazin erwachsenenbildung.at, 27. Vienna. Online: http://erwachsenenbildung.at/magazin/16-27/meb16-27.pdf (15/09/16).

Fine, Cordelia (2010). *Delusions of Gender: How Our Minds, Society, and Neurosexism Create Difference*. New York: W. W. Norton.

Fleck, Ludwik (1980 [1935]). *Die Entstehung und Entwicklung einer wissenschaftlichen Tatsache. Einführung in die Lehre vom Denkstil und Denkkollektiv*. Frankfurt/M.: Suhrkamp.

Foucault, Michel (2006). *Die Geburt der Biopolitik. Geschichte der Gouvernementalität II. Vorlesung am Collège de France 1978–1979.* Frankfurt/M.: Suhrkamp.

Freire, Paulo (1973). *Pädagogik der Unterdrü ckten. Bildung als Praxis der Freiheit.* Reinbek: Hamburg.

Freire, Paulo (1985). Reading the World and Reading the Word: An Interview with Paulo Freire. In: *Language Arts*, 62(1), pp. 15–21.

Götz, Judith (2014) (Re-)Naturalisierungen der Geschlechterordnung. Anmerkungen zur Geschlechterblindheit der (österreichischen) Rechtsextremismusforschung. In: FIPU (ed.): *Rechtsextremismus 1. Entwicklungen und Analysen.* Vienna: Mandelbaum, pp. 40–68.

Gramsci, Antonio (2003). *Selections from the Prison Notebooks of Antonio Gramsci.* Ed. Quintin Hoare and Geoffrey Nowell Smith. London: Lawrence and Wishart.

Haraway, Donna, J. (1988). Situated Knowledges: The Science Question in Feminism and the Privilege of Partial Perspective. In: *Feminist Studies*, 14(3), pp. 575–99.

Haraway, Donna J. (1991). *Simians, Cyborgs, and Women: The Reinvention of Nature.* New York: Routledge.

Harding, Sandra (2006). *Science and Social Inequality: Feminist and Postcolonial Issues.* Urbana: University of Illinois Press.

Haug, Frigga (2003). *Lernverhältnisse. Selbstbewegungen und Selbstblockierungen.* Hamburg: Argument.

Hodson, Derek (1999). Going beyond Cultural Pluralism: Science Education for Sociopolitical Action. In: *Science Education*, 83, pp. 775–96.

hooks, bell (1989). *Talking Back: Thinking Feminist, Thinking Black.* Boston, MA: South End Press.

hooks, bell (1994). *Teaching to Transgress: Education as the Practice of Freedom.* New York: Routledge.

hooks, bell (2010). *Teaching Critical Teaching: Practical Wisdom.* New York: Routledge.

Höppner, Grit and Schmitz, Sigrid (2014). Neurofeminism and Feminist Neurosciences: A Critical Review of Contemporary Brain Research. In: *Frontiers in Human Neuroscience*, 8. Online: http://journal.frontiersin.org/article/10.3389/fnhum.2014.00546/full (17/05/2014).

Hurlbert, Anya and Ling, Yahzu (2007). Biological Components of Sex Differences in Color Preference. In: *Current Biology*, 17(16), pp. R623–R625.

Jantz, Olaf and Rauw, Regina, eds (2001). *Perspektiven geschlechtsbezogener Pädagogik. Impulse und Reflexionen zwischen Gender, Politik und Bildungsarbeit.* Wiesbaden: Springer.

Jörke, Dirk (2011). Bürgerbeteiligung in der Postdemokratie. In: Postdemokratie? Aus Politik und Zeitgeschichte (APuZ 1–2/2011). Online: www.bpb.de/apuz/33562/postdemokratie (15/09/16).

McRobbie, Angela (2009). *The Aftermath of Feminism: Gender, Culture and Social Change.* Los Angeles: SAGE.

Mayer, Stefanie and Sauer, Birgit (forthcoming). "Gender Ideology" as an Empty Signifier: Political Discourse and Networking in Austria. In: David Paternotte and Roman Kuhar (eds), *Anti-Gender Crusades in Europe: Mobilizations against Equality.* Lanham, MD: Rowman and Littlefield.

Mendel, Iris (2015). *WiderStandPunkte. Umkämpftes Wissen, feministische Wissenschaftskritik und kritische Sozialwissenschaften.* Münster: Westfälisches Dampfboot.

Onnen, Corinna (2015). Studying Gender to Teach Gender. Zur Vermittlung von Gender-Kompetenzen. In: Juliette Wedl and Annette Bartsch (eds), *Teaching Gender? Zum reflektierten Umgang mit Geschlecht im Schulunterricht und in der Lehramtsausbildung*. Bielefeld: Transkript, pp. 83–102.

Oudshoorn, Nelly (1990). The Birth of Sex Hormones. In: *Journal of the History of Biology*, 23(2), pp. 42–83.

Pease, Allan and Pease, Barbara (2000). *Why Men Don't Listen and Women Can't Read Maps*. New York: Wellcome Rain.

Rajal, Elke and Schiedel, Heribert (2016). Rechtsextremismusprävention in der Schule. Ein ambitioniertes Programm. In: FIPU (ed.), *Rechtsextremismus 2. Prävention und politische Bildung*. Vienna: Mandelbaum, pp. 85–136.

Revelles-Benavente, Beatriz (2015). Materializing Feminist Theory: The Classroom as an Act of Resistance. In: Peta Hinton and Pat Treusch (eds), *Teaching with Feminist Materialism: Teaching with Gender: European Women's Studies in International and Interdisciplinary Classrooms*. Utrecht: ATGENDER. Online: http://atgender. eu/files/2015/12/Teaching_with_Feminist_Materialisms.pdf.

Rose, Hilary and Rose, Steven, eds (2001). *Alas, Poor Darwin: Arguments against Evolutionary Psychology*. London: Vintage.

Ruck, Nora (2014). *Schönheit als Zeugnis. Evolutionspsychologische Schönheitsforschung und Geschlechterungleichheit*. Wiesbaden: Springer VS.

Schiebinger, Londa (1993). *Nature's Body: Gender in the Making of Modern Science*. Boston, MA: Beacon Press.

Singer, Mona (2005). *Geteilte Wahrheit. Feministische Epistemologie, Wissenssoziologie und Cultural Studies*. Vienna: Löcker.

Sullivan, Shannon and Tuana, Nancy, eds (2007). *Race and Epistemologies of Ignorance*. Albany, NY: Suny Press.

Wagner, Thomas (2013). *Die Mitmachfalle. Bürgerbeteiligung als Herrschaftsinstrument*. Köln: PapyRossa.

6

SCREENING FEMINISMS

Approaches for teaching sex and gender in film

Felicity Colman and Erin K. Stapleton

In teaching feminist film studies for both practice-based and theoretical courses, engaging the student body in a critical politics of responsibility provides a useful entry into studies of feminism, diversity, and equity issues. As educators, we have to ask what we can do in concrete terms to address the gender and diversity inequities in the world without creating a competing grand narrative subscribing to the neoliberalist discourses of economic and ideologic "mastery", but instead by exploring different ways to conceive of the world together.[1] This can be taught through all areas of screen analysis: through cognizance of the technological platform involved, and the gendered production, distribution, and marketing of particular types of film; the plurality of ideologies, narratives, and themes; models covered by screen media; and in the appeal to and rejection of the situated body of the spectator and participant in that media. This approach to feminist film studies is heralded by feminist thinkers who engage technologies, notably Donna Haraway, whose entire body of work consists of an appeal to "making a difference" to the inequities of gender bias across societies.[2] The conceptualizations and representations that screen media produce and engage with offer readily identifiable sources, evidence, and archives of ideological biases in different cultural and political systems. Communicating the structures that screen media like film engages with enables both a political and cultural analysis of the screen text, and a collective reorienting experience for the student, a reorienting towards what Latour refers to as the "reassemblage of the social", and away from what Wendy Brown (2015) identifies as the "neoliberal political imaginary" where the student was recruited for enrolment in expensive higher education for economic and not for autonomous political reasons.[3] Students are engaged with interventions that disrupt the educational economy of student-as-consumer and educator-as-service-provider dynamic that the neoliberal university system articulates. We have found that students are encouraged by neoliberal educational institutions to expect to be given information, and to be served by the (contingent) educators in their classroom. In advocating a politicization of this educational process via a feminist ethics of relational responsibilities, the aim is to teach students how to learn to reclaim their political situatedness in order to seek out information, and to learn how to take an active role in knowledge production. However, in the current climate, as Anna Hickey-Moody and Mary Lou Rasmussen argue, when the "personal isn't just political: it's marketable", then an intervention is called for.[4]

In this chapter, we focus on the situated experience of the student body. In doing so we engage the notion of "responsibility", as feminists committed to tackling problems created by modes of oppression of different political communities through racial and gender profiling. Joining with Hannah Arendt, Karen Barad, Rosi Braidotti, Judith Butler, Donna Haraway, bell hooks, Gillian Howie, Luce Irigaray, Kara Keeling, Chandra Mohanty, Gayatri Spivak, and Iris van der Tuin, we advocate for a pedagogy of feminist film theory and philosophy that is informed by political feminist, postcolonial feminist, and feminist new materialist scholarship. In doing so, our aim is to reconsider the categories of oppression of minoritarian groups, and focus on the possibilities for new ontological sites, new creative methodologies, and new feminist genealogies. We find that we can locate actions of responsibility at individual, deindividualized, community, trans-species, and machinic levels of engagement. We also wish to acknowledge that the burden of responsibility, empathy, and welfare obligation disproportionately affects female educators. The notion of "emotional labour" can be deployed here to consider how female educators are made responsible for the welfare of their students in a manner distinct from the experiences of male educators.[5] This assumed responsibility extends to the political and feminist provocation of students, and all educators should question the inclusivity of their work in terms of a feminist education. This could easily be checked at the readiness levels of curriculum design or curriculum revision stages to ensure that an inclusivity of materials and a responsible ethical content, both adequate for an appropriate range of taught diversity issues, are inserted into the disciplinary canon – a canon in which critical attention is paid to the problems of structural patriarchal, political, ethnic, and social racism, and misogyny, *and* against negative "othering" so that an adequate space is set for the inclusion of positive imaginings in a site of life.

"We" are two inter-generational educators, both of whom have taught and shared responsibilities in the research, delivery, and reception of feminist film and screen media curricula since the early 1990s, teaching with students in predominantly South-East Asian Pacific and European cohorts. These shared curriculum experiences engage the fundamental "hard questions" for feminist politics, the aim of which is to confront the dominant discourses of masculinist inequalities, and heteronormative propositions, enabled through patriarchal masochistic power structures, and addressed through the mediating factors of technological platforms of various screen-based media. These questions include a confrontation with patriarchal systems, and an examination of aesthetic and ethical approaches to questions of identity politics, sex and gender essentialisms, education, health, and other social and philosophical questions.

This chapter examines the relationship between the changing location of the (non-)personal, the experiential and material, and the political, taking as central the intimate issues of the biologically sexed and the publicly and culturally gendered body; the question of the desire of sex and of gender, and the material forces that design the politics of that desire. These are not the only questions for a feminist curricula of screen cultures, but as provocations they provide a primary action point from and with which to engage with issues of the history of gendering, of new forms of relationship building, of the issues surrounding the tensions and resolutions between the essentialist and the conceptualist theoretical and lived feminist positions, and are a mandatory topic for media that in its majority has a focus on bodies on screen and the worlds they provoke and produce. Proposed is a three-stage model for teaching feminist film theory where the matter of the film image is engaged first in terms of the units of experiences it focuses upon, then examined for the kinds of forces engaged, and finally related in terms of temporal politics.

The chapter takes as its applied example the topics and images of French filmmaker Catherine Breillat, and in particular her film *Á Ma Sœur* (*Fat Girl*, 2001), although the chapter also draws on her films of the same period, *Sex is Comedy* (2002) and *Romance X* (1999). Breillat's films are about the isolation of women in a situation of "romance" (*Romance*), the condition of women in relation to the situation of men in society (*Romance*), women in competition (the mother and her daughters, and the two sisters in *A Ma Soeur*), rather than women and comradery. Other feminist films that seek to represent women's comradery or feminist solidarity would engender a different kind of feminist reading and critique from those of Breillat. However, the concepts and methods are applicable for any film that engages with the articulation of issues surrounding gender construction, feminist agency, and feminist genealogies produced under patriarchal structures.[6]

Methodology: forming a collective identity

In film and media studies, late twentieth-century feminist theories appeal to the personal experience of the spectator.[7] Second-wave feminist discourses around the "personal is political",[8] together with a self-reflexive awareness of the situation of the viewer's body and its empirical, racial, and psychological experiences in relation to the screen action,[9] created a subject-centred approach to screen analysis. Typical of this are screen theories that identify with a particular viewing position, a stand-point for a specific body which then provides the possibilities of a politics of alienation from particular screen forms or dominant narratives, sites for women designated as "non-being",[10] cross-identification,[11] oppositional or counter-readings,[12] or politicized female spectatorship[13] that simultaneously locate the spectator-as-subject, a specific identity unable to engage with material possibilities beyond the rigidity of identity location. While this specificity can be politically productive in providing a starting point for the possibility of community, it can also be exclusionary in terms of its identification of a specific race, gender, or sexuality, and often does not account for non-gendered and non-stratified sexual possibilities, such as the experience of queer sexualities, gender-fluid, gender-queer, and transgender sensations and bodies. Further, the singular position is incompatible with a feminist new materialist position that argues for the understanding of an intra-active dynamic field in which the matter of bodies are relationally constituted.[14]

If we assign this personal viewing body to the student as spectator, then we run the risk of assigning an already mediated, visualized identity politic to that body, which can become an "essentialist" position. For example: you are x, based on the ways in which you signify as x and not y or z. For the majority of students, learning *how* to learn to take an empathetic, ethical, and critical approach to images of identity clusters requires a shift of focus toward how one can identify at various points that are the result of collective, trans-subjective, non-individuated communities or groups and not be limited to the specifics of perception either in relation or comparison to surrounding bodies, or restricted in ideological focus to the dominant media and institutional narratives. What we want to emphasize as worthwhile in the classroom safe space is the identification of experiential moments of the recognition of difference, not the already conceptualized body as a singular object. Joining experiential perspective with academic knowledge, as bell hooks describes, can result in the creation of shared communities but it is not without the risks associated with the identification and voicing of positionality.[15] As every classroom educator knows, the risks inherent to inviting student voices to contribute require that a careful mediation take place. This is necessary in order to avoid allowing dominant voices to overpower discussion, as well as to enable and allow productive silences where reflection may occur. In this we would advocate a controlled space where equipment is limited, in order to allow the students to focus on thinking through the issues at hand.[16] The instructor learns to rein in the discussion and bring shade to the silences through the carefully set questions for each class. It is advisable that all students have watched the film example together and done the set readings prior to the class time, which is framed for the students as a point of responsibility to their classmates as well as to their own learning. Thus students already have a shared body of knowledge that provides recognizable points for discussion and debate. This classroom experience becomes a process of following the methodology advocated by the teaching of feminist materials, with the pedagogical focus being on using the individual experience of the shared screen to then form a collective set of concepts and knowledges produced by this experience.

In addition to thinking about the feminist politics at hand, a consideration of the gendered nature of the technological production of screen media, such as film, is requisite to forming a considered analysis of the material nature of technology and of all its implications. In this, we follow the teaching of Karen Barad, who, in following Donna Haraway's diffractive methodology, reminds us that an approach to understanding differences can be achieved through a "performative understanding of techno-scientific and other natural-cultural practices [where] knowing, thinking, measuring, theorizing, and observing are material practices of intra-acting within and as part of the world".[17] Within any given media form, what are the potentials for a community of multiplicity, rather than a community of exclusion? Engaging the students from the outset in a recognition of the uneven distribution of resources in the world, including access to privileged sites of narrative film as well as citizen screen-based journalism, requires a focus on the material conditions depicted on screen and their political mediation. Information concerning the context of the filmic production and its contextual distribution field further contribute to an engagement with the politics of the screen system, and with the economy of its production of the various points where trans-subjects can identify as such within shared, situated communities – where we take a community to mean an identification of commonalities and themes, not of commonalities of identities. Recognition of a student and a community body does not simply mean identification of an absolute standpoint, or concrete "fact" about the situation of that body and its epistemological and molecular constitution.[18] Rather, it is about appealing to the material factors of heterogeneities that comprise a community of knowledge, not the identification of homo-semiotic markers of normativity: "Location is not a listing of adjectives or assigning of labels such as race, sex, and class", Haraway argues, rather it is about being "in the action, be[ing] finite and dirty, not transcendent and clean" in a relationship or community of solidarity, not mimesis.[19] This understanding of "situated knowledge", as Haraway describes the field of scientific knowledge, requires a certain kind of participant that we can think of in screen media terms as the technological fields that generate not just a spectator, as described in film theoretical trends of the twentieth century, but a participant that also acts as "modest witness"; required to engage and activate a critical position in and of community-epistemology.[20]

Taking an initial "show and tell" approach, we ask students to recount their personal experiences of viewing a film, of the *how* of the story (the epistemic facts of image and story construction), and of the situated (technological, physical, experiential) viewing experience. The aim of the classroom recounting is to then enable the students to move towards taking a turn away from this personal experience and towards being a "modest witness". Becoming a collective involves moving away from a singular standpoint, towards a shared resource in order to critique not only the production and concepts of the film, but also how and what are the forces enabling a relatable "experiential" moment as individuals within a collective. In teaching the *how* of a critical framework for engaging with the filmic text, such experiences can become a set of critical epistemological methods of the ways and means by and in which discursive, performative, material, and technological moments engage in the formations of materials and concepts that are generated by new technologies.

The approach is thus: 1. Articulate and critique the situatedness of the viewing experience in material (including technological) and social terms; 2. Identify and critique the epistemology of the narrative and its images in political terms; 3. Determine and critique the temporally determined witness-participant of the technological specificity of different screen media.[21] In taking these steps the method being practised, which should also be discussed with the class, is one of a material relationality using the tools of pedagogic classroom-as-safe-space and as test-laboratory. To develop this further, we point the instructor to Latour's critical address of the social in pondering how to think more abstractly about individual experience within the larger frameworks that institutions such as higher education and global film practices put forward.[22]

Temporal politics: portraits of women on the market

The position of the student in the classroom should be one of a freedom that is nonetheless respectful of the diversity of communities within that site. Through initial exposure to feminist concepts in the set reading texts and discussion in the classroom, the political grammar of gendered differences begins to emerge, using a feminist language that teaches a political modality through attention to experiences and manifestations of difference. Observation and analysis of the materiality of the situated body of the on-screen lives performing their communal bodies, through specific conditions of life, provides a way for students to begin to appreciate the abstractions of knowledge that feminist theories can and have enabled. Luce Irigaray's essay "Women on the Market" can be read in relation to any screen media form, setting up the more complex terms for questioning and discussing the historical roles that women are forced to take up in societies organized through particular stratifications of the gendered production of labour and through gendered economies of life.[23] Taking the critical language of capitalism that Marx developed to address the circulation of women as commodities in the marketplace, Irigaray argues that "wives, daughters, and sisters have value only in that they serve as the possibility of, and potential benefit in, relations among men".[24] We can take this market positioning of women-as-commodity as a starting point for conversation. Describing screen media situations, conditions, and characters, students often pick out images or concepts that they can personally relate to. This allows the biases of ethnic, gendered, and institutionalized identity-knowledge to become shared in the group, providing a useful starting paradigm that enables intensive entry points for students into or outside of texts and enabling their communities to create alternatives. Such a project may then be critiqued in terms of the binary positioning of a narrowly conceived, stereotypical, or limited "subject" – in the complexities of the gendered framework into which this "woman" or "gender" or "sex" or "race" notion circulates – and the extent to which each is performed and "entangled" with the other may be identified and discussed.[25] Challenging stereotyping and seeking different ways of expressing the multidiscursive affects that different bodies can generate has become one of the pressing agenda items for feminist theorists engaged in feminist epistemologies.[26] Hinton and Treusch note with regard to teaching with a feminist agenda today that the feminist materialist work demonstrates that "'actors' in knowledge processes cannot be conceived of in solely atomistic or anthropocentric terms".[27] New materialist feminist critiques offer accounts of historical shifts through genealogical approaches,[28] and post-human critiques of the notion of singular "identities" demonstrate the importance of taking a bio-deconstructed approach to the social political body and its mediated forms.[29]

In film studies, the pedagogic frame of feminism is addressed through the film content, and sometimes through its technological modality. The film text (which may or may not be overtly articulated as "feminist") is screened for the class, chosen for its affective lesson – perhaps a "friendship" film (e.g. *4 Months, 3 Weeks and 2 Days*, Dir. Cristian Mungiu, 2007); or a film that addresses a "family" experience (e.g. *Wasp*, Dir. Andrea Arnold, 2003); or a "coming-of-age" theme (e.g. *Mustang*, Dir. Deniz Gamze Ergüven, 2015); or a social "revenge" film (e.g. *A Girl Walks Home Alone at Night*, Dir. Ana Lily Amirpour, 2014) – and also chosen for the fundamental theoretical lesson on how a personal situation enables a positional aesthetics that is both determined and determining of one's access, entry, and position within a community; the film text is also chosen for the affective nature of its political conditions. Appealing to the student's potentiality for consciousness of the political conditions of the screen media site through the examination of the situation, the inhabitants of the screen, and their mediation, the pedagogic screen narrative enables students to take up a responsive analysis in the first instance. Depending on the type and style of screen media experienced, the classroom can then diffract this reading into as many different possible positions as are conceivable within the contextual and technological frameworks.

Witnessing sex as a material politics: après ma mort, je m'ennuie encore

Feminist film critic Sophie Mayer addresses Breillat's film *À Ma Soeur*[30] in terms of a question that Molly Haskell asks in relation to the staging of sex scenes in teenage films: "whose sexuality is it, exactly?"[31] This is a question that reappears in the case of many staged versions of "female" sexuality on screen, for example the lesbian sex scenes in the film *Blue Is the Warmest Color* (Dir. Abdellatif Kechiche, 2013), which were critiqued as being representative of the silence of women against their use as sexual motivators for men (and derided and critiqued by lesbians on multiple online forums, most famously in a clip titled "Lesbians React to Sex Scenes in 'Blue is the Warmest Color'").[32] Mayer refers to *À Ma Soeur* as "scintillating and disturbing", addressing the ways in which the teen female body is used as a problematic site.[33] In *À Ma Soeur*, adolescent female sexuality is framed around the concept of virginity, and female virginity in particular, which is an aspect that Eugenie Brinkema relates directly to transgression and violence.[34]

Breillat's film focuses on the rigidity of the lives of two sisters, how they are shaped by the perception of those around them and the expectations that their physical presence produces. Breillat draws a stark comparison between them by framing one as a late twentieth-century commercially "beautiful" fifteen-year-old girl, Elena (played by Roxane Mesquida), and the other, twelve-year-old Anaïs (played by Anaïs Reboux), as the "fat girl". There is an ethical issue to be discussed in the casting and framing of competition between young women in this way, which could be a focus of a classroom discussion. In one intense scene, Elena invites a boy, Fernando (played by Libero De Rienzo), into the sisters' holiday house bedroom, and as Anaïs is ignored, the couple engage in extended, awkward foreplay. Fernando's heavy breathing can be heard over the conversation as he fondles Elena's covered breast. The girl's body, then, becomes a site that serves to refer back to the viewer's sexual encounters, as well as to communicate the tension between the strength of desire and the disappointing reality of such an experience.[35]

The relationship between sexuality, consumption, and desire is produced through the juxtaposition between Anaïs and Elena throughout the film, where Anaïs is designated as not being desirable because she eats, but Elena does not eat and is thus able to be consumed. In a precursor to the sexual encounter to follow, Elena and Fernando eat breakfast with the sisters' family. The topic of discussion rests on Anaïs' food. Anaïs' father comments on her heaped plate, and Elena continues the discussion by talking about Anaïs' weight and how she eats and does little else, which, in turn, puts Elena off her food. The film makes Anaïs eat to avoid being like her sister, being used by men. Anaïs fantasizes about exploiting men the way her sister is exploited by them: for example, while talking to herself in the pool, Anaïs kisses the railing. She envies, resents, and pities her sister as she watches during Elena's encounters with Fernando. That evening, the sisters lie in twin beds, and Elena applies lipstick while reclining. Anaïs asks her what she is doing, and she replies that as she can't escape the compound of the holiday house where they are staying, she has invited Fernando over. Anaïs is told that she sees, hears, and knows nothing, but will remain a witness to Elena and Fernando's sexual encounter. Here, Breillat produces a tension between adolescent sexual exploration, exploitation, and incestuous sexuality. Elena's moody, resolved teenage pout remains throughout. Fernando arrives and acknowledges the overbearing silence in the room by asking for music, a request that can't be accommodated because they must be quiet to avoid being caught. As a result, the sound of Fernando and Elena kissing is nauseatingly wet and breathy. Every movement is magnified by the crickets and silence. Elena (playfully) challenges Fernando on his desire for music, demonstrating the overanxiousness for men to desire her that Anaïs observes in the film's opening scene. Even music played in the background is a challenge or disruption to his desire, and represents the threatening competition for his attention that Elena fears.

The lack of ambient sound is further amplified when Elena and Fernando progress to his touching her breast while they kiss. The breathy groping becomes unbearable for the squeamish viewer as Fernando fumbles with Elena's bra. Elena asks Fernando how many girls he's "had" while he touches her breasts; she is matter-of-fact, even defiant, and clearly threatened by the thought of competition, but still obligingly stretches and offers her body to him. Not sleeping with him "makes a big difference", he says, as he gets out a cigarette, realizing she's a virgin. He smokes while telling her about a woman that wanted to sleep with him so much it made him "feel sick" and tells her how he tried to avoid having sex with her. "I got a kick out of dumping her like that", he laughs, as he ashes a cigarette in an ashtray he's placed on Elena's stomach, further demonstrating his disdain for women, and particularly for those who articulate their desires. This further reinforces for Elena that she is to be desired and not to desire autonomously. Elena asks whether Fernando would respect her, even if she slept with him; he replies that he would, although it is obvious from this exchange that he already does not.

Anaïs listens from her bed, picking at her nose, and covering her eyes with her hands, but watches through her fingers as Fernando has sex with her sister. He promises to only penetrate her "part of the way" and to not come in her, he tries to guilt her into allowing him to fuck her properly by threatening to fuck someone else instead, or directly afterwards. She replies that she loves him, but that she needs time. She looks away from his eyes, moving her head to avoid confrontation. He tries to fuck her anyway, and then tells her she's "spoiling" their relationship, and this strained negotiation extends for a considerable amount of time, made tedious through repetition.

Elena's desire to protect and mediate her virginity is a demonstration in opposition to Anaïs' assertion at the beginning of the film, that she wants her "first" to be "nothing" so that no man can claim (sexual) ownership over her. Fernando calls Elena a "little girl who looks like a woman" and continues to try to manipulate her into having sex with him. He touches her hip and vulva, and describes the encounter as "a demonstration of love" (her love for him, although that remains unclear). Throughout, the presence of Anaïs, witnessing from her bed, produces further illicit tension. The scene abruptly cuts to Anaïs' eyes as Elena grunts, and then cries out "stop" and groans. The audience infer the act through the fear on Anaïs' face. Elena is clearly in pain as Fernando penetrates her anally, following his explanation that women can still say that they haven't been with someone that way, which Elena designates "sick". Afterwards, she says "I feel like crying" and Fernando responds by telling her "that was a wonderful gift" and touches her face and won't stop in a way that is as oppressive for the viewer as it is for her. Fernando stays in Elena's bed until morning, still grabbing at her face and neck, closely, controlling. Before leaving, he asks Elena to fellate him, and Elena expresses concern that Anaïs is awake and jealous. Anaïs abruptly yells that she wants some sleep. As he leaves, Fernando designates their encounter sinister, not because of Anaïs, but, as he implies, because he has not had everything he wanted. Worried, Elena asks if he wants to break up, and then says "until next time" before fellating him at the garden gate.

The situation that Breillat sets up here makes overt the sexing of gender, and this community's conditioning of women and men clearly represents the senses of all performing as commodities in a given site. Indeed, film critic Linda Williams argues that *À Ma Soeur* "turns out to be a comparative study in the forms of humiliating sexual initiation and the damage they can do to young girls with no real power over their sexual fate".[36] The use of Elena's body as an object for penetration only denies her any agency for her own desire in the marketplace of bodies. The relationship between the body, its desires, and the condition of identity, or the self, is further complicated here as a site of constant movement. Breillat's narrative ending of this film provides an extreme rejection of the normative modes of female gendering that the film maps out when Anaïs' self, along with the notion of a body, and the body's sense of the self is refigured. Instead of a singular girl, sister, or daughter, the body is produced in ways that must be recognized through interaction with the material and representational world, in such ways that each recognition, experience, interaction, and moment is generative of a new body and a new self.[37] This generativity further complicates desire, particularly, as Braidotti has noted, the concept of desire as reliant upon a mastery of the self, to be defined in opposition to an other.[38] Desire becomes a site of the demarcation of privilege, where the possibility for the subject of desire is defined by the ability of the subject within a given political context to express it. As Braidotti writes, "desire is never a given", but the (sexual) expression of autonomy provided by the objectification of an other, and the provision of social and political recognition bestowed upon some bodies, forms, and sensations over others.[39]

Conclusion: communicating the political praxis

The concepts of sex, gender, and desire provide provocations for the classroom. Sex can be a confronting topic for students of all ages and orientations to address, as can their position on what constitutes gender, and how to articulate notions of desire. The cultural variations in what constitutes normative standards of behaviour in all such topics and related ideas, policies, and practices mean that cognitive, empirical, and semiotic methods for analysis of sound-images are limited in their address. Recent theoretical turns in post-psychological affect theory, in film studies in particular, have seen the address of the sensorial that the cognitive may have left out, but affective theories per se,[40] tend to repeat the same universalist errors that the "spectator" theories of first-wave feminist film theory made in addressing the "body" of the viewer.[41] Not all bodies are the same, and they certainly can't be ascribed any form of reactive change by another. In a theoretical turn towards a queer "sensuality", the argument that a "sensual figuration" created through filmic displays of sexual acts "cancel" semiotics by their "excess" requires further elaboration of what constitutes excess, and to whom. If the image is to be understood as being relationally productive for re-examining the situation of the political sphere, then the methods for analysis of the image must be adequate. The dictum "the personal is political" in the contemporary classroom brings with it the danger of becoming an emphasis on rigid identification categories within the realm of the personal and the authentic at the expense of the political and actionable.[42] In the feminist classroom, students often relate their personal experiences to ideas discussed, but it is not the relationship between existing feminist ideas and their own lives that is important but rather the question of how to mobilize that relationship between the personal, once identified, and the broader politics of the community at hand. The use of cultural examples and particularly films can assist with this mobilization as a clear way to motivate students to think beyond themselves and to queer a representation, following Patricia MacCormack's notion of queer as an approach to given material where "queer is a way of approaching the unfamiliar".[43]

The conception of normative forces and their critique can be established as "subjectivist" where the experience of life is "a detaching power" designed to separate the individual from the community and from communication.[44] The position of experiential normativity, which is constituted by the identification of the unremarkable for the student, is a position of habit. We read and relate to specific images, including moving images, as a comparative relation to a culturally and economically ascribed "normativity" that is composed by a repetition of recognition which produces this habit, a process that Claire Colebrook describes as "the stabilisation of the self through a repeatable norm".[45] Films that confront normative positioning and expectations (for example, *Baise-Moi*, 2002, dir. Coralie Trinh Thi and Virginie Despentes, 2002; *Spider Lilies*, 2007, dir. Zero Chou), or films that approach ideas of gender in a challenging or non-normative way (for example, *The Life and Times of Rosie the Riveter*, 1980, dir. Connie Fields; *Daughters of the Dust*, 1991, dir. Julie Dash; *All About My Mother*, 1999, dir. Pedro Almodóvar; *The Milk of Sorrow*, 2009, dir. Claudia Llosa) become tools for constructing a feminist pedagogy. The different forms and genres of feminist films also provide further tools.[46]

We advocate balancing images of popular culture feminism with a range of different local and delocalized feminist cultures so that a "normative" position (as Irigaray addresses) becomes questionable through the proliferation of images of different feminisms, thus providing a framework for a critical feminist pedagogy. This approach often exceeds textbook phrasing, and therefore prevents the discussion of feminisms from being confined to any specific location when seen and compared collectively.[47]

Teachers must be prepared to set up flexible but firm rules of debate at the start of classes, addressing the issues of safety of opinion, confidentiality within the classroom space, the concepts of different cultural mores and norms, and the temporally and culturally divisive arena of censorship. Students should be allowed to not participate in some of the screenings or areas of discussion if they feel unable to confront some of the topics broached, and alternatives for assessment processes should be arranged prior to the start of classes. Teaching the practice of inclusive formations of discourses of the self also means providing a grounding in the critical histories and theories of such practices – including Foucault's concept of care of the self, but also extending to recognition that a self-body is constituted across political histories that perform community requirements.[48] While some critique of the rise of the "trigger warning" is valid, the use of techniques like creating the concept of a "safe space" and warning students about challenging material in advance both allows access for participants who, for whatever reason, feel unable to engage with that material, but (perhaps even more importantly), it allows teachers to continue to present students with stimulating and provocative materials without censoring them for fear of undermining the mental health or cultural sensibilities of those at risk.

A political community is predicated on common goals, but it must also be an agreement or treaty between diverse bodies, an agreement to participate in the recognition of commonality and solidarity while engendering difference. This approach to feminist pedagogy has the potential to produce the most politically engaged, nuanced student experiences. In this chapter, we have mobilized a discussion of films made by Catherine Breillat to illustrate the possibilities for feminist film analysis in the classroom. In offering an alternative and critical approach to neoliberal feminist discourses that eschew the particularity of the material body for the sake of authentically located identity politics, Breillat makes an analysis of the affective political aesthetics of the screen site. Using the framework of "relational responsibilities" that is to be devised in the classroom and the tools of feminist second-wave (Haraway) and feminist materialist (Barad) theory, this chapter has established that there has been a fundamental change in the ways in which we can conceive of a personal-political, and how the relation between the personal-political might be renegotiated in the context of the analysis of screen media through feminist pedagogy. In this, we hope to re-engage students in the active, collaborative, and creative production of feminist epistemological thinking.

Questions

- What have been some of the historical roles women have played in society, culture, and politics? How are these roles depicted in contemporary film?
- How is the position of "woman" challenged or confirmed by contemporary film?
- How does the neoliberal economy produce a "feminism without women"?[49]

Suggested assignment

- Using specific examples, discuss the empowerment of women through the contemporary televisual and cinematic use of the female body as an active and creative site for the expression of sexuality and desire.
- Could we speak of a gendered temporality? Discuss with reference to film/television.
- In what ways can films and/or television programmes which foreground aspects of sexuality be read as subversive?
- What might constitute a feminist discourse of a counter language? Discuss with reference to films or television programmes which address the voice, language, sounds, and/or music of women.
- Discuss the political implications of pornography for women through an evaluation of different feminist positions on pornography.
- Is a woman's body her destiny? Argue this topic through at least two of the key concepts of feminist film theory.

Notes

1 Here we draw on the respective works of Donna Haraway, "Situated Knowledges: The Science Question in Feminism and the Privilege of Partial Perspective", *Feminist Studies*, 14, 3 (1988): 575–99; bell hooks, *Teaching to Transgress: Education as the Practice of Freedom* (New York: Routledge, 1994), 172;

and Wendy Brown, *Undoing the Demos: Neoliberalism's Stealth Revolution* (Cambridge, MA: MIT Press, 2015), 41 ff.

2 Donna Haraway, *Modest–Witness@Second–Millennium: FemaleMan©_Meets_ OncoMouse™: Feminism and Technoscience* (New York: Routledge, 1997), 16.

3 Bruno Latour, *Reassembling the Social: An Introduction to Actor-Network-Theory* (Oxford: Oxford University Press, 2007); Brown, *Undoing the Demos*.

4 Anna Hickey-Moody and Mary Lou Rasmussen, "The Sexed Subject in-between Deleuze and Butler", in *Deleuze and Queer Theory*, Chrysanthi Nigianni and Merl Storr, eds, 37–53 (Edinburgh: Edinburgh University Press, 2005), 39.

5 Karen Ramsay, "Women: Mothers and Others: Discourses of Women and Motherhood in Three Academic Departments", in *Challenges and Negotiations for Women in Higher Education*, Pamela Cotterill, Sue Jackson and Gayle Letherby, eds, 48–9 (Dordrecht: Springer, 2007).

6 For example, the film *Mustang* (Deniz Gamze Ergüven, 2015) would be equally well suited to such a reading, as are the film oeuvres of: Chantal Akerman; Ana Lily Amirpour; Andrea Arnold; Sadie Benning; Lizzie Borden; Jane Campion; Gurinder Chadha; Lisa Cholodenko; Sofia Coppola; Catherine Corsini; Julie Dash; Claire Denis; Maya Deren; Vivienne Dick; Cheryl Dunye; Marlene Gorris; Leslie Harris; Mary Harron; Todd Haynes; Joanna Hogg; Karyn Kusama; Clara Law; Samira Makhmalbaf; Marzieh Meshkini; Trinh Minh-ha; Tracey Moffatt; Kimberley Pierce; Monika Pellizzari; Sally Potter; Carolee Schneemann; Céline Sciamma; Susan Seidleman; Monica Treut; Rose Troche; Margarethe Von Trotta; Athina Rachel Tsangari; Agnes Varda – to name but a few examples.

7 Annette Kuhn, *The Power of the Image: Essays on Representation and Sexuality* (London: Routledge, 1985), 3; Martine Beugnet and Laura Mulvey, "Feminist Perspective", in *Feminisms: Diversity, Difference and Multiplicity in Contemporary Film Cultures*, Laura Mulvey and Anna Backman Rogers, eds (Amsterdam: Amsterdam University Press, 2015).

8 Carol Hanisch, "The Personal Is Political", in *Radical Feminism*, Anne Koedt, Ellen Levin, and Anita Rapone, eds (New York: Quadrangle Books, 1973), 113.

9 See bell hooks, *Reel to Reel: Race, Sex, and Class at the Movies* (London: Routledge, 1996); Minh-ha Trinh, *Cinema Interval* (London: Routledge, 1999); Laura Mulvey, "Visual Pleasure and Narrative Cinema", in *Film Theory and Criticism: Introductory Readings*, Leo Braudy and Marshall Cohen, eds, 833–44 (New York: Oxford University Press, 1999); A. Smelik, *And the Mirror Cracked: Feminist Cinema and Film Theory* (London: MacMillan, 1998).

10 Jane Gaines, "White Privilege and Looking Relations: Race and Gender in Feminist Film Theory [1988]", in *Feminism and Film*, E. A. Kaplan, ed., 351 (Oxford: Oxford University Press, 2000).

11 Mulvey, "Visual Pleasure and Narrative Cinema".

12 bell hooks, "The Oppositional Gaze: Black Female Spectators", in *Film and Theory: An Anthology*, Robert Stam and Toby Miller, eds, 510 (Malden, MA: Blackwell Publishers, 2000).

13 Mary Ann Doane, "Film and the Masquerade: Theorizing the Female Spectator", in *Film and Theory: An Anthology*, Robert Stam and Toby Miller, eds, 495 (Malden, MA: Blackwell Publishers, 2000).

14 See Rosi Braidotti, *Metamorphoses: Towards a Materialist Theory of Becoming* (Cambridge: Polity Press, 2002); Karen Barad, "Posthumanist Performativity: Toward an Understanding of How Matter Comes to Matter", in *Signs*, 28, 3 (2003): 801–31.

15 hooks, *Teaching to Transgress*.

16 For example, restricting the use of laptops and smartphones during class discussion, which can be discussed with students in relation to respecting and engaging with others, as well as a way of preventing the recording of discussion in a "safe space".

17 Karen Barad, *Meeting the Universe Halfway: Quantum Physics and the Entanglement of Matter and Meaning* (Durham, NC: Duke University Press, 2007), 90.
18 Haraway, *Modest-Witness@Second-Millennium*, 25–6.
19 Ibid., 2–3; 37.
20 In our forthcoming book on *Feminist Screen Media, Practice and Philosophy* we describe more fully this sense of the feminist epistemological community participant.
21 We use the term "witness" here on a number of levels, beyond the scope of this article, we refer readers to Haraway's sense of a "modest witness" as well as the use in observational and trauma film accounts, for example as discussed in Lisa Downing and Libby Saxton, *Film and Ethics: Foreclosed Encounters* (Abingdon: Routledge, 2010), 71–4.
22 Latour, *Reassembling the Social*.
23 See Maria Mies, *Patriarchy and Accumulation on a World Scale: Women in the International Division of Labour* (London: Zed, 1998 [1986]).
24 Luce Irigaray, "Women on the Market", in *This Sex Which Is Not One*, trans. Catherine Porter (Ithaca, NY: Cornell University Press, 1985), 172.
25 We engage the sense of a performance of identity and the entangled subjectivities it produced through readings of Barad, Butler, and Haraway: Barad, "Posthumanist Performativity"; Judith Butler, *Bodies that Matter: On the Discursive Limits of Sex* (New York: Routledge, 1993); Haraway, "Situated Knowledges".
26 Cf. Sara Ahmed's work on diversity, affect, and race within a feminist key in *On Being Included: Racism and Diversity in Institutional Life* (Durham, NC: Duke University Press, 2012); *Queer Phenomenology: Orientations, Objects, Others* (Durham, NC: Duke University Press, 2006); and the new materialist approach taken to generating feminist epistemology by Iris Van der Tuin, in her book *Generational Feminism: New Materialist Introduction to a Generative Approach* (Lanham, MD: Lexington Books, 2015).
27 Peta Hinton and Pat Treusch, "Introduction: Teaching with Feminist Materialisms", in *Teaching with Feminist Materialisms*, Peta Hinton and Pat Treusch, eds (Utrecht: ATGENDER, 2015), 3.
28 van der Tuin, *Generational Feminism*.
29 For examples of these critiques see Patricia MacCormack, *Posthuman Ethics: Embodiment and Cultural Theory* (London: Routledge, 2012); Rosi Braidotti, *The Posthuman* (Cambridge: Polity Press, 2013); and Rosi Braidotti, "Posthuman Affirmative Politics", in *Resisting Biopolitics: Philosophical, Political and Performative Strategies*, S. E. Wilmer and Audrone Zukauskite, eds, 30–56 (London: Routledge, 2016).
30 Which was re-titled *Fat Girl* for Anglophone cinematic release, reflecting the need for explicit explanations in Anglophone filmic consumption practices.
31 Haskell, cited in Sophie Mayer, *Political Animals: The New Feminist Cinema* (London: IB Taurus, 2015), 147.
32 See Manohla Dargis, "Seeing You Seeing Me: The Trouble with 'Blue Is the Warmest Color'", *New York Times*, 25 October 2013. See also Marlene Gorris' 1982 film, *A Question of Silence*. The video "Lesbians React to Sex Scenes in 'Blue is the Warmest Color'" can be found here: https://youtu.be/rIjJ_VtU9PA (accessed 10 September 2016).
33 Mayer, *Political Animals*, 146.
34 Eugenie Brinkema, "Celluloid is Sticky: Sex, Death, Materiality, Metaphysics (in Some Films by Catherine Breillat)", *Women: A Cultural Review*, 17, 2 (2006): 156.
35 A useful classroom reading to accompany the viewing and discussion of this film is found in Linda Williams' discussion of Breillat's films in her chapter

"Philosophy in the Bedroom: Hard-Core Art Film since the 1990s", in Williams, *Screening Sex*, 258–98 (Durham, NC: Duke University Press, 2008).

36 Williams, *Screening Sex*, 283.

37 L. Ayu Saraswati, "Wikisexuality: Rethinking Sexuality in Cyberspace", *Sexualities*, 16, 5/6 (2013): 587–603.

38 Rosi Braidotti, keynote lecture: "Vectors of Affirmation", London Graduate School Bloomsbury Lecture, Central St Martins and Kingston University, London, 2015.

39 Rosi Braidotti, "Interview with Rosi Braidotti: 'The Notion of the Univocity of Being or Single Matter Positions Difference as a Verb or Process of Becoming at the Heart of the Matter'", in *New Materialism: Interviews and Cartographies*, Rick Dolphijn and Iris van der Tuin, eds, 32 (Ann Arbor, MI: Open Humanities Press, 2012).

40 See Marie-Luise Angerer, *Desire after Affect*. Trans. Nicholas Grindell (London: Rowman and Littlefield, 2015 [2007]); Anu Koivunen, "The Promise of Touch: Turns to Affect in Feminist Film Theory", in *Feminisms: Diversity, Difference and Multiplicity in Contemporary Film Cultures*, Laura Mulvey and Anna Backman Rogers, eds, 97–110 (Amsterdam: Amsterdam University Press, 2015) for a summary.

41 See Susan Hayward, *Cinema Studies: The Key Concepts*, 343–9 (London: Routledge, 2000) for a summary.

42 Hanisch, "The Personal Is Political", 113.

43 MacCormack, *Posthuman Ethics*, 109.

44 Claire Colebrook, "Norm Wars", in *Revisiting Normativity with Deleuze*, Rosi Braidotti and Patricia Pisters, eds, 81–2 (London: Bloomsbury Publishing, 2012).

45 Colebrook, "Norm Wars", 90.

46 For just one example, see the discussion of feminist documentary film in Ilona Hongisto, *Soul of the Documentary: Framing, Expression, Ethics* (Amsterdam: Amsterdam University Press, 2015).

47 For example: we might look at the specific events and how different feminist groups respond to them in films by Nadine Labaki, Samira Makhmalbaf, or Andrea Arnold.

48 Michel Foucault, *The Care of the Self: The History of Sexuality*, Vol. 3, trans. Robert Hurley (New York: Vintage Books, 1988).

49 Braidotti, "Posthuman Affirmative Politics", 40.

References

Ahmed, Sara. *Queer Phenomenology: Orientations, Objects, Others*. Durham, NC: Duke University Press, 2006.

Ahmed, Sara. *On Being Included: Racism and Diversity in Institutional Life*. Durham, NC: Duke University Press, 2012.

Angerer, Marie-Luise. *Desire after Affect*. Translated by Nicholas Grindell. London: Rowman and Littlefield, 2015 [2007].

Barad, Karen. "Posthumanist Performativity: Toward an Understanding of How Matter Comes to Matter". *Signs*, 28, 3, 2003, 801–31.

Barad, Karen. *Meeting the Universe Halfway: Quantum Physics and the Entanglement of Matter and Meaning*. Durham, NC: Duke University Press, 2007.

Beugnet, Martine and Mulvey, Laura. "Feminist Perspective". In *Feminisms: Diversity, Difference and Multiplicity in Contemporary Film Cultures*, edited by Laura Mulvey and Anna Backman Rogers, 187–202. Amsterdam: Amsterdam University Press, 2015.

Braidotti, Rosi. *Metamorphoses: Towards a Materialist Theory of Becoming.* Cambridge: Polity Press, 2002.

Braidotti, Rosi. "Interview with Rosi Braidotti: 'The Notion of the Univocity of Being or Single Matter Positions Difference as a Verb or Process of Becoming at the Heart of the Matter'". In *New Materialism: Interviews and Cartographies,* edited by Rick Dolphijn and Iris van der Tuin, 19–37. Ann Arbor, MI: Open Humanities Press, 2012.

Braidotti, Rosi. *The Posthuman.* Cambridge: Polity Press, 2013.

Braidotti, Rosi. "Posthuman Affirmative Politics". In *Resisting Biopolitics: Philosophical, Political and Performative Strategies,* edited by S. E. Wilmer and Audrone Zukauskite, 30–56. London: Routledge, 2016.

Brinkema, Eugenie. "Celluloid is Sticky: Sex, Death, Materiality, Metaphysics (in Some Films by Catherine Breillat)". *Women: A Cultural Review,* 17, 2, 2006.

Brown, Wendy. *Undoing the Demos: Neoliberalism's Stealth Revolution.* Cambridge, MA: MIT Press, 2015.

Butler, Judith. *Bodies that Matter: On the Discursive Limits of Sex.* New York: Routledge, 1993.

Colebrook, Claire. "Norm Wars". In *Revisiting Normativity with Deleuze,* edited by Rosi Braidotti and Patricia Pisters, 81–97. London: Bloomsbury, 2012.

Dargis, Manohla. "Seeing You Seeing Me: The Trouble with 'Blue Is the Warmest Color'". *New York Times,* 25 October 2013. Retrieved from www.nytimes.com/2013/10/27/movies/the-trouble-with-blue-is-the-warmest-color.html?_r=0.

Doane, Mary Ann. "Film and the Masquerade: Theorizing the Female Spectator". In *Film and Theory: An Anthology,* edited by Robert Stam and Toby Miller, 495–509. Malden, MA: Blackwell Publishers, 2000.

Downing, Lisa and Saxton, Libby. *Film and Ethics: Foreclosed Encounters.* Abingdon: Routledge, 2010.

Foucault, Michel. *The History of Sexuality, Vol. 3: The Care of the Self,* translated by Robert Hurley. New York: Vintage Books, 1988 [1986].

Gaines, Jane. "White Privilege and Looking Relations: Race and Gender in Feminist Film Theory [1988]". In *Feminism and Film,* edited by E. A. Kaplan, 336–55. Oxford: Oxford University Press, 2000.

Hanisch, Carol. "The Personal Is Political". In *Radical Feminism,* edited by Anne Koedt, Ellen Levin, and Anita Rapone, 113. New York: Quadrangle Books, 1973.

Haraway, Donna. "Situated Knowledges: The Science Question in Feminism and the Privilege of Partial Perspective". *Feminist Studies,* 14, 3, 1988, 575–99.

Haraway, Donna. *Modest-Witness@Second-Millennium: FemaleMan©_Meets_OncoMouse™: Feminism and Technoscience.* London: Routledge, 1997.

Hayward, Susan. *Cinema Studies: The Key Concepts.* London: Routledge, 2000.

Hickey-Moody, Anna and Mary Lou Rasmussen. "The Sexed Subject in-between Deleuze and Butler". *Deleuze and Queer Theory,* edited by Chrysanthi Nigianni and Merl Storr, 37–53. Edinburgh: Edinburgh University Press, 2005.

Hinton, Peta and Treusch, Pat. "Introduction: Teaching with Feminist Materialisms". In *Teaching with Feminist Materialisms,* edited by Peta Hinton and Pat Treusch, 1–22. Utrecht: ATGENDER, 2015.

Hongisto, Ilona. *Soul of the Documentary: Framing, Expression, Ethics.* Amsterdam: Amsterdam University Press, 2015.

hooks, bell. *Teaching to Transgress: Education as the Practice of Freedom.* New York: Routledge: 1994.

hooks, bell. *Reel to Reel: Race, Sex, and Class at the Movies*. London: Routledge, 1996.

hooks, bell. "The Oppositional Gaze: Black Female Spectators". In *Film and Theory: An Anthology*, edited by Robert Stam and Toby Miller, 510–23. Malden, MA: Blackwell Publishers, 2000.

Irigaray, Luce. "Women on the Market". In *This Sex Which Is Not One*, translated by Catherine Porter, 170–91. Ithaca, NY: Cornell University Press, 1985 [1978].

Koivunen, Anu. "The Promise of Touch: Turns to Affect in Feminist Film Theory". In *Feminisms: Diversity, Difference and Multiplicity in Contemporary Film Cultures*, edited by Laura Mulvey and Anna Backman Rogers, 97–110. Amsterdam: Amsterdam University Press, 2015.

Kuhn, Annette. *The Power of the Image: Essays on Representation and Sexuality*. London: Routledge, 1985.

Latour, Bruno. *Reassembling the Social: An Introduction to Actor-Network-Theory*. Oxford: Oxford University Press, 2007.

MacCormack, Patricia. *Posthuman Ethics: Embodiment and Cultural Theory*. London: Routledge, 2012.

Mayer, Sophie. *Political Animals: The New Feminist Cinema*. London: I. B.Tauris, 2016.

Mies, Maria. *Patriarchy and Accumulation on a World Scale: Women in the International Division of Labour*. London: Zed, 1998 [1986].

Mulvey, Laura. "Visual Pleasure and Narrative Cinema". In *Film Theory and Criticism: Introductory Readings*, edited by Leo Braudy and Marshall Cohen, 833–44. New York: Oxford University Press, 1999.

Ramsay, Karen. "Women: Mothers and Others: Discourses of Women and Motherhood in Three Academic Departments". In *Challenges and Negotiations for Women in Higher Education*, edited by Pamela Cotterill, Sue Jackson, and Gayle Letherby, 48–9. Dordrecht: Springer, 2007.

Saraswati, L. Ayu. "Wikisexuality: Rethinking Sexuality in Cyberspace". *Sexualities* 16, 5/6, 2013, 587–603.

Smelik, A. *And the Mirror Cracked: Feminist Cinema and Film Theory*. London: MacMillan, 1998.

Trinh, T. Minh-ha. *Cinema Interval*. London: Routledge, 1999.

van der Tuin, Iris. *Generational Feminism: New Materialist Introduction to a Generative Approach*. Lanham, MD: Lexington Books, 2015.

Williams, Linda. *Screening Sex*. Durham, NC: Duke University Press, 2008.

7

DOUBT, EXCITEMENT, PLEASURE

Feminist practices of teaching and learning in art and education

Barbara Mahlknecht

Introduction

This chapter discusses how processes of teaching and learning in art education could productively draw on feminist thinking to make sense of affective
experiences such as doubt, excitement, and pleasure. Art and education are
two fields where affect plays a primary role: while art is firmly connected
to perception, the senses, and aesthetic experience, and therefore involves
both body and mind, feminist practices of teaching and learning aim at both
the transformation of the self as well as the conditions in which one learns.
Within the last two decades in the field of art and education, art educators,
teachers, theorists, and artists have been intensively working with language
and discourse as a central mode of the production, reflection, and distribution of knowledge.[1] At the same time, the sphere of feelings, emotions, the
body, and affects has not been taken into account so much. Learning processes always also involve affects. As this topic is still very young, and only
a few previous studies have explicitly drawn on affects within processes
of teaching and learning in art education,[2] I would like to contribute to
this emergent field of discourse by drawing on the nuanced and multifold
elaborations of feminist thinkers and teachers who have scrutinized the role
of affects, feelings, and emotions within learning processes. I am interested
in exploring the multifold and critical legacies of feminist thinking about
teaching and learning that relate to affect.

I argue that there are different reasons why – as art educators, thinkers, and practitioners – we have to critically examine the role and function of affects and work with emotions and feelings within the context of
art education. Firstly, in contemporary capitalism, affects are extensively
produced, distributed, organized, regulated, and maintained for the needs

of capitalism.[3] The necessity of critically examining affect in the thinking and practice of art pedagogy relates to the overall conditions of contemporary society as well as to art production. Precisely because affects are a primary source of processes of valorization in capitalism, and therefore represent a central aspect of contemporary culture and society, critical art pedagogies need to scrutinize and to work on the role of affects both as a generic subject of study as well as within the practice of art education itself. Secondly, because contemporary art is a field that is both intensively shaped and regulated by global capitalism, and therefore represents a "factory" for new ideas on the production and distribution of affects, this suggests that artists, curators, art educators, and theorists need to critically examine the interrelations of art, capitalism, and affects.

Thirdly, as Lauren Berlant (2007),[4] Ann Cvetkovich (2007), and Sarah S. Amsler (2015) have underlined, the relations of capitalism, colonial continuities, and racism are "affectively anchored" and "emotionally mediated regimes of power" (Amsler 2015, 110), as Amsler put it:

> Affect is equally significant in radical democratic politics. Whether we incline towards participation, withdrawal or domination; co-operation, individuation or competition; and receptivity, prejudice or dogmatism is an affective problem as much as it is an intellectual, social or economic one. Patriarchy, capitalism, colonial and neo-colonial systems of power, racism, xenophobia, bureaucracy, militarism, terrorism, political behaviour, collective action and scientific knowledge are affectively anchored and emotionally mediated regimes of power.
>
> *(Amsler 2015, 210)*

If we conceive art education as a radical and transformative practice that looks at and engages in how to both alter and create the conditions of learning, then we have to include affects as never isolated and purely subjective entities. On the contrary, affects are deeply embedded in the societal, political, economic, and institutional relations. And art education can respond to these conditions either by reaffirming and reproducing or by disrupting, questioning, and transforming them.

Feminist thinkers such as Sara Ahmed (2014) and Anne Cvetkovich (2012) are critical regarding the overemphasis that conceptualizes the affective turn as the rewriting of cultural theory through a paradigmatic shift to affect. Cvetkovich and others, for instance, have argued that the shift to affect in cultural theory does not fully recognize that the subject of affect has a long history in feminist research. Within the tradition of feminist thinking, affect emerges e.g. in relation to the private and public sphere.[5]

As the legacies of feminist thinking on affect in the context of teaching and learning represent a rich field of complex elaborations that tackle the production and function of affect in learning processes as well as the power relations inscribed into its material and bodily aspects, I argue that reconnecting to these critical elaborations is more than valuable. Feminist thinkers have scrutinized the productive role of affects and feelings within learning processes such as pleasure, excitement, doubt, uncertainty, and discomfort. Drawing on the materialist-feminist writings of Frigga Haug and the author, activist, and feminist bell hooks, I will explore doubt, excitement, and pleasure in feminist thinking. These elaborations are thought to contribute to the emergent field of studies on gender, affect, and art education and to the development of new strategies and practices in art education at universities and art academies as well as in the context of schools, art galleries, museums, and community arts projects.

Contemporary capitalism, the production of affects, relational and art pedagogical practices

The following section provides a cartography that tries to map some of the complex and multilayered relations between contemporary capitalism, policy papers, and the rise of relational and immaterial practices in art and art education. I will sketch these connections by drawing on a diverse field of studies and materials – the theorization of affective capitalism, the *UNESCO Roadmap for Arts Education*, the claim for the application of affects within art education by Howard Cannatella, as well as the emerging field of immaterial, relational art (pedagogical) practices. This trajectory aims at elaborating on the interconnections of capitalism, affect, art, and education in order to point out the problematic developments that call for new feminist concepts and practices resistant to the capitalist regimes re/producing the gendered and racialist hierarchies and relations of power that involve, produce, and regulate affect.

In contemporary global capitalism, affects play a crucial role. As recent studies on neoliberal regimes of affective capitalism have emphasized, affect-production, similarly to knowledge-production, is regarded as an exploitable resource.[6] In the context of new post-Fordist conditions of labor, the immaterial productivity of bodies gains importance, and both affective skills and affective sources of living labor are subjected to processes of valorization-by-capital. In his seminal text, *The Autonomy of Affect* (1995), Brian Massumi underlines the value of affect for capitalism: "The ability of affect to produce an economic effect more swiftly and surely than economics itself means that affect is itself a real condition, an intrinsic variable of the late capitalist system, as infrastructural as a factory. It is beyond infrastructural, it is everywhere, in effect". In this context, art education, because it is connected to the senses, to perception, feeling, emotion, and affect, can be regarded as a significant instrument for the development of "human capital".

For instance, the UNESCO World Conference that took place in Lisbon in 2006, entitled "The World Conference on Arts Education: Building Creative

Capacities for the 21st Century", shows a clear connection between a neoliberal politics aiming at "maximizing the reach and frequency of market
transactions" through bringing "all human action into the domain of the
market" and art education (Harvey 2005, 256). The *UNESCO Roadmap
for Arts Education*, published as an outcome of the conference, makes
claims about the "implementation of Arts Education at a policy and govern-
mental level". It elaborates on the aims and concepts of arts education, the
essential strategies for "effective" arts education, utilizing both research and
knowledge sharing and recommendations that address educators, parents,
artists, directors of schools, and training institutions as well as government
ministries:

> This Roadmap, therefore, aims to communicate a vision and develop
> a consensus on the importance of Arts Education for building a cre-
> ative and culturally aware society; encourage collaborative reflection
> and action; and garner the necessary financial and human resources
> to ensure a complete integration of Arts Education into education sys-
> tems and schools.
>
> *(UNESCO 2006, 3, 5)*

Moreover, the *Roadmap for Arts Education* suggests that art education can
contribute to the valorization of human capital by stimulating imagination,
aesthetic perception, and human intelligence as well as by mobilizing skills,
activities, and experiences. From this point of view, the investment in art
education emerges as a central instrument for the accumulation of capital.

Another of the Roadmap's arguments connecting arts education to affects
proposes that arts education is able to establish a "solid grounding of the
citizen" by fostering emotional development that "can bring about a better
balance between cognitive and emotional development" (UNESCO 2006,
5). Though these two arguments – the production of affect as related to
the development of human resources, and the production of emotion as a
solid ground of citizenship – might substantially differ, they both highlight
how affect and emotion are being conceptualized as primary sources for the
development and the utilization of "human capital" and "creative capital".

Similarly to the *UNESCO Roadmap of Arts Education*, philosopher
Howard Cannatella in a recent publication entitled *Why We Need Arts
Education* (2015) advocates in favor of "the happiness principle" in art education. For Cannatella, as found in John Stuart Mill's *Utilitarianism* (1863),
art education can contribute to augmenting human happiness. At the same
time, art education is a tool to regulate and calibrate emotions. According to
Cannatella, it enables us to "soften[s] our passions, infuse[s] and energize[s]
our feelings". Significantly, this understanding of the relation of art education and affects is utilitarian. While art education is an instrument, affects
represent its material source. Cannatella is examining how art education, as

a common good, can contribute to society: he suggests that affects and emotions can both enhance and decrease the quality of living and of sociability, and that art education has to calibrate affect and emotions while aiming at enhancing "happiness". In other words, art education offers tools and methods to provoke "good" feelings and to channel "bad" feelings. As a consequence, Cannatella's conception of happiness easily relates to a particular mode of the capitalistic valorization and regulation of affects that transforms subjectivity itself into a mode of productivity (Lazzarato 1996).

All in all, both the *Roadmap for Arts Education* and Cannatella's conception promote art education as an instrument that provokes, mobilizes, regulates, and channels affects and emotions with the purpose of serving a human-resource capitalism whose principal material of valorization is human potential. Through learning systems, human capacities are to be developed and capitalized.[7] For this purpose, affects and emotions are extensively produced and maintained for the needs of capitalism.

The immaterial modes through which contemporary capitalism produces, regulates, calibrates, and channels affects that become a source of the capitalistic valorization processes are related to the field of relational art (pedagogical) practices. Art theorists such as Claire Bishop (2006) have argued for the rise of immaterial and relational art practices that blur art and life and that produce a specific sociability. In the wake of the social turn in contemporary art, relational artistic practices are increasingly evaluated by their working processes and their models of collaboration. Moreover, affects such as discomfort and frustration that can be accompanied by "absurdity, eccentricity, doubt or sheer pleasure" can emphasize central aspects of an artwork's aesthetic impact (Bishop 2006, 181). Indeed, artistic practices, as well as the relations and structures they produce, resemble the relational structures of affective capitalism.

Taken together, the sketched relations between affective capitalism, the *UNESCO Roadmap for Arts Education*, Cannatella's claim for the application of affects within art education and the emerging field of immaterial, relational art (pedagogical) practices highlight the necessity for critical feminist approaches. Feminist practices of teaching and learning in art education elaborate on the interconnections of materiality, the body, and affect and examine the power relations inscribed into how we relate to ourselves, to each other, and to the world through affect, emotions, and feelings. In the following section, I would like to draw on the multifold elaborations of materialist-feminist Frigga Haug and the author, activist, and feminist bell hooks.

Pedagogical relations I: excitement, pleasure

bell hooks describes her early learning experiences in the United States of the 1960s that were marked by racial segregation, oppression, and exclusion as well as the black civil rights movement as empowering. In her book *Teaching to Transgress: Education as Practice of Freedom* (1994), hooks understands teaching and learning as practices of liberation and as tools of resistance. In examining her learning experience, hooks detects significant differences. Reflecting on her time as a student at the Western, white-dominated institution of Stanford University, she understands how learning can be a practice of submission and obedience, while she remembers her early learning experiences at the Booker T. Washington School in Hopkinsville, Kentucky, to be liberating. Departing from this experience, *learning* in hooks' examination emerges as a practice of intellectual resistance situated in the in-between of pleasure and danger: insofar as the possibility of transformation implies both the pleasure of being changed as well as it unsettles the subject in its stability and its values:

> I loved learning. School was the place of ecstasy – pleasure and danger. To be changed by ideas was pleasure. But to learn ideas did run counter to values and beliefs learned at home was to place oneself at risk, to enter the danger zone. Home was the place where I was forced to conform to someone else's image of who and what I should be. School was the place where I could forget that self and, through ideas, reinvent myself.
>
> *(hooks 1994, 3)*

This movement of blurring the subject's boundaries entails the experience of excitement – pleasure and danger. Excitement as transgression, enthusiasm, and tension can be linked precisely to the openness, the inconsistency, and fragility of processes of learning and teaching, processes that ultimately cannot be determined or controlled, and that may alter both teachers and learners. Excitement exceeds the limits of the pedagogical relationship, just as desire for excitement transgresses the conventional setting of the classroom: "Excitement in higher education was viewed as potentially disruptive of the atmosphere of seriousness assumed to be essential to the learning process. To enter classroom settings in colleges and universities with the will to share the desire to encourage excitement, was to transgress" (hooks 1994, 3). Based on respect and acknowledgment, hooks, in following radical critical educator Paolo Freire, understands education as a "practice of freedom" that addresses both learners and teachers. The practice of freedom includes self-empowerment as well as the radical self-exposure to one's own vulnerability and desire.

According to hooks, excitement and pleasure are related to teaching and learning. Pleasure, a term that draws from the Old French word "plesir", also "plaisir", as "enjoyment, delight, desire, will", means "sensual enjoyment as the chief object of life" and is recorded from the sixteenth century.[8] Pleasure is related to objects that affect us, but also to an encounter that can give us pleasure. We can take pleasure from others, and we can give plea-sure *to* others. The sensation or emotion of pleasure – to take and to give pleasure – can be passively experienced as well as actively given. Pleasure is relational, and it connects objects and subjects. Pleasure is related to the body, to the mind, and to objects.

To examine the role of pleasure within processes of teaching and learn-ing, we can draw on what Sara Ahmed writes in her text *Happy Objects* (2010, 31). Ahmed draws on John Locke's *An Essay Concerning Human Understanding* (1698) to explain how happiness is related to the "'what' in 'what happens' and the 'what' in 'what' that makes us happy" (Ahmed 2010, 31). Locke describes pleasure and pain as the primary affects. Pleasure is also, as Ahmed underlines, intertwined with touch, taste, hearing, feeling, and seeing, because pleasure is the proximity of objects and subjects. To explain this, Ahmed refers to John Locke's example that pleasure is related to an object that affects us positively, for example, grapes. For the one who loves grapes, pleasure is evoked by the grapes, or more precisely by eating grapes. Pleasure is not only about the object itself, but – e.g. in tasting the grapes – it is about the "sensuous proximity with the flesh of the body, as a meeting of the flesh" (Ahmed 2010, 31). Moreover, pleasure involves the memory of pleasure and, therefore, it can relate to an object that is absent.

But what is the role of pleasure in processes of teaching and learning? How can pleasure function as a catalyst for learning processes in art educa-tion? For hooks, pleasure is related to the "joy of learning" and to "eros as a motivating force" within pedagogical processes. She speaks about the excite-ment that is provoked through engaged pedagogy and collective learning. Hooks emphasizes that within the Western white hegemonic spaces of teach-ing and learning, students and teachers are "determined to erase the body":

> Entering the classroom determined to erase the body and give our-selves more fully to the mind, we show by our beings how deeply we have accepted that passion has no place in the classroom. Repression and denial make it possible for us to forget and then desperately seek to recover ourselves, our feelings, our passions in some private place – after class.
>
> *(hooks 1994, 192)*

Conversely to the repression of passion in the classroom, the experiences she had at black schools enabled hooks to bring forward a black feminist teach-ing practice where pleasure and excitement play a crucial role.

Excitement, in the sense of the "condition of mental and emotional agita-tion" that transgresses the boundaries between objects and subjects as well as in the sense of "encouragement", addresses a bodily experience of both pleasure and endangerment, enjoyment, and pain that creates and opens new perspectives and relations. Both pleasure and excitement can be understood as a vehicle in processes of teaching and learning. Pleasure and excitement, conversely to Cannatella's concept of art education as a tool to regulate and calibrate passions, are, in hooks' view, neither an aim in themselves nor a tool to enhance or decrease the quality of life. Rather, affects, emotions, and feelings are related to learning processes, and they represent the material conditionality of how the self is able to reorient itself to others and the world in new and unexpected ways that can sometimes be joyful and easy, and other times challenging and painful.

Now, I consider hooks' conception of pleasure and excitement as a very valuable source for thinking and working with affects, emotions, and feelings in the context of feminist practices of teaching and learning. Moreover, art education represents a particular field where teaching and learning with pleasure and excitement could be especially productive. Contemporary practices of art education, in departing from situated practices and strategies that enable us to work from and with affect and emotion and that involve the body, touch, hearing, seeing, and feeling, could engender new critical spaces of feminist teaching and learning. These practices could counter the hegemonic repression and exclusion of affect, emotion, and feeling from learning settings, while at the same time introducing them as a critical and emancipatory agenda that could resist its contemporary instrumentalization and commodification by processes of capitalistic valorization.

Pedagogical relations II: doubt, contradiction

While pleasure and excitement represent affects that open up multifold relations between the self, the other(s), and the world, and transgress the boundaries of a presupposed order of things, doubt appears as a contrasting concept. In the history of Western philosophy, doubt is a complex and multifold concept. Often, doubt is associated with the pure and abstract process of cognition, and it is related to René Descartes' *Meditations on First Philosophy* (1641). Descartes, in his *Meditations*, applies doubt as an epistemological method. Through radical doubt, the *Meditations* aim at indubitable grounds for the foundation of science. Descartes puts the fundamentals of the presupposed truth into question and takes the "*cogito ergo sum*" as the indubitable evidence. Conversely, Baruch de Spinoza conceptualizes doubt in relation to imagination: according to de Spinoza, impressions are themselves contradicting, and therefore they provoke the indecision of imagination. At the same time, doubts can themselves provoke affects such as fear, trust, confidence, despair, joy, and remorse. If doubt is resolved, affects can change. Doubt, according to de Spinoza, is both related to the contradictive impressions of perception and affects. Doubt is not itself an affect, but it is tightly related to affects that are either provoked or changed through doubt (Handwerker Küchenhoff 2006, 137 ff).

Unrest, discomfort, doubt, fear, experience, illusion, and contradiction are indeed substantial categories for the thinking of Frigga Haug, a feminist-materialist sociologist, philosopher, and teacher. In her book *Relations of Learning: Self-Movements and Self-Blockades* [Lernverhältnisse. Selbstbewegungen und Selbstblockierungen] (2003), she introduces her study on learning and teaching first of all through expressing a feeling of *vital unrest*. After many years of examining theories of learning and the way that other learners learn, Haug finds herself unsettled. Partly, this unrest relates to the desire oriented towards "re-leasing" learning rather than working on a "foundation" of learning. Haug writes: "I am unsettled by real people, by what they do, how they move, how they learn, and what difficulties they thereby experience, what solutions they find" (Haug 2003, 9). Moreover, her discomfort results from her irritation that Klaus Holzkamp's *Relations of Learning: Self-Movements and Self-Blockades* [Lernen. Subjektwissenschaftliche *Grundlegung*] (1993) neglects crucial issues of learning such as ideology, gender, and culture.[9]

Haug's multilayered and complex explorations aim to tackle learning as vital and dynamic processes that relate to the self, to others, and to the world. She conceives learning as part of societal conditions that either affirm and reproduce or question and transform these very same circumstances. Haug's examination focuses precisely on how learning can enable processes that disrupt rather than reconstitute the conditions in which one learns. Haug's exploration traces the interrelationships in the in-between of societal circumstances, learning, the transformation of the self as well as the conditions in which learning is embedded.

Haug's liberatory attitude, in following Gramsci as well as Marx, targets a critical intervention into social, political, and cultural relations. Marx, in his *Theses on Feuerbach* (1845), criticizes the materialist doctrine that perceives men as pure products of circumstances, and he emphasizes that changing conditions relate to and coincide with the human activity of "changing the self".

But how are doubt, experience, crisis, and contradiction particularly articulated in Haug's study of learning processes? And how are these learning processes themselves being shaped by the thinking-feeling of doubt, contradiction, and crisis? As her point of departure, Haug examines four different case studies of learning experience through the technique of what she calls "memory work" [Erinnerungsarbeit].[10] Working on memory indeed represents one of her central research methods. The memories she keeps of learning situations reveal experiences of different quality: both her memory of learning how to read and how to throw a ball recall feelings of inability, refusal, and blockade. The situation of a university seminar in which she tries to pose an intelligent question provokes insecurity, futility, and deception. Learning how to use the computer as an adult finally recalls the feeling of curiosity and self-determination as crucial to the experience of learning.

Contrary to Klaus Holzkamp's theory, which focuses on the success of learning and not on its failure, these experiences are being conceived as inhibition. There is failure, reluctance, uncertainty, shame, futility, delusion, inability, denial, and blockade. But, on the other hand, there are also experiences of the pleasure of learning, of curiosity, and of self-determination. Haug takes these personal experiences as a starting point to challenge the one-dimensional conception of learning as constant improvement, and to explore how learning processes involve the negotiations of habits, misjudgments, and contradictions.

In Haug's extensive and complex analysis of learning and teaching that she bases on her memories and the memories of her students, as well as on learning diaries and observations, negative affects, emotions, and feelings play a crucial role. Haug's interest is not to examine how these experiences can be transcended and transformed into higher individual competencies, but to investigate how "critique, intervention, ability, realization, and thought can themselves become pleasure and possible passion" (Haug 2003, 46). For Haug, joy, risk, and uncertainty are therefore very closely connected to each other.

Doubt is not the main subject in Haug's study, but it emerges from notions such as doubt [Zweifel], dialogue [Zwiegespräch], and twilight [Zwielicht] as well as ambiguity and ambivalence. Doubt, dialogue, and twilight in German include the syllable "zwie" which means "twofold". Affects, as one can derive from Haug's elaborations, are related to doubt and to ambiguity/ambivalence. Haug's reading of pleasure, passion, critique, change, and blockade suggests that they cannot and should not be separated from each other. It is precisely their close and mutual interrelation that enables processes of learning to disturb the self-evidence and self-affirmation of the learning subjects, as well as their reproduction of hegemonic societal conditions. Learning connects doubt, ambiguity, and ambivalence to pleasure, joy, and passion that together garner the necessary conditions of true self-change.

Towards feminist practices of teaching and learning at the intersection of art education

In the present conditions of capitalistic regimes that are characterized by hyperactivity, simultaneity, restlessness, affective exhaustion, and emotional exploitation (Tsianos and Papadopoulos 2006), critical and transformative practices of teaching and learning are needed. If, as Lauren Berlant has pointed out, we all develop skills for adjusting over time and for calibrating our affects to respond to the pressure of capitalistic precarity and contingency,[11] and if, as outlined, current policy papers and discourses on art education respond to this pressure of capitalistic precarity, critical and transformative feminist approaches are crucial.

Today, contemporary radical practices and discourses in art education often work with the legacies of emancipatory pedagogies conceptualized by thinkers, educators, and teachers such as Paolo Freire, bell hooks, Jacques Rancière, and others. Art educators, artists, teachers, and students seek to intervene in existing political, ideological, social, and cultural relations and to open up alternative collective spaces of agency. Education in the realm of art relates to a multiplicity of relations between people, things, information, artifacts, structures, and institutions that equally involve perception, reflection, cognition, and affect. Processes and practices of art education spawn new connections between material and immaterial, mental and bodily aspects. In turning away from the neoliberalist and utilitaristic model of art education that feeds into the instrumentalization and commodification of affects, I have suggested that contemporary radical practices and discourses in art education should be expanded through critical methods and approaches of feminist thinkers and teachers that have complicated the relations of affects, emotions, and feelings to processes and practices of learning and teaching.

If the present is a "mediated affect" (Berlant 2011) where affects, emotions, and feelings correspond with the contemporary condition of capitalism, and if art and education represent a particular field where affects are being shaped, then a critical and transformative feminist account of affects, emotions, and feelings in art education is more than urgent. In turning away from the neoliberalist and utilitarian model of art education that feeds into the instrumentalization and commodification of affects by processes of capitalistic valorization, I have elaborated on the complicated and multilayered formulations of learning and teaching that have been developed and continuously put under scrutiny by feminist thinkers and teachers. Of course, these practices and concepts cannot suspend the models by which global capitalistic economic conditions form contemporary subjectivities.

Bell hooks' conception of teaching and learning represents less an individual practice than a mutual relationship that engages teachers and students in a complex process provoking the transgression of their own presuppositions. Processes of teaching and learning require time and space as well as commitment. Drawing on a black feminist perspective, hooks emphasizes that bodily experiences play a crucial role within learning processes. In fact, she argues that the splitting of body and mind that is continuously reproduced in the hegemonic Western white classroom is a main instrument of repression. Similarly, according to Haug, in a society of dominance, the liberation from dependence is limited. As a consequence, subjects, to sustain their agency, deny contradictions and try to adjust to adverse experiences. Haug elaborates on how learning subjects are embedded in their own societal conditions and how they embody these very same conditions. To organize a learning process, therefore, means to bring experiences into crisis, to deconstruct illusions, to question the obviousness of knowledge leading to the allowance of conflicting experiences and perceptions: "To organize a process of learning means to bring experiences into crisis. To this end, students need teachers that challenge the seemingly self-evident ways of how we perceive ourselves and the world, and to constantly question the self-adaption/assimilation. Teachers have to disturb the harmony of contradicting experiences by students" (Haug 2003, 65).

To think of and work with conceptions and experiences of affect, feeling, emotion, and embodiment in processes of teaching and learning could open up a new arena of critical practices and thinking in art education. I consider the conceptions of both bell hooks and Frigga Haug of particular interest for current and future critical investigations for art educators, artists, art teachers, and theorists addressing the interrelations of affect, emotion, and feeling within processes and practices of learning and teaching.

Notes

1 I am referring here to the German-speaking discourse in art education. Drawing on Jacques Lacan, Eva Sturm was one of the first scholars that elaborated on a theory of art education by examining the acts of speech and acts of silence within art education. See Sturm 1996.

2 Most studies connect art education to affect from the perspective of neuroscience, focusing on "outcomes", or they relate to the creative turn within the arts. Very few elaborate on an emancipatory and critical account of affect in art education. See: e.g. Deepwell 2010; Settele 2014.

3 E.g. Negri and Hardt (1999) argue that affective labor is the hidden resource of capitalist accumulation. They here, for instance, draws on a central feminist materialist critique that was coined by feminists such as Mariarosa Dalla Costa, Leopoldina Fortunati, Selma James, Silvia Federici, and Brigitte Galtier in the 1970s. Federici in response has formulated a nuanced critique of their claim for affective labor. Federici criticizes the term "affective work" in particular – coined in the context of the debates on immaterial labour – since this term tends to re-mythologize reproductive work.

4 Berlant: affective mechanisms are always "deeply ambiguous, compromised and unstable" (2007, 297).

5 See Cvetkovich 2007 and Baier et al. 2014, 20–2. The editors of the anthology on affect and gender that comprises a collection of key texts newly translated into German underline that in the context of women studies from the 1970s onwards the private sphere has been critically examined as the site of gendered relations of labor. Moreover, Baier et al. stress that affects are always entangled with the gendered and racialized relations of power.

6 See e.g. Tero Karppi et al. forthcoming; Sauer and Penz 2016.

7 See: www.britannica.com/topic/human-capital#ref1181263.

8 www.dictionary.com/browse/pleasure.

9 The translation of the title of Holzkamp's book is by Barbara Mahlknecht. The seminal work on learning, published by Holzkamp, the founder of critical psychology, represents one of Haug's primary references. Another central reference is Antonio Gramsci's theory of hegemony. Although Haug renounces elaboration on how Gramsci's conception relates to her examination of learning, his theory of hegemony constitutes a significant source of inspiration for her thinking.

10 Haug's use of the term "memory work" includes both meanings: working *on* memory and working *through* memory. For an extensive elaboration on this feminist-materialist method see Haug 2001.
11 Berlant 2011, 8. Berlant describes the relation of attachment as "affective attachment to what we call the good life" (Berlant 2011, 27) that represents an optimistic fantasy that has survived from the social-democratic promises of the post-war period in the US and Europe. According to Berlant, affect is not something "natural" and individual, but is equally shaped by the conditions of present capitalism.

References

Ahmed, Sara. "Happy Objects". In *The Affect Theory Reader*, edited by Melissa Gregg and Gregory J. Seigworth. Durham, NC: Duke University Press, 2010.

Ahmed, Sara. *The Cultural Politics of Emotion*. New York: Routledge, 2014.

Amsler, Sarah S. *The Education of Radical Democracy*. London: Routledge, 2015.

Baier, Angelika, Binswanger, Christa, Häberlein, Jana et al. *Affekt und Geschlecht. Eine einführende Anthologie*. Vienna: Zaglossus, 2014, 20–2.

Berlant, Lauren. "Nearly Utopian, Nearly Normal: Post-Fordist Affect in La Promesse and Rosetta". *Public Culture* 19:2, 2007, 272–301.

Berlant, Lauren. *Cruel Optimism*. Durham, NC: Duke University Press, 2011.

Bishop, Claire. "The Social Turn: Collaboration and Its Discontents". *Artforum*, February 2006.

Cannatella, Howard. *Why We Need Arts Education: Revealing the Common Good: Making Theory and Practice Work Better*. Rotterdam: Sense Publishers, 2015.

Cvetkovich, Anne. "Public Feelings". *South Atlantic Quarterly* 106:3, Summer 2007.

Cvetkovich, Anne. *Depression: A Public Feeling*. Durham, NC: Duke University Press, 2012.

Deepwell, Katy. "Feminist Pedagogies". *n.paradoxa. International Feminist Art Journal* 26, July 2010.

Handwerker Küchenhoff, Barbara. *Spinoza's Theorie der Affekte: Kohärenz und Konflikt*. Würzburg: Verlag Königshausen und Neumann GmbH, 2006.

Harvey, David. *A Brief History of Neoliberalism*. Oxford: Oxford University Press, 2005.

Haug, Frigga. *Erinnerungsarbeit*. Hamburg: Argument Verlag, 2001.

Haug, Frigga. *Selbstbewegungen und Selbstblockierungen*. Hamburg: Argument, 2003.

hooks, bell. *Teaching to Transgress: Education as the Practice of Freedom*. New York: Routledge, 1994.

Karppi, Tero, Laukkanen, Anu, Mannevuo, Mona, Pajala, Mari, and Sihvonen, Tanja, eds. "Affective Capitalism". *Ephemera: Theory and Politics in Organization*, forthcoming.

Lazzarato, Maurizio. "Immaterial Labor", translated by P. Colilli and E. Emery. In *Radical Thought in Italy: A Potential Politics*, edited by Michael Hardt and Paolo Virno. Minneapolis: University of Minnesota Press, 1995, 133–47.

Massumi, Brian. "The Autonomy of Affect". *Cultural Critique* 31, Autumn 1995, 83–109.

Negri, Antonio and Hardt, Michael. "Value and Affect". *Boundary 2* 26:2, Summer 1999, 77–88.

Sauer, Birgit and Penz, Otto. *Affektives Kapital: Die Ökonomisierung der Gefühle im Arbeitsleben*. Frankfurt: Campus, 2016.

Settele, Bernadette. Mitteilen, was trifft. Diskurse, Affekte und das Wirken von Kunst in der Kunstvermittlung. *Verband Schweiter Lehrerinnen and Lehrer Bildnerische Gestaltung* I, March 2014.

Sturm, Eva. *Im Engpass der Worte. Sprechen über moderne und zeitgenössische Kunst*. Frankfurt am Main: Reimer, 1996.

Tsianos, Vassilis and Papadopoulos, Dimitris. Precarity: A Savage Journey to the Heart of Embodied Capitalism, 2006, http://eipcp.net/transversal/1106/tsiano-spapadopoulos/en.

UNESCO. *Roadmap for Arts Education*. Lisbon, 2006.

8

FEMINIST ETHICS OF RESPONSIBILITY AND ART THERAPY

Spanish art therapy as a case in point

Ángela Harris Sánchez and Adelina Sánchez Espinosa

In times of crisis, one becomes particularly sensitive to the urgent need to incorporate a politics of social responsibility as one of the essential ingredients of education. Just as we are giving the finishing touches to this chapter we are sad to find demonstration of this point on hearing the news that Brexit has triumphed. Britain is leaving the European Union for the worst reasons: out of fear of the other and in a selfish "Britain first" race. Misguided by an ultra-conservative-controlled media, Britons believed they had to choose between their own profit and solidarity with those refugees who are knocking on their doors in despair, refugees who are asking us all for help after having to leave their homes behind because of wars generated by Western capitalism and its greed. The surprising choice of 51 percent of the British population has been devastating. As we write this, nobody knows yet the long-term consequences of this terrible choice, but the short-term consequences are, unfortunately, already with us. The abject murder of MP Jo Cox, noted for her committed defense of diversity and the integration of immigrants in the UK, cannot be dissociated from the pro-Brexit hate campaign and its climactic display of an infamous anti-migrant poster on the very day of her killing.[1]

This introduction leads us to a crystal clear conclusion with which we would like to start our chapter: change in educational policies incorporating social commitment on a global scale cannot wait any longer. Europe must act quickly to face this need, and this volume, produced by a transnational European association and containing scholarly contributions from various European countries, seems to us a good platform to vindicate a basic argument in favor of social commitment, while also offering food for thought and good practices on how to conduct social change.

This chapter starts by looking at the need to incorporate an ethics of social responsibility in our curricula at the European level. It then turns its attention to new feminist approaches to affect and asks how this trend can illuminate our approaches to responsibility as activist teachers and practitioners in our respective fields. We then proceed to reflect on our own situations, and particularly on our perception of the oppressions and privileges which may mark the construction of our situated knowledges. Our contribution focuses next on the experience of art therapists in the Spanish academy, taking Spain as a case in point. We interview three prominent art therapists and explore the ways they position themselves in these feminist approaches to affect and to the ethics of responsibility, how this illuminates their everyday practice, and, in turn, how they think about the teacher training of future practitioners. In so doing we find that these art therapists enliven their field as a unique mingling of feminism, responsibility, and ethics, a very needed area for the promotion of social inclusion or marginalized sectors of population and the creation of new, more inclusive modes of citizenship. We conclude the chapter by highlighting a number of paradigms which can constitute a series of tools for future good practices and by offering a number of assignments to be used with people participating in art therapy sessions.

The incorporation of an ethics of social responsibility into the curriculum is one of the objectives of the European Union as shown by the 2010 "Charter on Education for Democratic Citizenship and Human Rights Education" adopted by the organization's 47 member states in the framework of Recommendation CM/Rec (2010)7, intended to "provide a focus and catalyst for action in the member states" and "disseminat[e] good practice and rais[e] standards throughout Europe and beyond".[2] The charter was prompted by recommendations frequently made by the European Council since the turn of the twenty-first century, recommendations which had, indeed, moved some member states to action. The Spanish experience can serve as a case in point here. The European Council's 2002 recommendation moved the socialist government under Jose Luis Zapatero to modify the primary and secondary school curricula in order to include an obligatory subject called "Educación para la Ciudadanía" ("Education for Citizenship") in 2007. According to the royal decrees regulating it, the new subject was based on the acquisition of "social and citizenship" competence through the "consolidation of self-esteem, personal dignity and responsibility and the formation of independent, respectful, participative and engaged citizens". The text also stated that these aims would be achieved by including content related to "human relations and affective-emotional education ... ethical theories and human rights ... conflict solving, equality between women and men ... respect for minorities and diverse cultures".[3] Unfortunately, the subject lived a very short life since it was withdrawn from the curricula after strong controversy when the government changed in 2011 and the conservative party, PP, passed a new educational law.

All this proves, once again, Donna Haraway's point that "knowledge is produced from particular positions that are always embodied, never 'innocent', and must be seen as part of a complex web of power relations" (McAlister 2010: 128). Indeed, we as feminists are not alien to the need to reconstruct knowledges from different positions, and the role played in this process by the politics of social responsibility. As feminists, we have all this in our DNA. As Sara Ahmed puts it, "Certainly, within the academy, feminist knowledges and pedagogy emerge as sites of transformation" (2000: 8). Any innovative approach to feminist pedagogy must have to do with ethics and social commitment, and this is what has inspired us to direct our attention to art therapy. The use of art as therapy for people who need help as victims of inequality processes (whether social exclusion, gender violence, etc.) is an arena where a social-feminist politics of responsibility has become salient. Its principles of social inclusion and the humanistic politics of ethics and affect are a common denominator between art therapy and feminism.

A new style of engaging with the social can motivate us to compromise in the actual materialization of change, building the bridge between classroom and society, between reflection and action, between social epistemologies and material realizations. As Marian López Fernández-Cao points out in one of her relevant contributions on the use of feminist methodologies in artistic creation, art is a tool for questioning and opening enquiries rather than providing absolute answers: "El arte abre puertas, plantea preguntas. Nunca las responde" (2014: 47), and this is what makes creativity possible. Our personal reaction to art and through art empowers us in the acquisition of situated knowledges which connect us with others, and which can be transferred to others in an interactive way, changing our approach. López Fernández-Cao's reflection on her class experiences is most illustrative here:

> I think that, above all, we must share with [our students] our knowledges, we share … our own desire to know, our passion for life and art … for the vision of artists who died long ago. To look with their eyes, to speak with their words, just like when we read out a written thought. To dare to think that thought again. To dare again from a different perspective.
>
> *(López Fernández-Cao 2014: 49)*[4]

The generation of affect through art is what generates our passionate desire to learn and then to share new knowledges.

Indeed, "affect theory" has become a key approach in twenty-first-century scholarship within many different fields, to the extent that the term "the Affective Turn" has been coined to refer to this trend. Since the publication of Brian Massumi's (1995) seminal work on the autonomy of affect in the 1990s, "affect" has opened up new paths for scholarship aiming to reconsider our place in the world and the way we "affect" and are "affected" by others. Feminist approaches within this "affective turn" have been many, with people like Sara Ahmed, Ann Cvetkovich, Clare Hemmings, Eve Kosofsky Sedgwick, Sianne Ngai, or Martha Nussbaum, to name but a few, offering very relevant contributions in reconsidering affects such as "shame", "guilt", or "happiness". In what concerns us here, Sara Ahmed's questioning of "happiness" has been particularly illuminating as a standpoint from which to construct and conduct art therapy practice. Ahmed starts by wondering whether compulsory happiness has become a social duty, which makes feminist questioning and protesting unpleasantly antisocial. Hence, Ahmed vindicates the need to become a "feminist killjoy":

> The feminist after all might kill joy precisely because she refuses to share an orientation towards certain things as being good, because she does not find the objects that promise happiness to be quite so promising. By not expressing happiness in response to proximity to such objects, the feminist becomes an affect alien; she "brings things down".
>
> *(Ahmed 2007: 127)*

What we find most inspiring here is the reconsideration of affects, the breaking-apart from the way they have gradually become socially accepted means of oppression and the empowerment of the very act of questioning them. A reconceptualization of affects can clearly be a very useful tool for responsible resistance.[5]

Art therapy appears to us as the ideal ground for the application of this new approach to affects since it uses the creation of art to reach into the emotional part in each one of us, connecting the unconscious and the intentional, bridging self-reflection and ethical rapport with the other.

Methodology

It was these ideas that caused us, the authors of this chapter, to team together. Ángela Harris Sánchez is a feminist researcher and practitioner in the field of art therapy and Adelina Sánchez Espinosa is a feminist scholar and the curriculum developer and coordinator of GEMMA: Erasmus Mundus Master's Degree in Women's Studies and Gender. We thought that exploring connections in our fields under the paradigm of a politics of responsibility and social commitment, and from a feminist standpoint, would be a fruitful and rewarding task and hence we started this investigation, a work still in progress and to be continued with further interviews to come not only in Spain but also in Italy and the Netherlands.

As feminists we find that our situatedness is most important when it comes to reflecting upon our methodology. We must start by highlighting that our collaboration is based on "affect": one, because we are connected through feminist activism; two, because we are mother and daughter, which makes working together easy, after so many years of living together and learning how to cope with the problem-solving situations of ordinary cohabitation. It is, indeed, important to do research from diverse but still imbricated perspectives, perspectives which are born from affective ways of relation with each other, mother–daughter, and with the ways of living with/through others. Our different positions regarding age and academic privilege have generated an understanding of each other's positions which we have also found most productive. Following Haraway we believe that "situated knowledges are particularly powerful tools to produce maps of consciousness for people who have been inscribed within the marked categories" (Haraway 1991: 187). Thus, including ourselves in our research has made us interpellate our positions in relation to those categories and reflect, not only on our areas of oppression, but also on those of privilege. In this sense our methodology of research tries to be responsibly feminist, since reflection on our positions is the basis of our response-ability.

As for the sample we have chosen: they have been conducted with three relevant individuals in the field of art therapy in Spain. The three of them, two women and a man, engage in the field of art therapy not only as scholars but also as practitioners. In order to keep their anonymity, we will be referring to them as AG, VM, and JR.

Inspired by the feminist scholarship on affect and ethics which we have briefly reviewed above, we created a set of questions whose answers could give us information on how the interviewees position themselves in terms of a feminist ethics of responsibility, on how this may or may not be part of their everyday practice and how, in turn, they teacher-train future practitioners. The specific questions asked were the following:

- What's art therapy for you? How did you introduce yourself in this field?
- Do you conceive of yourself as a feminist? If that's the case, how, when, and why did you become a feminist?
- It seems as if, just as some social movements that are traditionally linked to the left have become, in a certain way, contaminated by neoliberalism, art, and education are also at risk of becoming so. On this basis, we would like you to comment on some specific aspects: Do you think that the union between art therapy and feminism could help revitalize art and education?
- Do you think this union could help generate the dynamics of a more ethically committed society?
- Nowadays it seems as if ethics and social commitment are often dismissed as secondary. What connection do you find between art therapy and social compromise? How would/do you link them?
- There are many different ways of approaching education. In this specific case, we are talking about transmitting social compromise and generating social activism in the people we work with. To what extent is social

compromise a central point in your training practice? And what about feminism? Do you think they are part of your training/teaching experience? Why/why not?

- What actions do you think are necessary in education in order to approach this social compromise and multidirectional education that we have been talking about?

Analysis of the interviews

What follows are comments on the most significant attitudes and good practices which emerge from our analysis of the answers provided by our interviewees.[6]

To AG, what makes art therapy different from other therapies is its focus on the creative *process* rather than its product, and its focus on "health", a positive concept, rather than on "pathology", a negative one: "creativity is essential" she states, "so that people can find ways out, solutions to their own difficulties" which can make all the difference to the extent that "it can be decisive for survival, the finding of opportunities, the opting out of pathologies".[7]

The humanistic approach of art therapy finds its counterpart in feminist humanism, in her opinion. Feminism is a home, a position, a locus to inhabit which makes you a more humane person, which places you in contact with others, and so is art therapy. In times of crisis, she thinks, the tools of art education can be of use and creativity becomes essential, an attitude which all three interviewees share. To AG, creativity helps you fight the homogeneous thinking imposed by capitalism, since it opens up your mind to diversity and multiculturality.

AG finds the imbrication of feminism and art therapy obvious. Both are based on a compromise made in order to fight and dismantle biases and inequalities:

> The main aspects where a common dialogue between both is established can be the compromise to spot and dismantle the various biases, asymmetries in relationships, inequalities in access to resources which do not only produce a social gap but also make men stand in a position of privilege simply because they are men, while maintaining women in their subordinated place, only because they are women.

Feminist art therapy, specifically, concentrates on empowering women who have suffered psychological damage and on finding alternative spaces where they can recover a sense of their own self-worth. Hence, in her opinion, art therapy also intersects with feminism since it tries to de-pathologize women and connect health and affective life:

Feminism denounces the fact that women's self-images are shaped by social oppression and sexual discrimination. The feminist therapies within art therapy notice the psychological damage that sexism produces in women, and facilitates the construction of alternative spaces where they can discover their personal power and recover a sense of their own worth. In art therapy, images can be a way of self-exploration, they can be used to produce a personal transformation, as well as to produce a political or cultural change in the reality that frames these women's lives. Gender differences oppress and put pressure upon both women and men. They are a source of conflict and anxiety. But gendered social norms end up affecting women more than they do men, as proved by the differential clinicalization in the fields of general health and gender violence. These differential norms and constructions are reflected in the images and texts that surround us every day. It is important to learn how to recognize and expose them, so that we can deactivate and destroy them. Both in art therapy and in feminism, there is an emphasis on demonstrating to these people (women) that they are not neurotic, that they are simply people who have been negatively affected by irrational social structures and constructions. From this perspective, feminism and art therapy promote a brighter perception of the self-image inside society.

Interestingly, to AG both disciplines emerge as instruments to generate change in the "politics of subjectivity" which in turn could create synergies for transformation beyond the individual level. Caring about those on the margins of social acceptance creates the possibilities and conditions for social inclusion:

The process of art therapy must help women to understand, question, and challenge the social and cultural conditions which are responsible for this conception of women as "neurotic", "mad", or "deviant" … Hence we must unveil the relation between the centrality of affect and the recurrence of dissatisfaction and transmit the basic idea: that the more you feel the better your health gets … In other words, both disciplines emerge as instruments that make possible a shift in one's politics of subjectivity and the generation of synergic changes for transformation and social inclusion … Art therapy is a tool to construct the social spaces that systemic culture has failed to create because of its foundational biases. I think this is a fundamental point, because it promotes real paths for social inclusion.

AG, like the other two interviewees, vindicates the expressive potential of art when relieved of its neoliberal servitude. Appreciating art can illuminate us, help us see ourselves and then generate sympathy and sensitivity towards difference. The autoethnographic approach of the art therapist is what eventually helps her/him bridge the gap of difference and empathize with the other. Most interesting is that art can generate emotions which become universalized through their being felt by many different human beings:

> Besides, art is a marvellous vehicle for the construction of and education in values. In appreciating art, individuals can identify universal emotions that unite us as human beings. Also, art can act as a mirror for the person who can see her/his own social alienation when looking into it, so that the art work functions as a new psychic inscription. All this leads to the creation of new dialogues, analyses, and reflections from which the subject can conceive him/herself as such in harmony with his/her environment. Confronted with hegemonic culture, diversity plays a fundamental role in the conquest of social change since it is its activism and artistic practice that can promote the regeneration of the social tissue.

The experience of art places us in contact with the other and is, therefore, particularly prone to generating activism whether through artistic practice or spectatorship. All in all, when art is used as a democratic and interpersonal tool to help the other, rather than as a partner in crime promoting a neoliberal power game, it can generate an increase in self-awareness which can eventually lead to collective transformation.

To VM, art therapy is a *possibility*, and she emphasizes this word:

> It is a possibility, and I want to emphasize the word "possibility" to clarify the difference between this and any absolute statement. It is the possibility to rework intrapsychic conflicts via artistic creation. The potential of this is unique since it allows for the expression of issues which would be very difficult to raise on any other level.

Possibility is a word she likes. It is potential and multifariousness rather than absolute materialization. And this, we learn later on in the interview, is also feminism. The potential of art therapy in reworking conflict through artistic creation and helping bring trauma out makes it unique as a tool to help those in need.

VM is fully conscious of and experienced in the many facets of both art therapy and feminism, since she has been involved in political activism, trade unionism, in the health service, and also in art education. This places her in a unique multiperspectival position from which some very interesting reflections come out:

I reached feminism a long, long time ago. I was a militant in CC.OO,[8] in the healthcare section, I've worked in a hospital for nearly 19 years, and inside CC.OO there were colleagues who considered themselves feminists and this personal contact was crucial. We could say that this changed my life, that it changed the views I had about myself and about the world. Since then I could say that, well since I am so old now, I could say that my militancy in feminism has been constant for … say 40 years? Yes, 40 years … Basically, I think that [art therapy and feminism] revitalize the human being … My last lessons, in the years before my retirement, were devoted to the relation between art therapy and feminism. To me this meant connecting and confronting the possibilities that I would call "insurgent" in feminism with the more "academic" approaches of an art therapy master.

Art therapy and feminism act as revitalizers and activators of the human being, VM thinks. Feminism can add an insurgent component to the academic approach of a master's program in art therapy, hence activating the students who would, later on, become art therapists themselves. The union of feminism and art therapy is fruitful since it results in militant participation. To VM, what matters in feminist art therapy is its social aspect, the collective compromise on activism. It is this interpersonal networking side which makes art therapy a much more effective therapy than any other, according to her:

I do think, from my own research and experience, that the approach to art therapy from a feminist perspective is not so much about individual autoethnographic approaches, as some people would have it, but, on the contrary, it is based on militant and participant investigation. This is to say: it implies research-action and, especially, collective militant compromise. And this can make the difference since it becomes much more powerful than conventional therapies.

She maintains that in our mutual recognition of interdependence and our sharing of vulnerabilities to make living a collective concern rather than an individual burden, we are acting as feminists, we are exercising our own humane responsible commitment with others:

Basically the answer is that we must approach the issue from one of the most fundamental feminist contributions: the feminist recognition of the interdependence of all human beings, which is, in turn, very closely related to the recognition of vulnerability. This means taking care of life the way we do from feminism, from critical feminism, which has nothing to do with other approaches based on over-medicalization and on an excess of psychology … Feminist artistic therapy, on the other hand, obviously supports a totally different way to look at these personal characteristics. That is why, in my opinion, the latter are insurgent methods which can subvert and fully modify the therapy setting. Also, we must be careful not to place ourselves in the position of redeemers. I would say this is part of a very conservative approach, at the end of the day. If this is the case, well I don't consider myself redeemer of anything, not even of myself. This means, I don't need anyone to save me and I don't need to save anyone. I do think that the acceptation of common vulnerability is a most powerful weapon for solidarity, empathy, and caring for life. And this perspective, which in my opinion is utterly feminist, is where we must find the union with art therapy: linking them in this diagnosis of humanity.

VM concludes that the first step to take in order to change the politics of social compromise is the transformation of the educational system. Education must incorporate subversive feminist methodologies to change the conception of the classroom:

Unifying the educational system is the main thing to do here … and certainly we need a general pact on education. I find this essential. But apart from this political action we should also take social action, act on the adoption of these insurgent feminist methodologies and take them as a central starting point. If political action reinforces social action and vice-versa, if political and social compromise unite, teaching will be a totally different experience and the classroom will be a transformed space. You then start positioning yourself as an equal, someone who is there in order to learn in a collective way, you and the students learn together. From this new perspective we can open up new paths, new windows, for curiosity hence really touching and learning about the real interests and concerns of the students, rather than those of professor, as is often the case.

Thus, the classroom experience should be multidirectional, the learning experience should be shared by teacher and students, and this should transform the classroom into a totally different space.

Finally, to JR, art therapy as a discipline exists in its application to needed human and social contexts, and hence could be defined as: "approaches and strategies for the application of art to human and social contexts in need. Always with the purpose of development, improvement, growth, change, and ultimate transformation". He has personalized his own approach to art therapy by bearing in mind its interconnectivity with many other fields and by placing creativity as one of its central components:

Throughout my years of training and professional experience, from the very beginning, I have acquired a consciousness of the interrelations between various disciplines whose interplay is essential for art therapy. The concepts and practices of fields such as art, psychology and psychotherapy, education, creativity, in their mutual imbrication, have made me reflect on and personalize my own approach.

Interestingly enough, although he dislikes any sort of label, including that of feminism, JR is conscious that feminism is integrated in his practice: it is present in his openness to questioning and to the relativization of reality, his approach to the need to revise reality critically, to the construction of new identities, to the finding of mechanisms for empowering the underprivileged, for making-visible the invisible, etc.:

> I don't conceive myself as a feminist, the same as I don't consider myself many other things which, in fact, I am. I don't tag myself as a feminist. This said, I completely share the ways of understanding our culture, of constructing identities, of focusing on structures and power dynamics, of making visible the invisible, of finding mechanisms which convey critical revisions of reality, which problematize reality and make it more complex, which eventually are instrumental to its transformation, as is the case with feminism … As to the specific question on feminism, my answer is that it is integrated in my work and present in various ways. It is the questioning of gender models that are present in art and have become largely naturalized; the need to bring to light and reclaim the works, ideas, and identities of important women creators who have been traditionally neglected; the use of language; the revision and questioning of any gender aspects which may have been normalized around gender in cultural, educational, or artistic uses, on visual culture. It is also the questioning of the conventional models of creators.

To JR, art therapy adds the human component in the way it puts into practice ethics and aesthetics. It requires a new conception of the creator, and here the interview touches on one of his research concerns: the concept of "creativity". Art is no longer the production of the artistic genius isolated in his ivory tower but a transferable experience, the bridge between an individual and the world, and this makes art powerful since, from this new conception, it allows for the re-signification and re-shaping of this world:

> I think that, by definition, art therapy and social and human compromise are built together. I can see no other way. Art therapy is a way of putting into practice the integration between ethics and aesthetics, of rescuing art from the futility of ornament, good taste, or the mere

production of objects, from the "ivory tower" of the artistic genius. This can be used so that art can be transferred to a complex reality as another way, a very powerful way, of approaching the experience of yourself and the world. We can, in this manner, re-signify, retell, and transform this reality.

In our opinion, the most outstanding paradigm which comes out of this interview as regards our enquiry is the concept of creativity in its connection with an ethics of responsibility and with social compromise. There is an urgent need, he concludes, to build a real culture of creativity within the educational system because creativity, considered under this new light, is, ultimately, transformative.

Conclusion

Our analysis of the three interviews shows us certain paradigms in art therapy practice which can be described as feminist: self-reflection and autoethnography, while positioning ourselves in the world as a place which needs to be changed through joint action; multidirectional rather than monodirectional practices; choice for constant enquiry and interactive rapport rather than absolute answers; creativity as the shared, "distributed" capability constructed within the community rather than the peculiar gift of a few; the interpersonal sharing and coping with vulnerability through the construction of affective networks. All of these are, indeed, transgressive feminist acts of ethical social compromise.

Under the influence of their responsible practices and also inspired by our reading of "affect" as a useful tool[9] for education, we have started thinking about a possible toolbox for future practice based on paradigms such as empathy, self-reflection, humanism, inclusion, and activism which could function as instruments to generate and cultivate creativity through affect and eventually transform classrooms into spaces for interactive solidarity.

Suggested assignment

Based on the common paradigms highlighted above we propose the following assignments which consist of exercises and further reflection questions: From the perspective of the role played by emotions in the formation and development of creativity, we propose the following exercises:

- Participants are prompted to express six basic emotions: anger, fear, disgust, happiness, sadness, and surprise, by using rolls of paper (displayed in front of them as a sort of screen) and some paint. The person guiding the activity will name these emotions one by one so that participants come to the front when they feel the emotion and express it by using the materials (there are infinite possibilities that go from painting to the destruction of material).

- After this, we will attempt to feel emotions through the body of the others so that participants can understand that emotions are felt differently depending on the position we take. In pairs, participants will hold each other's arm/hand/finger … They will take turns in expressing the emotion by using this part of the other's body. The idea is that participants can exchange ways of living emotions and hence enhance their empathy.
- Recognizing emotions and how we can share them is something that we consider essential in order to develop creativity which is, at the end of the day, the expression of emotions and personal experiences felt vividly.
- Participants will be asked to reflect on: How do you recognize yourself through these emotions? Does it feel differently experiencing this from another body's perspective? How do you feel towards the other after this shared experience?

From the point of view of self-positioning, cultural introjections, and vulnerabilities, we would like to propose the following activities:

- Inspired by the *Siluetas* series by Ana Mendieta (1973–8), where Mendieta outlines her silhouette in nature or represents her semi-buried naked body on earth, we propose a self-positioning exercise. This is a freer activity, a reflection, where the participant will place her/his body in a natural space which he/she decides can help in escaping context and reflecting on cultural introjections. Here the participant will need to feel confident about the space chosen in order to ignore external input.
- Participants will be asked to reflect on: Why have you chosen that space? How does your body feel in it? What do you need to get rid of in order to feel that way?
- *Fingerprint, mirror, and mask*: This is a sequence of three activities which can follow the previous one. It starts with "fingerprint": the formation of artistic material drawn from a part of the body which helps the participant put him/herself in the center of consideration. "The mirror" follows this: participants will contemplate their reflections in a mirror and then start experimenting with colors, painting on the surface of the mirror. The premise is that our personal image is conditioned by the external gaze, relating both to the actual reflection and to the added paints which connect with it. Finally, with "the mask" we wish to reflect on cultural conditionings and how they generate vulnerability and influence the way we live our lives. Through the creation of a mask, we propose a reflection on the external visions of others and their resulting introjections. Aiming to express this we paint the outside and inside of the mask differently. The internal part is the one not shown and will be

used to reflect on what we don't communicate. The external part, on the other hand, is that which we consciously share with others.

Participants will be asked: how does the image that the others have of us affect and determine our actions and ways of experiencing life? What do you feel when you look at what is left of the reflection in the mirror? When you don't have your own reflection as a point of reference, what is there left? How do we communicate with others?

Notes

1 See, for instance, Alex Massie's article in the *Spectator* where he establishes the connections between the murder and the hate campaign and insists that "Events have a multiplier effect. So do feelings" (http://blogs.spectator.co.uk/2016/06/a-day-of-infamy; accessed 18 June 2016). Along similar lines *The Guardian* heads their obituary editorial as follows: "an attack on humanity, idealism and democracy" (www.theguardian.com/commentisfree/2016/jun/16/the-guardian-view-on-jo-cox-an-attack-on-humanity-idealism-and-democracy; accessed 17 June 2016). On the poster itself being reported to the police as breaching UK race laws and a "blatant attempt to incite racial hatred", see www.theguardian.com/politics/2016/jun/16/nigel-farage-defends-ukip-breaking-point-poster-queue-of-migrants (accessed 17 June 2016).
2 www.coe.int/en/web/edc/charter-on-education-for-democratic-citizenship-and-human-rights-education (accessed 24 June 2016).
3 "La Educación para la Ciudadanía tiene como objetivo favorecer el desarrollo de personas libres e íntegras a través de la consolidación de la autoestima, la dignidad personal, la libertad y la responsabilidad y la formación de futuros ciudadanos con criterio propio, respetuosos, participativos y solidarios, que conozcan sus derechos, asuman sus deberes y desarrollen hábitos cívicos para que puedan ejercer la ciudadanía de forma eficaz y responsible … Para lograr estos objetivos se profundiza en los principios de ética personal y social y se incluyen, entre otros contenidos, los relativos a las relaciones humanas y a la educación afectivo-emocional, los derechos, deberes y libertades que garantizan los regímenes democráticos, las teorías éticas y los derechos humanos como referencia universal para la conducta humana, los relativos a la superación de conflictos, la igualdad entre hombres y mujeres, las características de las sociedades actuales, la tolerancia y la aceptación de las minorías y de las culturas diversas" (www.boe.es/boe/dias/2007/01/05/pdfs/A00677-00773.pdf; accessed 25 June 2016).
4 "Creo que, sobre todo, más que compartir con [el alumnado] nuestro saber, compartimos … nuestro propio deseo de saber, nuestra pasión por la vida, por el arte … por la visión de artistas que hace mucho han desaparecido. Mirar por sus ojos, hablar con sus palabras, como cuando leemos un pensamiento escrito en voz alta. Atreverse a pensar de nuevo ese pensamiento. Atreverse a ver, de nuevo, desde otra perspectiva" (our translation).
5 A similar approach is adopted in Chapter 2 by Olga Cielemecka and Beatriz Revelles-Benavente in this volume. Their reading of Lauren Berlant's "cruel optimism" leads them to conclude that there is an urgent need to "challenge and rework" the idea of failure.
6 The space limitation of this chapter does not allow for the full transcript of the interviews but this can be found at: www.dropbox.com/s/whp8plednv59tyq/transcript%20.docx?dl=0.
7 For all quotes from the interviews refer to link provided in footnote 6.

8 Spanish trade union confederation or workers' commissions.
9 Here we have also found Monika Rogowska-Stangret's contribution in Chapter 1 most inspiring, particularly when she calls on a conversation between Foucault and Deleuze from which it emerges that "one of the key roles of an intellectual is to face the reality or even to treat theory as a 'box of tools' with which one can handle the challenges of the surrounding world and unpack power relations" (Deleuze and Foucault 1977: 208).

References

Ahmed, Sara. "Multiculturalism and the Promise of Happiness". *New Formations*, 63 (2007), 121–37.
Ahmed, Sara, Jane Kilby, Celia Lury, Maureen Mcneil, and Beverley Skeggs, eds, "Introduction: Thinking through Feminism", in Ahmed et al., *Transformations: Thinking through Feminism* (London: Routledge, 2000), 1–23.
Foucault, M., G. Deleuze, "Intellectuals and power: A conversation between Michel Foucault and Gilles Deleuze", in Donald F. Bouchard (ed.), *M. Foucault, Language, Counter-Memory, Practice: Selected Essays and Interviews* (Ithaca, New York: Cornell University Press, 1977).
Haraway, Donna. *Simians, Cyborgs, and Women: The Reinvention of Nature* (New York: Routledge, 1991).
López Fernández-Cao, Marian. "Aplicando metodologías feministas para analizar la creación: propuestas en educación artística desde la experiencia de las mujeres". *Dossiers Feministes*, 19 (2014), 31–55.
McAlister, Faber, "Donna J. Haraway", in Jon Simons (ed.), *From Agamben to Zizek: Contemporary Critical Theorists* (Edinburgh: Edinburgh University Press, 2010), 127–43.
Massumi, Brian. "The Autonomy of Affect". *Cultural Critique*, 31 (1995), 83–109.

9

(FOSTERING) PRINCESSES THAT CAN STAND ON THEIR OWN TWO FEET

Using wonder tale narratives to change teenage gendered stereotypes in Portuguese EFL classrooms

Alexandra Cheira

> One is not born a woman, but rather becomes one.
>
> *(Simone de Beauvoir)*

Teaching, gender, responsibility, crisis: teaching out of the (gendered) box

Being *female* and being a *woman* are two very different categories, which similarly entail distinctive orders of being.[1] In fact, on the one hand, the distinction between sex and gender precludes the attribution of women's social functions to "biological destiny". On the other hand, and arguably more significantly still, this division makes it impossible to meaningfully refer to "natural" or "unnatural" gendered behaviour since, as Butler concludes, "all gender is, by definition, unnatural"[2] because it is a cultural construct. Why then, one might ask, is it so easy to make pre-conceived assumptions based on biological sex? For instance, why do teenage boys shudder at the idea of wearing pink clothes? Why are girls expected to help their mothers around the house whereas their brothers are not? Why are boys supposed to enjoy watching football whereas girls are expected to prefer soap operas? The list could go on and on, since these stereotypes are so deeply rooted that many people believe gender roles are so natural that they do not feel the need to question them, let alone challenge them.

Hence, it is of paramount importance that the cultural construction of femininity as a specific gender identity which embodies society's understanding of what is "feminine"[3] and, consequently, of female powerlessness, can swiftly change outside of academia as well, in the context of preventing discrimination and violence against women at a time of political crisis

enhanced by associated social and economic crises. These practical concerns are even more urgent to consider in a country where, in the words
of a (woman) researcher, "men still continue to make a show of unaccept-
able machismo today".[4] In fact, Anália Torres, a professor at the Technical
University of Lisbon's Higher Institute of Social and Political Sciences, has
argued that the growing rates of male unemployment may have dramatic
domestic consequences, because many Portuguese men "base their masculinity on their wage-earning power, even though both men and women have
been working and supporting the family for a long time now in Portugal".
In a country where women tend to earn substantially less than men in the
same job, it is men who are most often laid off in areas such as education
and health (where men earn up to 20 percent more than their female peers)
"because they are more expensive", a situation that has caused many men
to "have suffered a strong blow to their self-esteem, because their masculinity is traditionally associated closely with supporting the family". Torres
claims this has had two perverse consequences in many households: on the
one hand, in the current economic crisis, "women face greater difficulties,
aggravated in cases in which their husbands are unemployed, because they
still have to take everything on their shoulders". In fact, Torres has added,
this is especially serious in Portugal since "if a woman has work and her
partner does not, she continues to do the housework, unlike what occurs in
other places, where men participate in the housework when they are unemployed". On the other hand, women are too often the target of violence
on the part of their (unemployed) partners, frequently with tragic results.
The figures are appalling: according to UMAR[5] (one of the largest wom-
en's organizations in the country), thirty women were killed in Portugal by
their partners or ex-partners between January and November 2012 (three
months prior to Torres' interview). According to Mario Queiroz, Torres'
interviewer, "that makes Portugal the country with the largest number of
femicides – gender-related murders – in the European Union, in proportion
to the population".

Even though as feminists we have learnt to deconstruct gender stereotypes, the fact still remains that the messages about the expected roles of
men and women we are literally bombarded with every day via the media
make it more difficult for our teenage and younger students to evade their
nefarious influence. As a feminist teacher, my concern is precisely whether
the way we teach affects the ways boys and girls interact with each other so
as not to perpetuate gender stereotypes and, therefore, gender discrimination
and violence – a transnational concern. School can be made more relevant
for students, I argue, if we address gender stereotypes via a gender-conscious
approach to teaching. Hence, in order to teach gender with pedagogical
responsibility/response-ability, the biological category "female" and the culturally constructed, gendered category "woman" must by all means be discussed precisely by debunking the "natural" legacy of the male-dominated

discourse about women, a discourse from which they have systematically been erased as subjects. It is my strong belief this can be done at all levels of teaching and in different subjects, with literature being my chosen instrument in the language classroom. Likewise, in the specific context of Portugal, I argue that teaching gender at school may help decrease the alarmingly high (and growing) rates of youth-dating violence our schools have been faced with for a long time, a phenomenon I have prioritized as in need of urgent intervention.

Dating violence in Portugal: research and prevention programmes

In recent years there has been a growing awareness of, and concern for, the socio-cultural phenomenon of dating violence in Portugal, which has taken the form of both academic research, such as monographs and masters' theses in psychology or health-related areas,[6] and field work carried out mainly through preventive campaigns that have increasingly targeted ever younger teens or tweens. On the one hand, the rising number of research publications on the subject of dating violence suggests that "nowadays there is a growing interest in gender violence issues and a subsequent increase in research as a means towards understanding, explaining and preventing it".[7] In these publications, the focus of research has been primarily directed at investigating "what is being done in Portugal to prevent gender violence among adolescents in school settings",[8] as well as inspecting the factors that most contribute to the development of gender violence and suggesting how such prevention should occur.[9] Legally categorized as a criminal offence within the wider framework of domestic violence, dating violence has thus been studied with the purposes of "(1) promoting the acquisition of knowledge about this problem; (2) enabling youths to recognize abuse in close relationships; (3) producing changes in cultural beliefs that support violence; (4) providing generic abilities to manage situations of dating violence; (5) informing about resources in the community".[10] The case studies presented in several theses[11] depict secondary school or university environments and aim to investigate the way "dating violence in teenagers can shape some of their behaviours in future relationships by influencing their beliefs and attitudes".[12] These theses aim to demonstrate that "the main risk factors are associated with inter-parental violence, violence among peers and socio-economic and demographic low resources".[13] The studies also emphasize the fact that the impact of dating violence on the victim has far-reaching consequences, namely "physical, social, emotional and sexual damage to the victim".[14]

Thus, the fact that most researchers are female suggests a gendered perception of the problem, which suggests its importance as part of a political strategy of a feminist politics of responsibility, regarding the creation of social awareness on this topic. It is also substantiated by the fact that, according to a report elaborated by APAV (the acronym for Associação Portuguesa de Apoio à Vítima, the Victim Support Association) regarding data from 2000 to 2012, a significant majority of violence victims are female. In fact, APAV figures show that, of the 58.8 percent of the cases reported involving violence against girls or young women in this time frame, 51.5 percent of them referred to girls aged 11 to 17 years old. With regard to the category of violence employed, domestic violence was the reason in 85.9 percent of the cases, in a total of 11,541 reported cases. However, these numbers may be substantially higher, as they only refer to official statistics, where unreported crimes which have not been prosecuted do not figure. In the specific context of dating violence, there is a gendered difference regarding the use of violence against the partner that can account for the prevalence of female victims.[15] In fact, some studies demonstrate that, although both boys and girls acknowledge rage as the primary reason for violent behaviour, girls resort to violence as self-defence whereas boys admit they are violent in order to control their partner. Boys also report higher levels of sexual violence against their partner than girls do (37 percent against 24 percent, respectively), whereas more girls report the use of physical violence against themselves than boys do (28 percent against 11 percent, respectively).[16]

On the other hand, the rising numbers of dating violence cases have made it necessary to take action in school environments, since it is now quite universally understood that the requirements for effective prevention efforts are to: 1) start early, 2) have a broad target, and 3) theorize gender.[17] Hence, CIG (the acronym for Comissão para a Cidadania e Igualdade de Género, a government entity responsible for gender equality in Portugal, under the supervision of the Secretary of State for Parliamentary Affairs and Equality) and APAV have commissioned recurring gender violence-prevention programmes which specifically target teenagers and dating violence by fostering healthy, violence-free dating relationships. These prevention campaigns have taken the form of short video clips, available on the webpages of CIG and APAV, which depict abusive relationships and encourage male and female teenage victims to stop them by walking away from the abusers. APAV's 2012 campaign "Cut Off Violence: if they don't respect you, they don't deserve you"[18] and CIG's 2008 campaign "Dating violence is not love"[19] are two examples of successful campaigns that appeal to teenagers by their emphasis on the need for self-respect and self-assurance in the context of dating relationships.

In these campaigns, a multidisciplinary team composed of health and mental health service professionals, social workers, and APAV hotline workers go to schools to explain the different kinds of violence that abusive relationships often involve, at the same time urging teenage victims to stop the violence by leaving the abuser and reporting them to the police. Although students understand the concepts of physical, sexual, verbal, psychological, and social abuse, they normally have different opinions when discussing specific examples: whereas beating your date or calling him or her names is universally disparaged as abuse, controlling the way they dress or their time with friends is taken as either jealousy or wanting very much to spend as much time as possible with the loved one, and thus (mistakenly) regarded as a proof of love.[20] In the ensuing discussion, such pervasive, twisted myths are deconstructed since students realize that abuse really means trying to force the other to do something he or she doesn't want to do. Students are then encouraged to ask questions. At this point, since the team is never judgemental, merely guiding the discussion so students can find the answers for themselves, students are relaxed enough to ask the things they really want to know.

Suggested assignment

- Role-play one of the situations. Ask a boy student and a girl student to enact the chosen scenario. Encourage them to share their feelings with the class. Ask the class to comment on what they have witnessed. Ask the class what they would do if they witnessed this situation in real life.
- Show students the collected data on gender violence in Portugal. Ask them to comment.
- Play short video campaigns on promoting teenage awareness regarding violence and discrimination. Promote class discussion.

Feminist politics of responsibility: theorizing gender through literature in order to prevent teenage dating violence

A memorable question, prompted by a female 14-year-old student, arose a few years ago in one of these sessions: the girl wanted to know if the fact that she had dated a succession of boys in a relatively short time could in any way make them think she was "easy", a situation she felt would not occur had she been a boy. Bravely put in a room full of derisive peers, this question about how a male student would be treated in the same situation brought up in class by the worried female student directly addressed a form of gender inequality quite uncontested by most teenagers. In fact, regardless of their gender, family background, or academic inclinations, most Portuguese teenagers do not question the gendered double standard regarding accepted behaviour. Several studies on the relationship between gender roles and dating violence demonstrate that gendered stereotypes are associated with dating violence.[21] As many teenagers have traditional beliefs about male and female gender roles in relationships, this is a risk factor for their developing violent relationships.

As an English as a Foreign Language (EFL) teacher working at the high school level with teenage and young adult students, I have had a growing concern over the years that most of them do not question the double-standard discourse regarding gendered stereotypes still pervasive in Portuguese youth culture. In the long run, these stereotypes will make it more difficult for heterosexual romantic relationships to be "a site where both young men and young women learn new relational skills, skills not gained in the earlier gender-segregated friendships".[22] My ongoing personal campaign to change accepted gendered stereotypes had so far mostly taken place informally in class when the occasion arose, or in private talks normally requested by afflicted girls with regard to dating problems. The fact that the school where I have taught English for the past ten years had been seriously campaigning for healthy, violence-free dating, coupled with my personal belief in the potential of literature for fostering change, prompted me to do my part in attacking the double standard that echoes so loudly among teenagers. In addition, it inspired me to choose stories which could help my students understand that love and friendship do not equal complying with requests out of fear of being left out. I feel it is my responsibility (and my privilege) as a teacher to foster a consistent sense of self-worth in my students, so that they will be able to become their own gendered-stereotype-free person. Therefore, in order to accomplish that goal within the EFL classroom, I decided to teach wonder tales as extensive reading in my 8th and 9th grade classes. In the process of teaching wonder tales, I have confirmed that these narratives can indeed help students grow and become their own person by encouraging critical thinking, exposing sexist social conditions for what they are, and providing a model which allows students to reshape gendered expectations.

In my year as a trainee teacher, I made three important discoveries that have since shaped my teaching practice. The first was that a book on my desk would be a silent reminder that reading was a pleasant activity and would thus be much more eloquent than any words on the subject. The second was that students reacted better to literary texts than they did to adapted texts. The third was that teachers who are enthusiastic about literature will spark their students' interest as well. In my experience, a useful teaching tool in teaching short stories in the EFL classroom is to divide the text in parts and conclude each part at a particularly interesting moment. By not giving students the whole text at once as a reading chore, they will want to know what happens in the next instalment, instead of complaining about how much they have to read. Therefore, when I decided to start teaching wonder tales at English levels 4 and 5 (for students typically aged 13 and 14 years old) I was already armed with the knowledge that literary texts will find their way into the hands of even the most unwilling students if the teacher does not seem to be the one who is pushing them in their direction.

A personal campaign against gendered stereotypes in the EFL classroom: the uses of wonder tale narratives

Wonder tale scholar Marina Warner calls this genre "a magical elsewhere of possibility".[23] Commenting on the popularity of wonder tales, folklorist Jack Zipes declares that "everywhere one turns today fairy tales and fairy-tale motifs pop up like magic",[24] ranging from literature to theatre, opera, film, and TV series. Although most students have never read Tolkien's *The Lord of the Rings* or J. K. Rowling's *Harry Potter* novels, they are quite familiar with the film adaptations, as well as with the TV series *Once upon a Time* and *Grimm*. These wonder tale visual spectacles share, however, one important feature which was central in the students' understanding of the wonder tales they read in class, namely the fact that they were not intended for children.

That was the reason why, in order to teach the short story that is part of the academic curricula at every EFL level from level 2 to level 8, I decided in 2012 not to teach the stories that came with my 8th and 9th grade students' textbooks. Instead, I chose two wonder tales which challenge "the conservative ideologies of gender that often seem embedded in the very form of fairy tales".[25] I wanted my students, boys and girls alike, to question the established *status quo* in traditional wonder tales with regard to gender roles in order to make them think about the way expected gender roles in real life feed the double standard. More importantly still, in the framework of the ethics of teaching and learning response-ability that I believe is a key factor in education, I wanted to make my students responsible for changing biased perceptions regarding gender by confronting these with fictitious relationships whose gender issues nevertheless mirror real-life teenage dating situations so they could ultimately use what they learnt in their own dating contexts. Wonder tales were thus used in the EFL classroom so as to destabilize gendered misconceptions and lead to behavioural change in my students' daily lives. Thus, for my 13-year-old, 8th grade level 4 students, I selected "Melisande, or Long and Short Division" by E. Nesbit,[26] a well-aimed satire at stereotypes of female beauty magnified by the male imagination written by a Victorian woman writer. For my 14-year-old, 9th grade level 5 students, I opted for "The Princess who Stood on Her Own Two Feet" by Jeanne Desy,[27] a feminist wonder tale which, in Zipes' words, is "commensurate with alternative forms of child rearing that lead to encouraging the self-worth of an individual".[28] Research has demonstrated the extent to which beliefs in traditional gender roles, the subordination of women to men, the restrictions of women's rights, and the support of male domination are related to the tendency to blame the victim, to legitimize the aggressors' behaviour, and to maintain myths around gender violence.[29] Therefore, I wanted my students to understand that no one has the right to define them under the guise of loving them. Both stories fit quite well into the units "Teens" and "Teenagers' problems" that I wanted to teach during the first term.

As preparation, the books on my desk shifted from what I was really currently reading to texts I had already read but wanted the students to believe I was currently reading. The first was my battered but long-loved copy of Tolkien's *The Lord of the Rings*.[30] As it is the English edition and, moreover, compiles the trilogy in a single volume, I knew it would not fail to catch the students' attention. So it did: they flocked around my desk, exclaimed over the thickness and number of pages of the volume and wanted to know why I was rereading it. Was reading such a long book once not enough, they wondered, especially since I did not have to because of the films.

In the next few weeks, there was a steady stream of wonder(ful) books on my desk in order to set the mood. There were original and rewritten tales from contemporary writers like Angela Carter's *The Bloody Chamber and Other Stories*,[31] A. S. Byatt's *Elementals: Stories of Fire and Ice*,[32] and *The Djinn in the Nightingale's Eye: Five Fairy Stories*,[33] and feminist writers whose tales were collected by Jack Zipes under the title *Don't Bet on the Prince: Contemporary Feminist Fairy Tales in North America and England*,[34] among many others. While they perused the books, my students asked me why I was reading wonder tales. Was I not, as they delicately put it, too much of a grown-up already to still appreciate those kinds of tales? I truthfully told them that I have always loved wonder tales, adding that I had already researched a little on that topic for my MA and was considering a PhD where I could further study them. Then I took the opportunity to tell them a little of the history of the wonder tale before we actually started working. So that they could understand that wonder tales were not primarily told to children, I outlined the tradition of oral wonder telling. I explained to them that an adult storyteller would tell tales filled with wondrous and marvellous elements to an adult audience so that stories were told in order to promote the listeners' sense of belonging to a community.

Before they actually started reading the story, we had already discussed much of what I wanted them to focus on in seemingly casual conversations at the beginning of class. Thus, we examined the helplessness of several traditional wonder tale heroines such as Snow White, Cinderella, or Sleeping Beauty, and the way they depend on Prince Charming to rescue them. These constructions of femininity were then compared with filmic wonder tale revisions, such as *Mirror Mirror, Snow White and the Huntsman*, and the television series *Once Upon a Time*, in which Snow White sheds her passivity and becomes the saviour rather than the saved one. We also inspected the roles of stepmothers and fairy godmothers, as well as the fates of mothers in these tales. We commented on the way that magic and metamorphosis always go hand in hand in wonder tales. In teaching the stories I used the following strategy: I divided the tales into sections, making each part finish immediately before a particularly important revelation was made in order to lead the students to anticipate what was coming next. Each part had its own comprehension, vocabulary, and grammar exercises. When the entire story was read, I asked my 8th and 9th graders to comment on the choices that the princess had made and to detail their favourite moment in the story, as well as the part they had most disliked. Finally, as a writing assignment I asked them to rewrite the story from the point of view of the prince.

As formal preparation for the story, I decided to recreate a story-telling session in the classroom. We moved to the theatre room and I asked them to sit in a semicircle on the floor while I stood in front of them with a book in my hands to read them a story. As "Melisande" rewrites Sleeping Beauty's sleeping curse as a curse of baldness, and then subverts Rapunzel by smothering the princess under heavy layers of hair, I wanted to read my 8th grade students a new rendering of those tropes so that they could become aware that "[t]he fairy-tale gives form and coherence to formless fears, dreads and desires. Recognising a fairy tale motif, or an ancient myth, Cinderella or Oedipus, in the mess of a life lived or observed gives both pleasure and security and the sense – or illusion – of wisdom".[35] At the same time, I wanted them to understand the metamorphic life of tales, what novelist and wonder tale writer A. S. Byatt terms "telling a story in a new-old form".[36] Hence, I settled on two modern versions of "Little Red Riding Hood", James Thurber's "The Little Girl and the Wolf"[37] and Roald Dahl's "Little Red Riding Hood and the Wolf".[38] My students were highly entertained with the alternative endings they heard in the versions and of which they knew nothing. Both versions provide alternative ways of dealing with male violence and rewrite Little Red Riding Hood as a savvy, active heroine capable of protecting herself. Thurber has the little girl shoot the wolf dead with an automatic weapon she takes out of her basket, the moral being that "[i]t is not so easy to fool little girls nowadays as it used to be",[39] whereas Dahl has the girl shoot the wolf and make a wolfskin coat for herself.

With my 9th grade students, I also sat on the floor while I asked for a volunteer to tell us the tale of Snow White. When one of the girls finished telling the story, I stood up and read them an alternative Disney version translated into Portuguese, in which the story is told from the point of view of the queen. Folklorist Jack Zipes cautions against what he sees as Disney's worldview, a Manichean dichotomy between good and evil in which one can never become the other, and what he terms Disney's lack of character development "because all characters must be recognizable as types that remain unchanged throughout the film".[40] Hence, the queen's narrative highlights her good intentions regarding Snow White, in which all the hard work she put Snow White through at the beginning of the tale was really meant to make her beloved stepdaughter have a healthy lifestyle as she was getting too chubby and unfit.[41] The queen's narrative, aided by the drawings in which she is always tenderly smiling at Snow White, construes her motives as acting in Snow White's best interests. With this version, I wanted my students to realize that "[t]he literary fairy tale is a wonderful, versatile hybrid form, which draws on primitive apprehensions and narrative motifs, and then uses them to think consciously about human beings and the world".[42]

Then we started working in earnest. Before I handed them the copies of the stories, in the 8th grade classroom I projected the third and final illustration in the story,[43] depicting the princess crouching in a scale while her hair was in the other to be weighed, while the prince watches the scene with a somewhat menacing countenance and his sword in his hand. I then asked the students to interpret the image and wrote their suggestions on the board, telling them they would only know whether they had guessed when they had read the whole story. I quite distinctly remember one of the boys reading the image as an anticipation of gender violence against the female figure: the princess was about to be beheaded, he assumed, probably for having cheated on the prince. Before I had the time to ask him to elaborate, two of the girls had already reacted by saying that that was a soap opera solution quite in dissonance with the universe of the wonder tale, and asking him if he believed it was fair to kill a woman for infidelity. There was quite a heated discussion after that, until a girl posed a question which focused the discussion on gender inequality specifically regarding sexual politics: could the reverse be true, that is, would a man be killed either in a wonder tale or in real life because he had been unfaithful to his wife? Then, I told them the fictional story of Scheherazade, one of world fiction's most charismatic heroines of all time and the woman who cleverly triumphed over the king after he had been betrayed by his wife. I told my students about Shahryar's wife's death at his hands and his subsequent revenge on all his one-day wives, finally brought to an end by Scheherazade through her intelligent story-telling which postponed her own death for 1,001 nights in a row, and then conquered the king's pardon as well as his love for this different woman. We finally discussed the Islamic sexual politics that allows for male polygamy and the different construction of adultery in Western societies as a consequence.

In the 9th grade classroom, I wrote the title of the story on the board and asked my students to make informed guesses on its meaning. What could "a princess who stood on her own two feet" mean? And why would she do that? Interestingly enough, it was a boy who deciphered the metaphorical allusion to someone standing their ground. Then I asked them if they thought traditional princesses like Cinderella or Snow White stood on their own two feet. When they commented on their passiveness, I asked them to imagine a context in which these princesses could have stood on their own two feet. Confronting their stepmothers head on was the most voted situation. What about the princes, I insisted? Would Cinderella and Snow White need princes to rescue them if they had faced their stepmothers? Then, I asked them to choose from a list of adjectives and recorded the ones they thought could apply to the princess in this story based only on what they could infer from the title. Adjectives such as "brave", "honest", "reliable", and "self-confident" made the top of the list. Finally, I asked them if they thought any of these adjectives could be gender-specific, or more expected in one gender. The only adjective the majority of the students believed was more a male attribute than a female one was "self-confident", thus reinforcing my conviction that this particular story might teach them all different.

Afterwards, I distributed the first instalment of Nesbit's "Melisande" and Desy's "The Princess who Stood on Her Own Two Feet" and told my students to read it silently. As I had not warned them that the story was not finished, I wanted them to ask me about the rest, which they did in quite a baffled manner. The result was that, in both classes, instead of complaining that it was too much to read, they complained that it was too little after the fastest readers had looked at me in a puzzled way before they asked me where the end of the story was. I told them that "Melisande" had been divided into four sections and "The Princess who Stood on Her Own Two Feet" had been divided into three sections.

During the two weeks it took to teach the stories, many of my students tried to make me tell them if their hypotheses with regards to what came next were correct before they read the next instalment. The 8th grade students had a lot of fun trying to anticipate what the next funny episode in Melisande's life would be and how her problem would ultimately be solved. My 9th grade girls, however, were indignant that the princess had complied with the prince's wish that she would not stand taller than him by not standing up; that she would exist to be seen and not heard by never speaking again; and that her beloved pet, a talking dog, would sacrifice itself for her sake because the prince did not like it. They rejoiced when she found true love in a shorter prince who loved her for who she was and they could not agree more than "a Princess says what she thinks. A Princess stands on her own two feet. A Princess stands tall. And she does not betray those who love her."[44] They talked about the stories long after we had finished them, and the writing assignments were exceptionally good since my students really put their hearts into the task at hand. Regarding these, I had to ask a very incensed female student to cross out expressions like "I'm such a jerk!" in her written assignment. However, this was not due to the fact that the prince was not the embodiment of misogyny, because he was (we completely agreed on that point). The fact was that, since the prince was supposed to be telling the story through his own eyes and he clearly had not realized that he was completely biased gender-wise, he could not acknowledge that fact. Again, this was quite an interesting exercise in their fully realizing the importance of the narrator's point of view.

Suggested assignment

- Carefully select your texts for the language classroom. What your students read can either perpetuate or attack gender stereotypes, so choose storylines which actively engage in debunking stereotypes or provide alternative lifestyle options.
- Consider to what extent wonder tale narratives give students a platform for investigating, discovering, and discussing gender roles and expectations.
- Consider to what extent wonder tales can subvert gender roles, even when they assume questionable models like patriarchy.

Conclusion: fostering a gender violence-free school environment by developing female students' sense of self-worth

Feminist scholars[45] have tracked down "natural" gender expectations to their source, namely the legacy of the patriarchal ethos of dichotomous oppositions which have characterized Western philosophical thought ever since the Enlightenment. In fact, these scholars have productively challenged the framework of the metaphysical logic of binary oppositions, the poles masculine/feminine, culture/nature, reason/emotion, rational/irrational, by exposing the relationship of dominance and dependence which cancels out the difference these poles convey. Hence, they have unmasked the way in which one of the polar limits is systematically regarded as the presence of a certain attribute which is valued and consequently positive, whereas the other is deemed as the absence of that attribute, therefore negative. They have denounced the way man is "naturally" associated with culture, reason, and rationality as positive poles, while woman is related to nature, emotion, and irrationality as negative poles.

This discussion has furthermore paved the way for a major feminist breakthrough into the male-dominated discourse over women from which they had historically been erased as subjects. Consequently, history has indeed been male for a very long time – "his story", the story of male achievements written down by male historians. It was thus high time "her story" told another tale, and it has: feminist scholars and activists have consistently challenged the patriarchal argument in which "the qualities that women possess as a result of their biological sex become indistinguishable from those that they are told they should possess in order to be 'feminine'".[46] Thus, women should no longer be faced with the two fallacious alternatives of talking like women and being "feminine" but irrational, or talking like men and being rational but "unfeminine".[47] In fact, I argue that school acts as a catalyst for change as well as a potential equalizer with regard to gender by fostering equal opportunities for boys and girls as well as encouraging equal expectations for boys' and girls' academic achievement. Empirical evidence has demonstrated that educa-tion has played a vital role in women's lives all over the world, since educated girls "are less likely to marry early and against their will; less likely to die in childbirth; more likely to have healthy babies; more likely to send their own children to school; and better able to protect their children from malnutrition, HIV and AIDS, trafficking, and sexual exploitation".[48] Incidentally, the last time I taught "The Princess", Malala was proudly referred to by girl students as a real-life role model, a teenage princess who stands on her own two feet by insisting on the right to female education, a fact that made all students reflect as well on the different status of school as unquestionable, a universal right, and a gender-specific, restricted privilege.

In the specific context of teaching gender by encouraging students to reflect on the role of stereotypes in their daily life, namely with regard to teenage dating violence, this was such a gratifying teaching experience that I have taught these tales twice since then, with similar results. Not least, we as readers become implicated in the text's own politics of initiation and change, as gendered roles and expectations are primarily mediated through the female protagonists' response to the pressure of conforming to or evading them. Likewise, when reading the two tales in the EFL class-room, 8th and 9th grade students were forced to continuously revise their assessment of gendered stereotypes by investigating what happens when people change, and what happens when they do not. For this reason, I believe that wonder tales are indeed a particularly fit teaching tool in a classroom filled with teenage princesses trying to discover who they are and learning to stand on their own two feet with regard to their love relationships.

Suggested assignment

- Make a list of real-life and fictional "princesses who stand on their own two feet" with your students. Encourage them to explain their choices.

Notes

1 Marina Warner convincingly argues that fairies do not always make an appear-ance in this kind of tale. However, the wondrous element is always present, which accounts for Warner's preference for the designation "wonder tale" rather than "fairy tale". For this reason, I will use Warner's term throughout this chapter. See Marina Warner, ed., *Wonder Tales: Six Stories of Enchantment* (London: Vintage, 1996), 5.
2 Judith Butler, "Sex and Gender in Simone de Beauvoir's Second Sex", *Yale French Studies* 72 (1986): 35.
3 Susan Hekman, "The Feminist Critique of Rationality", in *The Polity Reader in Gender Studies*, ed. Anthony Giddens et al. (Cambridge: Polity Press, 1994), 50–61.

4 Anália Torres, "Portuguese Women Stand Up for the Family in Times of Crisis" (interview with Mario Queiroz), *Interpress Service*, 22 March 2013. All subsequent quotations refer to the same interview until further notice.

5 UMAR, the acronym for União de Mulheres Alternativa e Resposta, Alternative and Answer Women's Union, is a women's association formed in 1976. Represented in the consulting council of CIDM (Comissão para a Igualdade e Direitos das Mulheres, the Commission for Equality and Women's Rights) since 1977, the association is known for its socially engaged feminism and is committed to awakening feminist awareness in Portuguese society. For further information on UMAR, visit www.umarfeminismos.org/index.php/quemsomos.

6 See Rita Borges, A prevenção da violência de género em jovens e em contexto escolar: um olhar sobre a intervenção da CIG (Mestrado em Psicologia, Universidade de Lisboa, Faculdade de Psicologia, 2011), iii; Cristina Veríssimo et al., *Prevenir a Violência no Namoro: (N)amo(o) (Im)perfeito – Fazer Diferente para Fazer a Diferença* (Coimbra: Escola Superior de Enfermagem, 2013), 44–53; Marlene Matos et al., "Prevenção da Violência nas Relações de Namoro: Intervenção com Jovens em Contexto Escolar", *Psicologia: Teoria e Prática* 8 (1) (2006): 55–75; Ana Filipa Fernandes, Programas de sensibilização de violência no namoro: Impacto nos jovens (Mestrado em Psicocriminologia, Lisbon, ISPA, 2013).

7 Borges, *A prevenção da violência de género em jovens e em contexto escolar*, iii.

8 Ibid.

9 Veríssimo et al., *Prevenir a Violência no Namoro*, 44–53.

10 Matos et al., "Prevenção da Violência nas Relações de Namoro, 55–75.

11 See Borges, *A prevenção da violência de género em jovens e em contexto escolar*; Joana Andrade Oliveira, *Violência no Namoro Adaptação de um Programa de Prevenção em Jovens Universitárias* (Mestrado em Psicologia Clínica e da Saúde, Universidade da Beira Interior, Faculdade de Ciências Sociais e Humanas, 2013); Fernandes, *Programas de sensibilização de violência no namoro*.

12 Fernandes, *Programas de sensibilização de violência no namoro*, iii.

13 Ibid.

14 Ibid.

15 L. Hickman, L. Jaycox, and J. Aronoff, "Dating Violence among Adolescents: Prevalence, Gender Distribution, and Prevention Program Effectiveness", *Trauma, Violence and Abuse* 5 (2) (2004).

16 Associação Portuguesa de Apoio à Vítima (APAV), "Estatísticas APAV: Crianças e Jovens Vítimas de Crime (2000–2012)", www.apav.pt/apav_v3/images/pdf/CriancasJovensVCV_2000_2012.pdf.

17 E. L. Zurbriggen, "Understanding and Preventing Adolescent Dating Violence: The Importance of Developmental, Sociocultural, and Gendered Perspectives", *Psychology of Women Quarterly* 33 (2009): 31.

18 Associação Portuguesa de Apoio à Vítima (APAV), Campaign: "Corta com a Violência: Quem não te respeita não te merece", uploaded on 10 January 2012, https://youtu.be/b8vXfb80gF4.

19 Comissão para a Cidadania e Igualdade de Género (CIG), Campaign: "Namoro Violento não é Amor", 2008, https://youtube/BAdPTsXrRNA.

20 Fernandes, *Programas de sensibilização de violência no namoro*, 14–17; Oliveira, *Violência no Namoro Adaptação de um Programa de Prevenção em Jovens Universitárias*, 19–20.

21 See Hickman et al., "Dating violence among adolescents"; M. A. Straus, "Prevalence of Violence against Dating Partners by Male and Female University Students Worldwide", *Violence against Women* 10 (7) (2004): 790–811; A. Teten

et al., "Considerations for the Definition, Measurement, Consequences, and Prevention of Dating Violence Victimization among Adolescent Girls", *Journal of Women's Health* 18 (7) (2009): 923–7; J. W. White, "A Gender Approach to Adolescent Dating Violence: Conceptual and Methodological Issues", *Psychology of Women Quarterly* 33 (2009): 1–15.

22 Zurbriggen, "Understanding and Preventing Adolescent Dating Violence", 31.

23 Marina Warner, *Once Upon a Time: A Short History of Fairy Tale* (Oxford: Oxford University Press, 2014), 22.

24 Jack Zipes, *Breaking the Magic Spell: Radical Theories of Folk and Fairy Tales* (Lexington: University Press of Kentucky, 1979), 1.

25 Nina Auerbach and U.C. Knoepflmacher, eds, *Forbidden Journeys: Fairy Tales and Fantasies by Victorian Women Writers* (Chicago, IL: University of Chicago Press, 1992), 17.

26 E. Nesbit, "Melisande, or Long and Short Division", in *Forbidden Journeys: Fairy Tales and Fantasies by Victorian Women Writers*, ed. Nina Auerbach and U.C. Knoepflmacher (Chicago, IL: University of Chicago Press, 1992), 177–91.

27 Jeanne Desy, "The Princess who Stood on Her Own Two Feet", in *Don't Bet on the Prince: Contemporary Feminist Fairy Tales in North America and England*, ed. Jack Zipes (New York: Routledge, 1986), 39–47.

28 Jack Zipes, ed., *Don't Bet on the Prince: Contemporary Feminist Fairy Tales in North America and England* (New York: Routledge, 1986), 33.

29 See L. Berkel, B. Vandiver, and A. Bahner, "Gender Role Attitudes, Religion and Spirituality as Predictors of Domestic Violence Attitudes in White College Students", *Journal of College Student Development* 45 (2) (2004): 119–33; A. Mullender, *La violencia doméstica. Una nueva visión de un viejo problema* (Barcelona: Paidós, 2000).

30 J. R. R. Tolkien, *The Lord of the Rings* (London: Harper Collins Publishers, 1993).

31 Angela Carter, *The Bloody Chamber* (London: Vintage, 1995).

32 A. S. Byatt, *The Djinn in the Nightingale's Eye: Five Fairy Stories* (London: Vintage, 1995).

33 A. S. Byatt, *Elementals: Stories of Fire and Ice* (London: Vintage, 1999).

34 Jack Zipes, ed., *Don't Bet on the Prince: Contemporary Feminist Fairy Tales in North America and England* (New York: Routledge, 1986).

35 A. S. Byatt, "Fairy Stories: The Djinn in the Nightingale's Eye", in *Essays by A. S. Byatt*, 1999, www.asbyatt.com/Onherself.aspx.

36 Ibid.

37 James Thurber, "The Little Girl and the Wolf", in *Fables of Our Time* (New York: Harper & Row, 1983), 3.

38 Roald Dahl, "Little Red Riding Hood and the Wolf", in *Revolting Rhymes* (London: Jonathan Cape, 1982), 47–54.

39 Thurber, "The Little Girl and the Wolf", 3.

40 Jack Zipes, *Happily Ever After: Fairy Tales, Children, and the Culture Industry* (New York: Routledge, 1997), 93.

41 Teresa Figueira, trans., *A Minha Versão da História: Branca de Neve/ A Rainha* (Rio de Mouro: Everest Editora, 2006), 5–6.

42 Byatt, "Fairy Stories".

43 The illustrations are part of Nesbit's story in Auerbach and Knoepflmacher's anthology, but there is no reference as to who the illustrator was.

44 Desy, "The Princess who Stood on Her Own Two Feet", 46.

45 See Catherine Belsey and Jane Moore, eds, *The Feminist Reader: Essays in Gender and the Politics of Literary Criticism* (Cambridge: Blackwell, 1989); Anthony Giddens, ed., *The Polity Reader in Gender Studies* (Cambridge: Polity Press, 1994).

46 Hekman, "The Feminist Critique of Rationality", 51.

47 Ibid.
48 UNICEF, "Girls' education and gender equality", www.unicef.org/education/
bege_70640.html.

References

Associação Portuguesa de Apoio à Vítima (APAV). "Estatísticas APAV: Crianças
e Jovens Vítimas de Crime (2000–2012)". www.apav.pt/apav_v3/images/pdf/
CriancasJovensVCV_2000_2012.pdf (accessed 11 April 2016).
Associação Portuguesa de Apoio à Vítima (APAV). Campaign: "Corta com a
Violência: Quem não te respeita não te merece". Uploaded on 10 January 2012.
https://youtu.be/b8vXfb80gF4 (accessed 11 April 2016).
Auerbach, Nina and U.C. Knoepflmacher, eds. *Forbidden Journeys: Fairy Tales
and Fantasies by Victorian Women Writers*. Chicago, IL: University of Chicago
Press, 1992.
Belsey, Catherine and Jane Moore, eds. *The Feminist Reader: Essays in Gender and
the Politics of Literary Criticism*. Cambridge: Blackwell, 1989.
Berkel, L., Vandiver, B., and Bahner, A. "Gender Role Attitudes, Religion and
Spirituality as Predictors of Domestic Violence Attitudes in White College
Students". *Journal of College Student Development* 45 (2) (2004): 119–33.
Borges, Rita. *A prevenção da violência de género em jovens e em contexto escolar:
um olhar sobre a intervenção da CIG*. Mestrado em Psicologia. Universidade de
Lisboa: Faculdade de Psicologia, 2011.
Butler, Judith. "Sex and Gender in Simone de Beauvoir's Second Sex". *Yale French
Studies* 72 (1986): 35–49.
Byatt, A. S. *The Djinn in the Nightingale's Eye: Five Fairy Stories*. London: Vintage,
1995.
Byatt, A. S. *Elementals: Stories of Fire and Ice*. London: Vintage, 1999.
Byatt, A. S. "Fairy Stories: The Djinn in the Nightingale's Eye". In *Essays by A. S.
Byatt*, 1999. www.asbyatt.com/Onherself.aspx (accessed 14 July 2014).
Carter, Angela. *The Bloody Chamber*. London: Vintage, 1995.
Comissão para a Cidadania e Igualdade de Género (CIG). Campaign: "Namoro
Violento não é Amor". 2008. https://youtube/BAdPTsXrRNA (accessed 11 April
2016).
Dahl, Roald. "Little Red Riding Hood and the Wolf". In *Revolting Rhymes*, 47–54.
London: Jonathan Cape, 1982.
Desy, Jeanne. "The Princess who Stood on Her Own Two Feet". In *Don't Bet on the
Prince: Contemporary Feminist Fairy Tales in North America and England*, edited
by Jack Zipes, 39–47. New York: Routledge, 1986.
Fernandes, Ana Filipa. *Programas de sensibilização de violência no namoro. Impacto
nos jovens*. Mestrado em Psicocriminologia. Lisboa: ISPA, 2013.
Figueira, Teresa, trans. *A Minha Versão da História: Branca de Neve / A Rainha*. Rio
de Mouro: Everest Editora, 2006.
Giddens, Anthony, ed. *The Polity Reader in Gender Studies*. Cambridge: Polity
Press, 1994.
Hekman, Susan. "The Feminist Critique of Rationality". In *The Polity Reader in Gender
Studies*, edited by Anthony Giddens et al., 50–61. Cambridge: Polity Press, 1994.
Hickman, L., Jaycox, L., and Aronoff, J. "Dating Violence among Adolescents:
Prevalence, Gender Distribution, and Prevention Program Effectiveness". *Trauma,
Violence and Abuse* 5 (2) (2004): 123–42.

Matos, Marlene et al. "Prevenção da Violência nas Relações de Namoro: Intervenção com Jovens em Contexto Escolar". *Psicologia: Teoria e Prática* 8 (1) (2006): 55–75.

Mullender, A. *La violencia doméstica. Una nueva visión de un viejo problema.* Barcelona: Paidós, 2000.

Nesbit, E. "Melisande, or Long and Short Division". In *Forbidden Journeys: Fairy Tales and Fantasies by Victorian Women Writers*, edited by Nina Auerbach and U.C. Knoepflmacher, 177–91. Chicago, IL: University of Chicago Press, 1992.

Oliveira, Joana Andrade. *Violência no Namoro Adaptação de um Programa de Prevenção em Jovens Universitárias.* Mestrado em Psicologia Clínica e da Saúde. Universidade da Beira Interior: Faculdade de Ciências Sociais e Humanas, 2013.

Straus, M. A. "Prevalence of Violence against Dating Partners by Male and Female University Students Worldwide". *Violence against Women* 10 (7) (2004): 790–811.

Teten, A. et al. "Considerations for the Definition, Measurement, Consequences, and Prevention of Dating Violence Victimization among Adolescent Girls". *Journal of Women's Health*, 18 (7) (2009): 923–7.

Thurber, James. "The Little Girl and the Wolf". In *Fables of Our Time, 3.* New York: Harper & Row, 1983.

Tolkien, J. R. R. *The Lord of the Rings.* London: Harper Collins Publishers, 1993.

Torres, Anália. "Portuguese Women Stand Up for the Family in Times of Crisis". Interview with Mario Queiroz. *Interpress Service*, 22 March 2013.

Veríssimo, Cristina et al. *Prevenir a Violência no Namoro: (N)amo(o) (Im)perfeito – Fazer Diferente para Fazer a Diferença.* Coimbra: Escola Superior de Enfermagem, 2013.

Warner, Marina, ed. *Wonder Tales: Six Stories of Enchantment.* London: Vintage, 1996.

Warner, Marina. *Once Upon a Time: A Short History of Fairy Tale.* Oxford: Oxford University Press, 2014.

White, J. W. "A Gender Approach to Adolescent Dating Violence: Conceptual and Methodological Issues". *Psychology of Women Quarterly* 33 (2009): 1–15.

Zipes, Jack. *Breaking the Magic Spell: Radical Theories of Folk and Fairy Tales.* Lexington: University Press of Kentucky, 1979.

Zipes, Jack, ed. *Don't Bet on the Prince: Contemporary Feminist Fairy Tales in North America and England.* New York: Routledge, 1986.

Zipes, Jack. *Happily Ever After: Fairy Tales, Children, and the Culture Industry.* New York: Routledge, 1997.

Zurbriggen, E. L. "Understanding and Preventing Adolescent Dating Violence: The Importance of Developmental, Sociocultural, and Gendered Perspectives". *Psychology of Women Quarterly* 33 (2009): 30–3.

10

THE CASE OF TUMBLR

Young people's mediatised responses to the crisis of learning about gender at school

Jessie Bustillos

This chapter presents data collected in an ethnographic study, both online and offline. The focus of my research is young people, and so I carried out most of my observations in schools; both in classes and outside of formal learning school settings. The chapter explains processes of schooling and online engagements by young people as entanglements of learning and identity construction, particularly the ways in which schooling and online learning can be co-constructive, and can permeate the learning and self-expression of gender online. My ethnography develops explanations transversal to the increasing correlations between the expansion of youth technology use and a perceived learning problem, one where the institution of the school and its politics are constructed as being in crisis, out of touch, or unrelated to everyday life. Youth around the globe frequently use various Social Networking Sites (SNSs) such as Facebook, Twitter, Instagram, YouTube, and Tumblr. These platforms intensify the possibilities of visibility, searchability, spreadability, and durability of content online.[1] They also act as mediated mirrors of social surveillance, accessible to anyone in possession of a computer and an internet connection, or any connected mobile technology, which radical accessibility marks them as belonging to the public domain, and also blurs our preconceptions about the limits between public and private in everyday life. Due to the popularity of SNSs and the seeming ease with which young people engage with these platforms, I argue that they have become a site of struggle, possibility, and responsibility in which young people are constantly renegotiating their everyday lives and resisting some elements of social life. In discussing these issues, online encounters are understood within the realm of social surveillance, but also as sites of escape from and struggle with social surveillance. Similarly, social networking sites and the virtual as a neoliberal space are also put to work by young people to resist and redeploy school learning. In this article, I will therefore explore ways in which a specific student, Danielle, actively uses her online engagements to renegotiate constraining gender relations as experienced in school, and how she resists her school's social surveillance of gender by writing herself online.

I argue that Danielle engages with SNSs to reimagine and to re-enact a different kind of feminist response-ability, one that seeks to resist the constraining and highly surveilled gender politics of schooling. Deleuze and Guattari's notion of assemblages will be used to theoretically configure the ways in which the virtual, the non-virtual, the social, and the cultural entangle in Danielle's narrative.[2] I will elaborate on these arguments by drawing on empirical data collected in early 2016, as part of a doctoral research project conducted in London secondary schools. As part of my ethnographic work in schools I spent two years in frequent contact with students and teachers while developing my fieldwork. This ethnographic phase then continued and became a virtual ethnography for over six months; during this period I further developed my fieldwork by following selected research participants online on various SNSs. The description of this experience and the results of my ethnographic research are presented in three parts: firstly, a section on how SNSs have a surveillant nature but are also used by young people to respond to stifling gender learning and identity construction, which both exposes and makes possible different opportunities of learning which exist on a continuum with schooling practices and experiences; secondly, a section explaining the theoretical constructs used to analyse the data and to think about how young people's learning is becoming increasingly mediated on SNSs; and lastly, a section on the ethnographic data, both from the offline and the online phases of my research. This chapter focuses primarily on online encounters on Tumblr, a microblogging site, and also seeks to explore how the technology itself allows for particular digital affordances which, in the case of Danielle, were enabling and reconstitutive of gender relations across offline and online spaces.

Social surveillance and social media

The adoption of social media by young people has enabled a different kind of exposure and increased visibility, which in everyday interactions closely resembles surveillance. In this article, surveillance refers to the "covert, sustained and targeted collection of information about an individual or group".[3] Crucially, with reference to the networked and entangled nature of social media technologies, surveillance also becomes an organisation of relations.

For instance, social media sites such as Tumblr – a microblogging platform where people post text and multimedia in highly customisable and often very artistic blog form and follow other people's blogs – organise peer relations through the careful surveillance of online friendships, blogs, re-blogs, and the creation of profile content online. These interactions are all part of how surveillance occurs online, by users watching over each other, and this means that the nature of peer relations becomes more surveillant.[4]

Similarly, the kind of surveillance experienced online is social, since it creates a particular kind of youth sociality and interaction, whereby relations fall within a normalised set of expectations which shape the everyday lives of youths and reflect societal tenets. With reference to social surveillance, this article seeks to explain through Danielle's experiences how young people's online and social media encounters work in myriad ways; how they differ from platform to platform, with some platforms enabling more rigorous and traditional surveilling practices amongst peers, and others affording them a virtual landscape in which to escape and to reimagine themselves against particular politics of schooling. Therefore, the notion of social surveillance is theorised in this article as polymorphous: both enabled by the emergence and popularity of social media platforms, and also used by young people to extrapolate affordances that allow them to resist and contest, particularly in Danielle's case, some aspects of the gender politics of schooling. To this effect, there is a need to understand that social media virtual spaces as they are discussed here have an "architecture, very much like the architecture of physical spaces", an architecture enabling "particular modes of interaction".[5] This article therefore focuses on Tumblr because the key features of the site – re-blogging, liking blogs, and creating blogs tailored to interests – allow for power affordances that create close-knit online communities based on a digital feeling of camaraderie and solidarity, normally centred on a chosen interest. As explored in other parts of this volume, feminist politics occupy and are enacted in numerous spaces which before seemed to be closed off. In this chapter I explore how, for young people, social networking sites (specifically Tumblr) have become a reclaimed space where they can develop a response to constraining gender politics of schooling as a community, where they can develop response-abilities to the specificities of school experience which demarcate their everyday experiences of learning. With this in mind, in this chapter there will be tracings of gender actualisations which have become mediated on Tumblr by my research participant; gender is perceived as being what McNay called "lived social relations",[6] and an important function of my article is to situate how my respondent inhabits and renegotiates these lived social relations in Tumblr digital locales.

Whilst the arguments constructing social networking sites as emerging places of social surveillance are persuasive,[7] and to some extent true, they do not allow for further explorations into how they might also afford young people opportunities for self-expression and resistance. Danielle's case offers insights into how this is actualised on SNSs through the activities involved in identity work, the participation in community web culture, and the creation of online content that evidences her learning and resistance to schooling. Theoretically, this article develops a Deleuzean-Guattarian analytical lens by unravelling the lived social relations of Danielle as an assemblage of experience between school and online spaces. The notion of assemblage, to be discussed in the next section, therefore allows the narration of lines of continuity between school cultures, experience, and the digital affordances embedded within the locale of Tumblr. Another important part of the argument in this chapter is the notion of *mediatisation*, which serves to explore how an ever increasing part of being young is actualised online. In the next section I will begin to trace how these theoretical notions are configurative to the ways in which young people engage with social media.

Suggested assignment

• Young people are increasingly exposed to digital platforms, including social media, and there is a great deal of learning happening on these platforms and a great deal of information that is exchanged through them. Pedagogically, social media platforms are ready-made structures inviting analysis; discussing with students how these various platforms work through key features and interactions based on their own experience is a way to analyse these platforms more critically.

Gender assemblages of mediatisation

The philosophical notion of assemblages[8] is one which analytically binds together and harnesses the experiential and the affective, the temporal and the transformative scenes in the processes of engagement through which young people become mediatised. The notion of assemblages also allows for the development of a more refined approach to understanding the particularity of youth online sociality as a cyber-social composition of organic and non-organic, technological and affective happenings which go beyond individualised positions. The potentiality of the notion of assemblages has also been utilised in other studies, e.g. Coleman and Ringrose,[9] which explores the potential of Deleuzian philosophical notions in investigating aspects of practice across a variety of fields such as education, pedagogy, and art. Kofoed and Ringrose[10] have also utilised a Deleuzian-Guattarian framework to explore issues of cyberbullying in teenagers' lives. In my own study the notion of assemblages helps me maintain a recognition that mediatisations on social media have a particular durability and continuity which does not solely exist within individual subjective experiences, nor do they only reside in external factors, technologies, or trends, but rather the durability and continuity of social media mediatisations extend and become threaded and entangled among many units which compose the experience of something.

This chapter, through assemblage theory, proposes to go beyond focusing solely on the individual or on the structure of digital technologies to address Danielle's networked and shared nature of experience on Tumblr. This post-Cartesian approach could map out the interconnectedness between young people, digital technologies, and what they allow the individual. This approach is post-Cartesian in that it is not solely subjective, nor is it solely objective, and it is trying to push beyond binary oppositions between individuals and technology as well as the more traditional binary between agency and structure. French philosopher Gilles Deleuze, working in collaboration with Félix Guattari, elaborated on the notion of "machinic assemblage", defining these fusions and intermingling of elements in this way:

> On a first, horizontal, axis, an assemblage comprises two segments, one of content, the other of expression. On the one hand it is a mechanic assemblage of bodies, of actions and passions … On the other hand it is a collective assemblage of enunciation, of acts and statements of incorporeal transformations attributed to bodies. Then on a vertical axis, the assemblage has both territorial sides and reterritorialized, which stabilise it.[11]

Consequently, assemblages are transformative happenings, open coalitions between, in the case of my study, the young people themselves and the external elements encountered, explored, used, and internalised whilst using technologies. With reference to the earlier part of the quote above, on assemblages comprising "two segments, one of content, the other of expression" I point to how, through assemblage theory, I can uncover not just the ways in which young people use social media platforms or digital technologies but also the ways in which these materials and technologies have generated new ways of seeing and acting in their world. Moreover, on the assemblage having "both territorial sides and reterritorialised", I point to how Danielle has assembled-with the new fields of power that Tumblr uncovers in order to respond differently to her school culture and to her everyday experiences of schooling.

Therefore, assemblage theory asks us to think about new human becomings which open up new possibilities. In the case of this chapter, the offline and online tracings in the narrative of Danielle's experience materialise new response-abilities in the field of gender actualisation, amongst many other factors. The somewhat subversive culture of Tumblr, the intermingling of online content creation and the experiences of school cultures with opportunities for actualising cyber-resistances, all compose the "assemblage Danielle". These sensitisations of human experience through assemblage theory create a multidisciplinary openness which I want to use to understand Danielle's experiences.

Another important part of the analysis presented here involves dealing with the notion of "mediatisation", yet in doing so it is important to differentiate between "mediation" and "mediatisation". The notion of *mediation* comprehends the ways in which meaning is constituted. We live in a mediated world which becomes primarily mediated through language, but which also is increasingly re-mediated through digital technologies that permeate everyday life, as argued by Pink.[12] Increasingly, "there is no question that many, even all, dimensions of society are now *mediated* by digital networked technologies in ways that matter".[13] When youths enter online spaces and share their interests, personal details, and preferences, they are mediating themselves online; they are writing themselves an organised identity within an already-organised digitally-structured technology[14] and a publicly surveilled space which can be utilised in many ways by the individual, but which can also become utilised.

Yet, there is another important process, *mediatisation*, and this process underwrites the way in which online communication becomes appropriated by a certain group and not just how communications happen or become circulated. Arguably, the notion of mediatisation differs sharply from mediation, as mediatisation involves a "wider transformative logic or mechanism that is understood to do something ... (that is, to mediatize)".[15] The term "mediatisation" then comprises an understanding that involves a socially and culturally transformative process of becoming which characterises young people's cultural life through media.

As part of this article, "mediatisation" is conceptualised as a "process whereby communication media become in some respect more 'important' in expanding areas of life and society [and, specifically ...] how institutionalized technologies of communication expand in extension and power".[16] In the case of Danielle, her experiences of gender actualisation were crucially mediatised on Tumblr; that is, they were increasingly and substantially effectual online. Therefore, the notion of mediatisation is "a sensitizing concept that offers a general sense of reference and guidance in approaching empirical instances, sensitizing the researcher about where to look rather than defining precisely what exists in advance of social scientific investigation".

I therefore propose that the mediatisation of youth is characterised by Winfried Schulz's[17] four core dimensions of mediatisation – mediatisation as extending human capacities for communication through time and space, mediatisation as substituting prior or direct social activities or experiences with mediated ones, mediatisation as amalgamating primary and secondary (or interpersonal and mass-mediated) activities, and as accommodating social activities and institutions to media logic. The phenomenon of being young is increasingly mediatised; online friendships, online learning, entertainment, and gaming are only a few examples of this, and in the case of

Danielle, important acts of resistance and gender actualisation are possible because of the ways in which these aspects of youth have assembled with digital technologies.

These human-cultural-technological entanglements suggest that it is "becoming increasingly complex to separate bodies, gender and sexuality from the technological networks that give them form and meaning".[18] New media technologies are not apprehensible if we do not contextualise them within the embodied and gendered cultures that permeate them with new fields of power which then become appropriated by young users, and this is also a part of mediatising/ed assemblages. I argue that this contextualisation then raises serious questions about the traditionally gendered human subject whose boundaries are understood to be contained and explained by the subject's subjectivity and agency. Firstly, there is a need to explore response-abilities generated by new digital media more closely, since they can be very varied and highly responsive to specific events. As we shall discuss, Danielle's response-abilities are intrinsically conjunctional to school politics; Danielle's response-abilities are then extended and evidenced in her Tumblr engagements as I will discuss. Her sense of agency and her subjective experience is entangled with the online but is also responsive to what she perceives are restrictive school politics; however, these politics of schooling have also enabled her to develop innovative responses to assert her own identity through digital learning and online identity work.

Secondly, where does the human body end and the technological body begin? Given the inextricable relations between humans and machines that are in this study represented by new media technologies, other questions arise when we consider that the experience of gender and the performance of gender can now extend into spaces other than concrete physical environments. Where then is embodied subjectivity located? Is it possible to continue to speak of a contained subject with a singular human agency? It is perhaps more useful to ground understandings of the subject within ideas of distributed agency "which recognises agency as a process that is allocated to humans as well as non-human actors who depend on each other … it might be productive to approach online social practices as belonging to a larger assembly of everyday post-human activities".[19] This has also been suggested by Rogowska-Stangret in Chapter 1, where she calls for an analysis of individualisation that tries to explore how subjectivity is relational. I argue that by recognising the potential of gender actualisations online as performed by Danielle, we can see that there is a de-territorialisation of gender practices which goes beyond the territory of an agent, or of a self-governing human body as they become assembled and mediatised on the digital space of Tumblr, yet, all this is still harnessed to the organic realities of schooling.

Tumblr and enabling affordances of resistance

Danielle is female, 15 years old, and from London; she attends a mixed secondary school in south west London. I conducted an ethnography at Danielle's school for over a year, both in classes and out of classes; this phase then progressed into an ethnographic interview with Danielle after she volunteered to participate in the research. The ethnographic phase continued online, whereby I kept in contact with Danielle online via various platforms, including Tumblr, for a period of three months. Danielle is an avid Tumblr user; she engages by using all the key features that the site offers, which include microblogging as well as following, liking, and re-blogging other people's blogs. As I will argue, many of Danielle's media-tised resistances are found on Tumblr. As an SNS, Tumblr has a certain streak of virtual oddity surrounding it, partly because the user-generated content is perceived as edgy or cutting-edge, with features that seem to facilitate supportive and encouraging networks. To this effect Gross writes about Tumblr, "a mysterious new culture has been born. We are like ancient Egyptians. We communicate with pictures, we worship cats, and nobody understands us."[20]

This paraphrases a post that was re-blogged many thousands of times on the blogging site Tumblr. While the site doesn't have pyramids, pharaohs, or slaves, it does indeed have a distinct cultural identity setting it apart from networks like Facebook and Google+. Danielle also finds Tumblr distinct from other media and describes it as, "weirdly wonderful":

> I love it … I've had it since I was twelve. You can post GIFs, video edits, pictures, you can pretty much do anything on Tumblr, it's like weirdly wonderful, I post more original stuff on there than I do on Twitter but I also re-blog people's things. It's basically like a blog website, but maybe more public, less private than a blog. They're mainly for fandoms, photography or flaunting weird interests maybe.

For Danielle, Tumblr is an "awesome" platform; one which compensates for missed learning opportunities at school and one which also becomes a site for resistance, as we will explore later. Danielle's first comments on Tumblr point to how she perceives the site as a place where she has learnt; she explains: "It's really important to me, I've learnt a lot, like a lot, from being online and from people online, like school falls short". Youth online learning has been a developing topic in academic educational research.[21] Interestingly, digital learning goes beyond understanding the act of learning as something that occurs only cognitively; it seeks to explain how the very digital means through which learning happens on connected networks, mediated activity, and communication affordances reshapes individual learning.[22]

With regard to young people, the digital tools channelling and enabling digital learning, such as laptops, tablets, and mobile phones "are embedded in the contemporary youth cultures as mediators that promote unique learning opportunities".[23] This is delineated in Danielle's narrative about Tumblr when she says; "I'm on it a lot, because I've got the app on my phone, so it's like, so immediate and fun". The accessibility and portability of this mobile technology affords Danielle numerous cyberspatial opportunities, opportunities which have value to her because of how much she feels she has learnt on this platform. When I enquired further and asked Danielle what she has learnt on Tumblr, she replied:

> My school is … teaching things about … like, PSHE stuff, they feel that we don't really need to know any of this stuff, I've learnt almost everything from Tumblr because they have lots of, like, sexuality posts … anti-homophobic, and anti-sexist blogs, there are lots of feminists on Tumblr too. I use it a lot, like everyday I'm on it, it's like a sort of cool place to air your opinions and rant a little bit. I rant about school because PSHE stuff is so pointless. My friend follows me on Tumblr and she runs her blog on this sort of stuff, because she's pansexual and she posts things along those lines, she's made me think a lot about this.

Danielle expressly talks about her disappointment that school falls short when teaching about or discussing issues around sexism, homophobia, and sexuality. Danielle's learning on the platform of Tumblr is directly oppositional to that of her school's. As Danielle perceives it, she has been exposed to this content online, and it is this online content, including her friendships within the network, that have helped her to reflect on these issues. As a consequence, Danielle has become more critical of her own school practices; this is evident when she says, "I think … it's helped me quite a bit because … it's taught me things like, I've learnt things, which have also made me think about myself, and … question school a bit more about, things my school hasn't taught me". Danielle has both internalised and mediatised some of her virtual discoveries in this participatory web culture.

In Danielle's experience there is an obvious rupture between the sociocultural landscapes of school and of Tumblr, a rupture marked by the failings of school to address issues around gender, sexuality, homophobia, and sexism. To this effect, Ringrose argues that "both online and school spaces are shaped through commodified gendered and sexualized norms and idealizations, which 'striate' the space".[24] The striation of space indicates the relational states that characterise a place and implies that something happens in a particular way: "striated spaces are hierarchical, rule-intensive, strictly bounded and confining".[25] In Danielle's experience the striation of school occurs within a relation of power that she finds disempowering and neglectful, yet the online (i.e. her Tumblr engagement) recontextualises, re-addresses and enhances her ability to respond to these striations of space. This is further evidenced in Danielle's narrative; as she says, "my school is rubbish at teaching anything in relation to this. They haven't even started to brush against issues around consent, bisexuality, homosexuality … and that sort of thing and I've learnt it all from Tumblr." In understanding these issues it is important to map out the continuity of these lines of resistance, criticality, and experience as they occur offline within the school context and become extended and transformed online, within social media cultures.

Furthermore, as a site of mediatised resistance for Danielle, Tumblr digitally sustained ways and affordances which problematised her own identity but which also helped to materialise it in direct opposition to her school approximations around gender and sexuality. Danielle discusses some of this in the next extract:

> we haven't even been taught this, we were just told once that there was straight and there was gay and there's nothing in between … I thought that doesn't actually really apply to me … Tumblr taught me even things, like, transgender, pansexual, panromantic, biromantic, gender fluid … So … it's changed the way I look at myself but it also … shows up how other people feel awkward about this sort of stuff.

In this respect, Van Doorn[26] explains that "online articulations of gender, sexuality and embodiment are intricately interwoven with people's physical embeddings in everyday life, as well as the new media technologies they employ to extend digital experiences into digital locales". For Danielle, the everyday school culture which she experiences as limiting and undermining her own gender identity, described by her as being "biromantic asexual", has become digitally entangled with Tumblr, enabling her to digitally and materially interface her resistance to school politics through this gendered mediatisation of "coming out" on Tumblr, as illustrated in Figures 10.1 and 10.2. Danielle's older profile from June 2015 only displayed her name and her profile nickname on Tumblr, under a picture of her favourite YouTuber Dan Howell. Conversely, in later profile posts from November 2015 and early 2016, Danielle blogged a short five-lined passage which mediatised her gender identity as "bi" (see Figure 10.1); this is also rematerialised in her profile details as they appeared in early 2016 (see Figure 10.2).

There is a tangible relationship between the digital and physical instances of Danielle's materialisation of her gender identity on Tumblr. Danielle encountered a politics of schooling which, when interjected with her Tumblr online engagements, seemed constraining and restricting, since Tumblr offered the capacities that she was looking for to express her own views on gender and on her own identity, as we can see from Figures 10.1 and 10.2. The later online actualisations, digital learning, and interactions on Tumblr served as an example of the "immaterial potential of the virtual": the

FIGURE 10.1 Danielle's Tumblr post on her identity, November 2015

possible-online which did not seem possible offline, which in Danielle's narrative became "materially actualised in the form of digital objects"[27] such as pictures, text, and imagery – in the form of her post, her profile changes, and her online identity work. This identity work is by no means static, nor finished, and continues online and offline; it continues in a space that Danielle retraces and striates with friends and family:

> everyone on Tumblr is like accepting and stuff, so I can be more open about stuff. I've great friends on Tumblr. Like my mum says that this stuff is unreal, how much I know and the words I come up with. So lately we've talked about me being biromantic asexual and she's also learning from me.

This mediatisation of resistance to school politics and gender materiality online became embodied on the digital space of Tumblr, yet these mediatisations are also entanglements of school culture, the affordances of Tumblr, and Danielle's experiences. This mediatised assemblage has relationalities, temporalities, and intensities which traverse both school and

FIGURE 10.2 Danielle's Tumblr online profile, January 2016

online socio-spatialities in Danielle's story. Through the "specific time/space events" as explored in the article it is possible to explore how "the internet, including instant messaging and social networking sites, appears to intensify existing affective relations"[28] which encompass the actualisation of gender in Danielle's experience. The online content on Tumblr and her own identity work have opened up new response-abilities for Danielle to resist constrained learning at school, access feminist knowledge online, and forge an identity for herself which seemed at odds with her school's culture.

Suggested assignment

- The chapter lends itself to being discussed in schools and in educational environments where the teaching of issues around gender and sexuality might be opaque or neglected. The content might be openly discussed with an audience of young people who are familiar with using social media platforms, such as Tumblr.
- In order to generate lively analyses and debates, students can be split into two groups; with one group to be asked to discuss and list the

ways in which social networking sites might be used as instruments of social surveillance and the other group to discuss and list the ways in which social networking sites might be liberating, informational, and empowering.

- Further questions might include: what kinds of knowledges are disseminated online on the social media networks known or used by students? How are these various knowledges disseminated through the various networks? How do these knowledges vary from the systems of knowledge as experienced in educational institutions?

Notes

1 danah boyd, *It's Complicated: The Social Lives of Networked Teens* (New Haven, CT: Yale University Press, 2014), 11.
2 Gilles Deleuze and Félix Guattari, *Anti-Oedipus: Capitalism and Schizophrenia* (Minneapolis: University of Minnesota Press, 2008).
3 Daniel Trottier, "Interpersonal Surveillance on Social Media", *Canadian Journal of Communication* 37 (2012): 320.
4 Ibid., 320.
5 Zizi Papacharissi, "The Virtual Geographies of Social Networks: A Comparative Analysis of Facebook, LinkedIn and ASmallWorld", *New Media and Society* 11 (2009): 200.
6 Lois McNay, "Agency and Experience: Gender as a Lived Relation", in *Feminism after Bourdieu*, ed. Lisa Adkins and Beverley Skeggs (Oxford: Wiley-Blackwell, 2004).
7 Daniel Trottier, *Social Media as Surveillance: Rethinking Visibility in a Converging World* (Farnham: Ashgate, 2012).
8 Deleuze and Guattari, *Anti-Oedipus*.
9 Rebecca Coleman and Jessica Ringrose, *Deleuze and Research Methodologies* (Edinburgh: Edinburgh University Press, 2013).
10 Jette Kofoed and Jessica Ringrose, "Travelling and Sticky Affects: Exploring Teens and Sexualized Cyberbullying through a Butlerian-Deleuzian-Guattarian Lens", *Discourse: Studies in the Cultural Politics of Education* 33 (2012), 5.
11 Deleuze and Guattari, *Anti-Oedipus*, 88.
12 Sarah Pink, *Situating Everyday Life* (London: Sage, 2012).
13 Peter Lunt and Sonia Livingstone, "Is 'Mediatization' the New Paradigm for Our Field? A Commentary on Deacon and Stanyer (2014, 2015) and Hepp, Harvard and Lundby (2015)", *Media, Culture & Society* 38 (2016): 463.
14 Jennifer Corriero and Liam O'Doherty, "Digital Expressions and Networks Shape Intercultural Opportunities for Youth", *Intercultural Education* 24 (2013): 494.
15 Nick Couldry, "Mediatization or Mediation? Alternative Understandings of the Emergent Space of Digital Storytelling", *New Media and Society* 10 (2008): 376.
16 Johan Fornäs, "Mediatization of Popular Culture", in *Mediatization of Communication: Handbooks of Communication Science*, vol. 21. ed. Knut Lundby (Berlin: De Gruyter Mouton, 2014), 484.
17 Wolfgang Schulz, "Reconstructing Mediatization as an Analytical Concept", *European Journal of Communication* 19 (2004): 89.
18 Niels Van Doorn, "Digital Spaces, Material Traces: How Matter Comes to Matter in Online Performances of Gender, Sexuality and Embodiment", *Media, Culture & Society* 33 (2011): 536.
19 Ibid., 536.

20 Michael Gross, "What Makes People Click?", *Current Biology* 23 (2013): 1.
21 Sandra Calvert and Barbara Wilson, *The Handbook of Children, Media, and Development* (Chichester: Wiley Blackwell, 2008).
22 Elaine Tan, "Informal Learning on 'YouTube': Exploring Digital Literacy in Independent Online Learning", *Learning, Media and Technology* 38 (2013).
23 Asli Ünlüsoy, Mariëtte De Haan, Kevin Leander, and Beate Volker, "Learning Potential in Youth's Online Networks: A Multilevel Approach", *Computers & Education* 68 (2013): 523.
24 Jessica Ringrose, "Beyond Discourse? Using Deleuze and Guattari's Schizoanalysis to Explore Affective Assemblages, Heterosexually Striated Space, and Lines of Flight Online and at School", *Educational Philosophy and Theory* 43 (2011): 602.
25 Maria Tamboukou, "Machinic Assemblages: Women, Art Education and Space", *Discourse* 29 (2008): 360.
26 Van Doorn, "Digital Spaces, Material Traces", 532.
27 Van Doorn, "Digital Spaces, Material Traces", 534.
28 Ringrose, "Beyond Discourse?", 602.

References

boyd, danah. *It's Complicated: The Social Lives of Networked Teens.* New Haven, CT: Yale University Press, 2014.

Calvert, Sandra and Wilson, Barbara. *The Handbook of Children, Media, and Development.* Chichester: Wiley Blackwell, 2008.

Coleman, Rebecca and Ringrose, Jessica. *Deleuze and Research Methodologies.* Edinburgh: Edinburgh University Press, 2013.

Corriero, Jennifer and O'Doherty, Liam. "Digital Expressions and Networks Shape Intercultural Opportunities for Youth", *Intercultural Education* 24 (2013): 493–7.

Couldry, Nick. "Mediatization or Mediation? Alternative Understandings of the Emergent Space of Digital Storytelling", *New Media and Society* 10 (2008): 373–91.

Deleuze, Gilles and Guattari, Félix. *Anti-Oedipus: Capitalism and Schizophrenia.* Minneapolis: University of Minnesota Press, 2008.

Fornäs, Johan. "Mediatization of Popular Culture". In *Mediatization of Communication: Handbooks of Communication Science*, vol. 21, edited by Knut Lundby. Berlin: De Gruyter Mouton, 2014.

Gross, Michael. "What Makes people Click?", *Current Biology* 23 (2013): 1–4.

Kofoed, Jette and Ringrose, Jessica. "Travelling and Sticky Affects: Exploring Teens and Sexualized Cyberbullying through a Butlerian-Deleuzian-Guattarian Lens", *Discourse: Studies in the Cultural Politics of Education* 33 (2012): 5–20.

Lunt, Peter and Livingstone, Sonia. "Is 'Mediatization' the New Paradigm for Our Field? A Commentary on Deacon and Stanyer (2014, 2015) and Hepp, Harvard and Lundby (2015)", *Media, Culture & Society* 38 (2016): 462–70.

McNay, Lois. "Agency and Experience: Gender as a Lived Relation". In *Feminism after Bourdieu*, edited by Lisa Adkins and Beverley Skeggs. Oxford: Wiley-Blackwell, 2004.

Papacharissi, Zizi. "The Virtual Geographies of Social Networks: A Comparative Analysis of Facebook, LinkedIn and ASmallWorld", *New Media and Society* 11 (2009): 199–220.

Pink, Sarah. *Situating Everyday Life.* London: Sage, 2012.

Ringrose, Jessica. "Beyond Discourse? Using Deleuze and Guattari's Schizoanalysis to Explore Affective Assemblages, Heterosexually Striated Space, and Lines of Flight Online and at School", *Educational Philosophy and Theory* 43 (2011): 598–618.

Schulz, W. "Reconstructing Mediatization as an Analytical Concept", *European Journal of Communication* 19 (2004): 87–101.

Tamboukou, Maria. "Machinic Assemblages: Women, Art Education and Space", *Discourse* 29 (2008): 359–75.

Tan, Elaine. "Informal Learning on 'YouTube': Exploring Digital Literacy in Independent Online Learning", *Learning, Media and Technology* 38 (2013): 463–77.

Trottier, David. "Interpersonal Surveillance on Social Media", *Canadian Journal of Communication* 37 (2012): 319–32.

Trottier, David. *Social Media as Surveillance: Rethinking Visibility in a Converging World*. Farnham: Ashgate, 2012.

Ünlüsoy, Asli, De Haan, Mariëtte, Leander, Kevin, and Volker, Beate. "Learning Potential in Youth's Online Networks: A Multilevel Approach", *Computers and Education* 68 (2013): 522–33.

Van Doorn, Niels. "Digital Spaces, Material Traces: How Matter Comes to Matter in Online Performances of Gender, Sexuality and Embodiment", *Media, Culture and Society* 33 (2011): 531–47.

11

ON THE ROAD

Feminist alliances across Europe

Verònica Gisbert Gracia

Introduction

The austerity crisis has posed significant challenges to the conception of the humanistic subject as self-governing, independent, and liberal; to put this point another way, austerity has forced us to question that representation of the humanistic subject's ability to live himself, to live his own life free and autonomously, under his own decisions, to be sovereign. Our organic vulnerability, understood as a constitutive precariousness due to our interdependent sociality, bases our primary dependence on other lives and cultural contexts at all times. For those who are affected, their body has become a precarious body.

The current management of the crisis "is established as the only rational and viable mode of governance"[1] and neoliberal economic policies are constructed as a prudent and measured response, or as the duty of a responsible citizenry, which "thus renders critical thinking and acting redundant, irrational, and ultimately unpatriotic".[2] What austerity conceals is the ideological dimension of the crisis, that is, the shift from the modern social model to a government of the precarious[3] achieved through the destruction of increasingly fragile social bonds. Analyses of the impacts of austerity policies reveal that the intensification of *precarity*[4] is intersected by gender, race, sex, and class issues. Nonetheless, these excluded and precarious bodies have come together on "the common", through alliances, and are organizing strong resistance against neoliberal and patriarchal policies even at the risk of violence and death, "they are themselves [the precarious bodies] modalities of power, embodied interpretations, engaging in allied action".[5]

In this chapter, I will focus on one of these alliances, which in turn includes additional feminist alliances: the 4th International Action

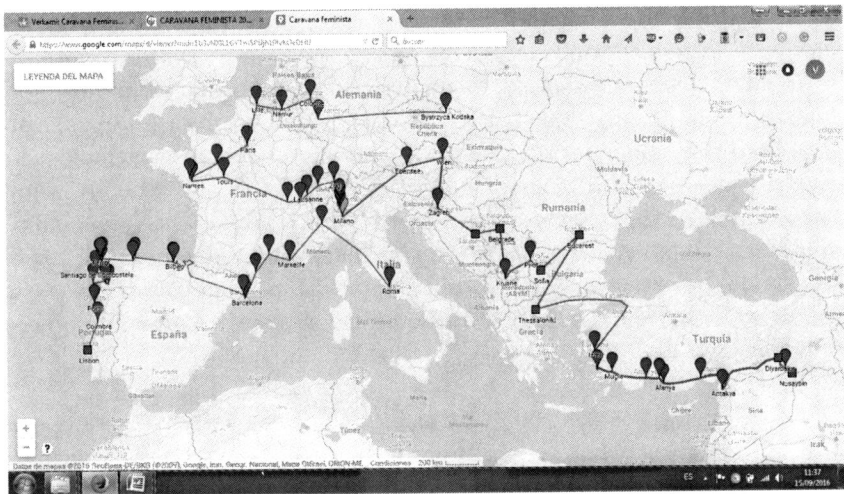

FIGURE 11.1 The route of the Feminist Caravan

of the World March of Women, which in Europe took the form of the Feminist Caravan.[6] This original form of action consisted of a physical caravan (one or more vehicles) which crossed parts of Europe, starting on 6 March in Kurdistan and lasting until 17 October 2015, ending in Portugal (Figure 11.1).

Some of the experiences reported by these women in their travel diaries will be analysed in the last part of this chapter to show the importance of solidarity beyond identities, and the challenge these feminist resistances to capitalist dynamics make possible.

Precariousness, *precarity*, and governmental precarization

We live in a body, our body, although it is not ours exclusively, and this means that as biological creatures who seek to persist we are necessarily dependent on social relations and institutions that address our basic needs for food, shelter, and protection from violence, to name a few. Furthermore, this shows us a new frame for analysis: interdependence. The body tells us about our vulnerability and our mutual dependence. The recognition of commonly shared precariousness could then go hand in hand with the recognition of the connection with others and thus would become the foundation for a political, rather than an individualized, independence that must fend off the negatively connoted dependency of others.

In addition, no body whose life is effective is autonomous, either in childhood or at any other moment of our existence. Our interdependence is radical and constitutive, it is impossible to deny. As a result, "precariousness is coextensive with birth itself (birth is, by definition, precarious), which means that it matters whether or not this infant being survives, and that its survival is dependent on what we might call a social network of hands".[7]

To move towards increasing the material conditions that extend the possibilities of life through the differential distribution of precariousness, material conditions made possible by the adoption of dynamic epistemological, ontological, and ethical policies with a commitment to a new bodily ontology will involve the mandatory rethinking "of precariousness, vulnerability, injurability, interdependency [to others, human and non-human], exposure, bodily persistence, desire, work, and the claims of language and social belonging".[8] Indeed, the body of this ontology is always exposed to others, in Butler's words:

> The "being" of the body to which this ontology refers is one that is always given over to others, to norms, to social and political organizations that have developed historically in order to maximize precariousness for some and minimize precariousness for others. It is not possible first to define the ontology of the body and then to refer to the social significations the body assumes. Rather, to be a body is to be exposed to social crafting and form, and that is what makes the ontology of the body a social ontology.[9]

Therefore, this precariousness defines our existence, although always in articulation with social and political implications which redistribute unequal and differentiated strategies of *precarity* which are at once a material and a perceptual issue. This means that some lives are more valuable than others; some lives can be mourned and others cannot; some lives are allowed to express mourning and others are not. Therefore, we must reflect deeply on current normative mechanisms to show how precariousness is distributed differentially and hierarchically, how to give recognition and to provide material conditions of life to some bodies without sacrificing the lives of others. Indeed, the normative, in the sense of political *precarity* exposed by Butler, is based essentially on an implementation of injustice and inequality; it is contrary to the conditions of fair, equal, and free life.

At the confluence that becomes through the combination of the bodily character of existence (the body as a place from which we feel the social) and its inherent exposition (the other's need to sustain embodied life), it is necessary to emphasize a characteristic of the ontological condition, although it has been suggested previously in the text: vulnerability. Thus, vulnerability does not refer to certain conditions of life marked by need, inequality, violence, and all that in one way or another would prevent a dignified life. In contrast, vulnerability, in a deep sense, is an inherent ontological dimension to the human condition itself.

At this point in the analysis of Butler's social and bodily ontology, we can affirm that:

[p]recariousness and *precarity* are intersecting concepts ... *Precarity* also characterizes that politically induced condition of maximized precariousness for populations exposed to arbitrary state violence who often have no other option than to appeal to the very state from which they need protection. In other words, they appeal to the state for protection, but the state is precisely that from which they need protection.[10]

Consequently, for the author, Butler's work offers not only a new bodily ontology but also the starting point for a renewed progressive or leftist politics.

This recognition of constitutive and shared precariousness would favour governments committed to implementing policies that facilitate the universal basic rights of subsistence such as: food, housing, health, and other necessary conditions to persist and thrive. Moreover, these policies would reduce the unequal distribution of wealth, and consequently, the exposure to violence of some populations that are marked as "lives that are not quite lives, cast as 'destructible' and 'ungrievable'. Such populations are seen as 'lose-able' ... rather than as living populations in need of protection from illegitimate state violence, famine, or pandemics".[11]

Unfortunately, contemporary political will remains distant from Butler's proposal, as Isabell Lorey asserts: "precarization can be seen as a neoliberal instrument of governance".[12] Precarization cannot be considered (as Butler[13] confirms in the preface to Lorey's book) a temporary condition, it is not an episode in contrast to the fundamental characteristics of contemporary societies, in which the neoliberal imaginary predominates as mythical reference. As a matter of fact, precariousness has become the hegemonic way in which we are governed and self-governing, "precarization is currently in a process of normalization".[14] Nonetheless, despite the normalization of precarization, we cannot say that we live in societies of insecurity but in societies governed through precarization. According to this form of government, the state continues to manage ancient insurance institutions, increasingly limited to discourses and practices of police and military security. Thus, the new pairing of neoliberal governance is no longer freedom and security but freedom and insecurity, "the state has not as its main purpose neither limitation of freedom or the fight against insecurity, but both turn in the ideological precondition to precarization as governance technique".[15]

As a consequence, the society we live in is by no means an insecurity society, it is indeed still a security society, but it is one that can be controlled through social insecurity, that is to say, all sociopolitical institutions within neoliberal logic are forced to juggle to manage a maximum of precarization, while controlling a minimum social assurance to ensure social peace. In any case, the process of normalizing precarization does not mean equality in insecurity; inequalities are not abolished. For neoliberal logic, inequality is central to government, and we could affirm that it is *useful*. Put differently, neoliberal logic dictates that government should find the bearable balance among different normalities; between a normality of poverty and a normality of wealth.[16]

Given the political and social global outlook in which we are mired, both authors propose new coalitions or alliances to overcome unequal neoliberal macro-politics, in Butler's words "those forms of legalized violence by which populations are differentially deprived of the basic resources needed to minimize precariousness".[17] These alliances should be supported on "the common", which means that we should build networks through different identities, opening extensive processes that can be named as a result of experience shared and imaginary life from other ethical and political criteria. From this perspective, we have to think of these alliances as an open movement, where certain kinds of ongoing antagonisms among its participants persist, valuing such persistent and animating differences as the sign and substance of a radical democratic politics.[18]

Bodily mobilization: interdependency and feminist alliances

Neoliberal policies are mainly austerity policies, which seek to strengthen the subject's individualism and consequently fail to deal with the material conditions set to meet basic needs like housing, food, health, and education. Nevertheless, we can find new political global collectivities seeking to reclaim democracy from capitalism and corporate power. If we consider the normalization of precarization, then we can observe:

> the need to confirm the importance of alliances and cohabitation across established categorizations of identity and difference, beyond the very polarity of identity/difference. The heterogeneity of precarious bodies, actions, frameworks, and affective states invites and requires the continuous political work of engagement, translation, and alliance, work that veers away from essentialized understandings of identity and representation, and, of course, that effectively opposes nationalist discourses and practices.[19]

However, we cannot forget that "the battle against induced *precarity* ought to be simultaneously a battle against racism, nationalism, anti-immigrant politics, misogyny, homophobia, and all forms of social injustice".[20]

In this sense, Butler and Athanasiou encourage the alliance of "the common" between sexual, racial, and religious minorities, and between feminist, gay, transgender, and queer people; alliances between lifestyles based on interdependence, and which can articulate a policy based on responsibility and ethical decisions, against war, state violence, and, ultimately, against the differential allocation of *precarity*.

Likewise, these alliances of "the common" should be built on the one hand through *slow*[21] *policy*, that is to say, through a policy that invites us to think and act beyond economic issues, to ask what is necessary to live a livable life, and to create a policy where attention and learning allow the discovery of what every experience has in common. Given our condition of vulnerability we share these more or less elaborate social bonds, whether we like it or not, with others. Moreover, in *slow policy*[22] the focus is the process, becoming the gerund in a political verb; societies are transformed through listening, learning, feeling, criticizing, and debating. Resistances from *slow policy* are constructed from everyday life; slow policy's goal is not taking power but transforming the world.[23] In brief, *slow policy* develops an active, conscious, and critical citizenship. On the other hand, it is an imaginative policy[24] that does not remain what it is, but generates other ways within social relations. In both cases, it is necessary and vital to build resistance from political experience rather than from fixed identities.

Feminist Caravan to link women's alliances

The Feminist Caravan analysed in this chapter is an example of these kinds of alliances from "the common" which were created over 212 days (7 months) on the road, with 163 feminist public events across Europe, 147 feminist art events, and 89 protests in the streets.

Preparatory meetings for this ambitious action took place in late 2014. Where possible, national coordinators of the World March of Women organized meetings with different local, regional, or national feminist organizations in order to plan activities to be carried out during the course of the caravan. This project was funded through crowdfunding, where the organization team achieved its goal in just one month. The caravan dream team, which is how they signed their statements, needed the money "to have a powerful caravan".[25] Its budget was 40,000 euros, of which 12,000 were obtained through Verkami; this was the initial budget to kickstart the caravan, especially for food and fuel. Moreover, the feminist caravan wanted to show that capitalist-alternative ways of living are possible, and for this reason they called for solidarity that would facilitate them in terms of material support such as food and shelter.

The feminist adventure started in Kurdistan, Turkey with a big opening event organized by the Kurdish women's movement and the Turkish Coordination of the World March of Women. Then, the caravan took the road through Greece (Thessaloniki) until the end of March, to the Balkans, and then to Italy and Switzerland. There they crossed into the north of France, Belgium, and Germany and stopped in August in Poland for an International Feminist Camp. Finally they returned south through Hungary and Austria to Italy, continued to the south of France, and went to Catalonia, the Basque Country, and Galicia in Spain before finally arriving in Portugal for a big closing event.

Women were part of this action through meetings, teambuilding days, interviews, and life/collective experiences. The feminist cross-border caravan drew a cartography of the different resistances of women collectives around Europe and made visible some of the feminist European struggles against injustice, against violence, and against poverty, racism, individualism, the sexual division of work, patriarchy, and heteronormativity; in other words, against the dominant accumulation model based on the appropriation of nature, control over women's bodies and lives, and the appropriation of social movements. Despite the different realities of life, the several levels of *precarity* attending the intersection of race, sex, gender, and class issues, even the different levels of violence exercised by states across Europe, this action has created the basis "for an alliance focused on opposition to state violence and its capacity to produce, exploit, and distribute *precarity* for the purposes of profit and territorial defence".[26] The feminist caravan showed the world that as women, we have the power to change and we have alternatives to share.

Resistances for the common goods

This feminist activism, conscious of our constitutive and shared vulnerability and consequently of our interdependencies, based a large part of their resistance on common goods and the appropriation of nature. The management of the global crisis, based on austerity, is privatizing the commons (water, housing, energy, territory, nature, etc.) and destroying social and labour rights. This irreversible project is transferring wealth from the poor to the rich. Through their struggles to defend or reappropriate the commons, women collectives try to change power relations and the model of production and consumption, which also involves a change in reproductive roles and gender equality.

On 12 March, the feminist caravan went to the village of Ahmetler (Turkey), where women's activism was at the forefront of the struggle to protect their territory against the building of a hydroelectric power plant which would destroy access to resources for 320 nomadic people. For villagers it was a question of survival: the power plant would have destroyed the canyon, polluted the water, and destroyed the whole mountain. Therefore, agricultural activities and farming would have been made impossible with the pollution of the water and of the eco-system. That is why people resisted: to save their territory, their lives, and the lives of their children (Figure 11.2). The fight was not easy. The village's strategy was a siege to prevent the company from bringing machines to the site; this action brought serious physical violence to the neighbourhood, according to Butler:

> To attack the body is to attack the right itself ... Although the bodies on the street are vocalizing their opposition to the legitimacy of the

FIGURE 11.2 Feminist activists in Ahmetler

state, they are also, by virtue of occupying that space, repeating that occupation of space, and persisting in that occupation space, posing the challenge in corporeal terms. … The persistence of the body calls that legitimacy into question, and does so precisely through a performativity of the body that crosses language without ever quite reducing to language.[27]

Women's struggles to protect their village and their water resources have lasted two years under both political and economic pressures, but they saved their territory. Now the valley is protected by national environmental protection, suggesting that the value of the site has finally been recognized.

Another stopover of feminist action was Bucharest, and here the caravan had the chance to meet some members of an evicted community who were resisting in the streets of Bucharest, organized in a camp, and waiting to be provided with a decent home by the municipality. This community is known as "Vulturilor 50",[28] the name of the street where they used to live before the evacuation (Figure 11.3). Around 13 families, more or less 60 people including children, have been occupying public space since 15 September 2014 while waiting for a house. Though they are receiving legal help from non-governmental organizations and logistical help from other citizens and neighbours, the resistance is hard, especially in wintertime.

Most of the members of this "Vulturilor 50" community are Roma, so in this meeting they had the opportunity to discuss women's situation in Roma communities in Romania, early marriages, and Roma women's grassroots

FIGURE 11.3 Meeting with members of "Vulturilor 50"

activism work with Roma women and with militants. Some of these women are activists from the Common Front for the Right to Housing, who explained the recent and ongoing struggle to discuss the difficulties Roma people have in gaining access to housing due to institutionalized racism and discrimination.

Women against war

When we affirm the precarious condition of life, we are confirming its finitude and destroying "our radical substitutability and anonymity in relation both to certain socially facilitated modes of dying".[29] Thus, it is war, without a doubt, which is the social and political condition which maximizes *precarity* for some people while minimizing it for others. War is built through interpretative frameworks which differentiate between those populations on whom life and existence depend, and those populations who represent a direct threat to my life and existence, and as a result we do not feel the same horror and indignity over the loss of the latter population's lives. Faced by state violence, our responsibility as interdependent beings is a response from indignation. Recognition of these lives lost by the violence of the state forces us to an open and public mourning, and this has enormous political potential.

FIGURE 11.4 Feminist from Vienna playing a song in Mauthausen

During their trip, the caravan stopped in several countries where the pop-ulation, women more specifically, have suffered the horror of war, and in consequence different acts were organized for memorial recognition (public mourning) of the people who died in these armed conflicts. On 8 May, the feminist caravan was in Mauthausen-Gusen Concentration Camp where, year after year, feminists and lesbians from Austria and Germany meet at the concentration camp to "commemorate all those who were 'unfortunate' enough to be different and unsuitable and thus were killed by the atrocities of the Nazi regime"[30] and work to ensure that fascist atrocities are never forgotten (Figure 11.4).

During the ceremony to commemorate the victims, feminists remem-ber the crimes committed against women in this camp and in other camps: Mauthausen-Gusen consisted of 32 barracks, and barrack 1 was used for prostituting women inmates. Women that were brought to this camp were "offered" by Nazis to be used for prostitution and in return they "promised" them freedom after six months. Women were used by every-one: by male inmates, because Nazis claimed that it was a good strategy to increase the productivity of prisoners by providing what they perceived as "entertainment", then by soldiers and by high-ranking SS officers. This is not part of the camp's official history, and accordingly, feminists and lesbians placed a memorial plaque in front of barrack 1 which tells the Mauthausen-Gusen women's stories.

Another act of public mourning took place in Srebrenica, where on 11 July 1995 more than 8,000 men and boys were massacred by the Serbian military forces of Bosnia. Their remains were put in mass graves and some bodies were dislocated in order not to be found again. On the same day, women divided from these men were brought to concentration camps and systematically raped by Serbian soldiers. Therefore, women participating in the caravan used their visit to Srebrenica to denounce the situation: the conditions of life which people are living in 20 years after the genocide and the rise of fascism all over Europe. This memory work is important, because it is the only way to prevent the re-emergence of nationalistic aspirations, fascist politics, and war.

These are some of the struggles and resistances the caravan found on the road, and following Butler and Athanasiou, we believe that "these resistances are an opportunity to create new social bonds and forms of collective struggles, overcoming the limits of self-sufficiency and redefining our relational and interdependence character as an answer to dispossession".[31]

Economics and bodily self-governance through solidarity

In this chapter we have seen that *precarious* lives have political agency, and thus "even after the public sphere has been defined through their exclusion, they act. Whether abandoned to *precarity* or left to die through systematic negligence, the concerted action still emerges from such sites."[32] Precarious life relationships are taken as a starting point for political struggles in order to find the possibilities of political practices in neoliberal conditions.

The occupation of public spaces is a powerful form of protest and struggle, but the truth is that to carry out this kind of action we must have gained specific rights beforehand, at least the right of free movement: "we take to the streets because … we can pass through that space without obstruction, harassment, administrative detention, fear of injury or death. … Mobility is itself a right of the body, but it is also a precondition for the exercise of other rights."[33] Indeed, occupations of public space, which means taking over a space that has already been defined by state powers, and therefore, public protests illuminate the relationship between public space and the existing regime. In other words, bodies on the street redeploy the space of appearance in order to contest and negate existing forms of political legitimacy.

On 10 March the feminist activists of the caravan stopped in Antakya (Turkey) to meet with Kampüs Cadilari (Campus Witches; see Figure 11.5), which is an organization created by female students to enable women to self-organize, shed light on, and fight violence against and harassment of women in Turkish universities. These feminist and anti-capitalist activists lead actions against rape, the murder of women, control over women's bodies, street harassment, and so on. They denounce sexism in education and the university system and work to build solidarity between women and to create spaces for women to denounce these different forms of violence. They participate visibly and dynamically in feminist demonstrations, and they organize action in the streets.

FIGURE 11.5 Kampüs Cadilari's poster

As I discussed earlier, austerity policies imposed by global governments have maximized the *precarity* in people's lives. In response to this precarious situation, many families have self-organized to occupy factories and save them from looting and destruction in order to start production again. That is the case of Vio.Me in Thessaloniki (Greece) where feminist activists of the caravan went to learn from the project and express their solidarity. Vio.Me's workers in Thessaloniki stood up against unemployment and poverty by leading a long struggle to self-manage the occupied factory in very adverse conditions. For three years, they have been producing and selling organic cleaning products. This project has a solidarity committee which involves in the decision process not only factory workers but also citizens and consumers. In assembly, they decide what their next actions will be and how to carry them out, thereby challenging capitalist power dynamics.

Nevertheless, from my point of view, the extraordinary characteristics of these feminist collectives I am analysing in this chapter are not only new forms of political struggle, but they also offer new perspectives on *precarity*, such as the fact that these collectives kept on travelling, and crossed again and again the apparently so-distant boundaries between culture and politics. Several European feminist collectives have queered the seemingly disparate fields of the cultural and political. Thus, these feminist actions show us that the exchange of the subversive knowledge of precariousness, the communicative search for common ground to make a politically constituted body possible, has not taken place within political or university contexts but with striking frequency within cultural institutions and social self-government centres[34] like the Women's House of Thessaloniki (Greece), the Casa de la Dona of Barcelona (Spain), or the Hunsrück women's community (Germany).

The Women's House of Thessaloniki was born from an initiative of women against debt and austerity measures. Their aims were to form a front, together with other movements, which will resist the neoliberal attack on their society. Under austerity circumstances the Greek population, in particular women, were living in deprivation and poverty, not even having substantial means to live and bring up their children (food, heating, health checks, etc.). In these conditions they set up a solidarity venue, a women's venue, addressing all women and especially single-parent families and single women. It is an "open" place where all of them can have their own voice heard, so that via self-organization they are able to resist the changes imposed by the International Monetary Fund and find answers to their problems in a collective way. This women's house provides legal advice on matters of domestic violence and health issues and also organizes direct action concerning upcoming problems due to the policies of memorandum decided by government (electricity cuts, house foreclosures, etc.).

In summary, the feminist caravan action shows us that another world is possible: one where women can encounter each other between cultures and different world views, between social classes, countryside and city, between women with differing abilities and life realities, where we can learn about each other and change our lives.

Suggested assignment

*   Having the concept of *Slow policy* in mind, ask yourself: Do you know any collective in your university or neighbourhood that practises a *slow policy*? Argue your answer.
*   Following the policy ontology of Butler, ask yourself: Could you indicate the most important difference between precariousness and *precarity*?

Notes

1 Judith Butler and Athena Athanasiou, *Dispossession: The Performative in the Political* (Cambridge: Polity Press, 2013), 149.
2 Ibid., 149.

3 Isabell Lorey, *Estado de inseguridad. Gobernar la precariedad*, 1st ed. (Madrid: Traficantes de Sueños, 2016). Available at: www.traficantes.net/libros/estado-de-inseguridad.

4 Beyond our shared existential precariousness, some lives slide into *precarity*, which is how public policies manage our vulnerabilities: they delve into the vulnerability of certain bodies and groups, hindering their chances of life, in order to reduce the precariousness of other bodies and groups, who live in privileged positions, in which their lives enrich and strengthen.

5 Judith Butler, "Bodies in Alliance and the Politics of the Street". Lecture held in Venice, 7 September 2011, in the framework of the series *The State of Things*, organized by the Office for Contemporary Art Norway, European Institute for Progressive Cultural Politicies), www.eipcp.net/transversal/1011/butler/en.

6 The website of Caravana Feminista can be found here: www.caravanafeminista. net.

7 Judith Butler, *Frames of War: When Is Life Grievable?* (London: Verso, 2009), 14.

8 Ibid., 2

9 Ibid., 2–3.

10 Ibid., 25.

11 Ibid., 31.

12 Isabell Lorey, "Becoming Common: Precarization as Political Constituting", *e-flux Journal* 17 (June–August 2010), www.e-flux.com/journal/becoming-common-precarization-as-political-constituting.

13 Judith Butler, Preface to Lorey, *Estado de inseguridad*, 13.

14 Lorey, "Becoming Common".

15 Lorey, *Estado de inseguridad*, 73–4.

16 Ibid., 75–6.

17 Butler, *Frames of War*, 32.

18 Ibid., 32.

19 Butler and Athanasiou, *Dispossession*, 154.

20 Ibid., 154.

21 The term *slow* was introduced in the field of critical policy by the Degrowth Movement. This movement was described by Serge Latouche, one of its greatest exponents today, as a set of theories that aim to criticize or struggles for growth encouraged by capitalism, in "Pour une société de décroissance", *Le Monde Diplomatique*, November 2003.

22 See in this volume Ester Conesa Carpintero and Monika Rogowska-Stangret (Chapters 3 and 1, respectively), where a critical approach to the resistances of the Slow Science Movement, requiring time to think, read, discuss, and build knowledge is developed.

23 To extend this idea: John Holloway, *Change the World without Taking Power: The Meaning of Revolution Today* (London: Pluto Press, 2002).

24 Silvia L. Gil, "Debates en la teoría feminista contemporánea: sujeto, ética y vida en común", *Quaderns de Psicologia* 16 (1) (2014), www.quadernsdepsicologia. cat/article/view/v16-n1-lgil.

25 All information about the crowdfunding: www.verkami.com/projects/10679#question_answers-10679.

26 Butler, *Frames of War*, 55.

27 Butler, "Bodies in Alliance and the Politics of the Street".

28 For more information about this community see https://jurnaldinvulturilor50. org/.

29 Butler, *Frames of War*, 14.

30 On its website, Caravana Feminista, "Women Struggles in Europe", "Feminist Caravan in Mauthausen Concentration Camp", www.caravanafeminista.net.

31 Butler and Athena, *Dispossession*.

32 Butler, "Bodies in Alliance and the Politics of the Street".
33 Judith Butler, "Bodily Vulnerability, Coalitions and Street Politics", in *Differences in Common: Gender, Vulnerability, and Community*, ed. Joana Sabadell-Nieto and Marta Segarra (New York: Rodopi Publishing, 2014), 168.
34 Lorey, "Becoming Common".

References

Butler, Judith. *Frames of War: When Is Life Grievable?* London: Verso, 2009.
Butler, Judith. "Bodies in Alliance and the Politics of the Street". European Institute for Progressive Cultural Politicies, 2011. Available at: www.eipcp.net/transversal/1011/butler/en (accessed 22 June 2016).
Butler, Judith. "Bodily Vulnerability, Coalitions and Street Politics". In *Differences in common: Gender, Vulnerability, and Community*, edited by Joana Sabadell-Nieto and Marta Segarra, 99–120. New York: Rodopi Publishing, 2014.
Butler, Judith. Preface to *Estado de inseguridad. Gobernar la precariedad*, by Isabell Lorey, 13–16. 1st ed. Madrid: Traficantes de Sueños, 2016. Available at: www.traficantes.net/libros/estado-de-inseguridad (accessed 23 May 2016).
Butler, Judith and Athanasiou, Athena. *Dispossession: The Performative in the Political*. Cambridge: Polity Press, 2013.
Caravana Feminista. "Women Struggles in Europe", 2015. Available at: www.caravanafeminista.net/ (accessed 3 April 2016).
Gil, Silvi L. "Debates en la teoría feminista contemporánea: sujeto, ética y vida en común". *Quaderns de Psicologia*, 16 (1) (2014). Available at: www.quadernsdepsicologia.cat/article/view/v16-n1-lgil (accessed 25 June 2016).
Holloway, John. *Change the World without Taking Power: The Meaning of Revolution Today*. London: Pluto Press, 2002.
Latouche, Serge. "Pour une société de décroissance". *Le Monde Diplomatique*, November 2003.
Lorey, Isabell. "Becoming Common: Precarization as Political Constituting". *e-flux Journal* 17 (June–August 2010). Available at: www.e-flux.com/journal/becoming-common-precarization-as-political-constituting/ (accessed 19 June 2016).
Lorey, Isabell. *Estado de inseguridad. Gobernar la precariedad*. 1st ed. Madrid: Traficantes de Sueños, 2016. Available at: www.traficantes.net/libros/estado-de-inseguridad (accessed 23 May 2016).

INDEX